CHURCH HISTORY 4

CHRISTIANITY WORLDWIDE

AD 1800 ONWARDS

TEF Study Guides

This series was first sponsored and subsidized by the Theological Education Fund of the WCC in response to requests from Africa, Asia, the Caribbean, and the Pacific. The books are prepared by and in consultation with theological teachers in those areas. Special attention is given to problems of interpretation and application arising there as well as in the West, and to the particular needs of students using English as a second language.

General Editors: Daphne Terry and Nicholas Beddow

IN PREPARATION

TEF Study Guide 22

CHURCH HISTORY 4
CHRISTIANITY WORLDWIDE
AD 1800 ONWARDS

LOUISE PIROUET

with contributions from
Ian Breward; Chang Sik Lee with H. D. Beeby
V. E. W. Hayward and T. Hawthorn; Enrique Dussel;
Otto Meinardus; T. V. Philip; and John Roxborogh

First published in Great Britain 1989
SPCK
Holy Trinity Church
Marylebone Road
London NW1 4DU

The photographs in this book are reproduced by courtesy of
The Basel Mission (p. 19a),
The World Council of Churches (pp. 19b, 175c),
The Council for World Mission (pp. 35a, 131c, 193b, 206b),
Photos-Service Vivant Univers (pp. 35b, 88c, 114a & c, 142b & c, 156c),
The Baptist Missionary Society (pp. 62a, 75b, 175a),
The Mansell Collection (pp. 62b, 221a),
The Methodist Church Overseas Division (pp. 62c, 75a, 156b, 193a, c & d),
The United Society for the Propagation of the Gospel (pp. 62d, 88a, 175b, 206a),
The Overseas Missionary Fellowship (pp. 88b, 95b & c),
Lee/Dennis Methodist Information (p. 95a),
The Church Missionary Society (pp. 131a, b & d),
Camera Press Ltd (p. 142a),
Tony Barr (p. 175b),
The Rev. John Ewington (p. 206c),
The Mill Hill Missionaries (p. 206d).

British Library Cataloguing in Publication Data

Pirouet, Louise
    Church history.
    4: Christianity Worldwide
    AD 1800 onwards
    1. Christian church, to 1975
    I. Title
    270

    ISBN 0-281-04361-2 (net edition)
    ISBN 0-281-04360-4 (non-net edition for
    Africa, Asia, S. Pacific and Caribbean)

Printed in Great Britain by
Latimer Trend & Company Ltd, Plymouth

Contents

Series Editors' Preface

This fourth volume in the TEF Guide to Church History, carrying on the story from 1800 where Volume 3 left off, is not intended to be an all-inclusive in-depth account of the Church in the modern era. Since World War II especially, the study of Church History, like that of history in general, has undergone an explosion. An immense amount of research has been done, and detailed studies have been produced in nearly every area, on the history of Christian missions, and of the now mostly autonomous Churches they helped to establish. The research continues, but there is no dearth of such material available within the various regions.

Despite today's vastly increased facilities for international communication and opportunities for ecumenical exchange, however, a striking degree of 'mutual ignorance' still seems to exist as between the Churches in one part of the world and those in another, and even, in some cases, between the different denominations within a single country.

Our aim here, therefore, has been to provide a sort of 'overview', of the worldwide contextual background, from which readers may gain an appreciation of what goes on in other parts of the Church, and perhaps come to a clearer understanding of the detailed historical studies carried out in their own areas.

Following the method which worked well for the Guide to Religions in the series (a subject of equally worldwide scope), this volume is planned as a sort of symposium. Specialists in modern Church History from different parts of the world were asked to contribute summary accounts of the expansion of Christianity over the past two hundred years in their particular regions, where so many new Churches have developed and come to maturity.

The material on North-East Asia comes from Dr Chang Sik Lee of Hankuk Theological Seminary in Korea, with additional contributions from Dr Victor Hayward (China), Dr H. D. Beeby (Taiwan) and the Reverend T. Hawthorn (Hong Kong); and that on the Indian Sub-Continent, Sri Lanka and Nepal from Dr T. V. Philip, Director, Senate of Serampore College in West Bengal. South-East Asia was originally to have been covered by Dr Alan Thomson, author of Volume 3 of this Guide, but his transfer to new duties made this impossible, and Dr John Roxborogh of Seminari Theologi Malaysia kindly took on the responsibility. Latin America and the Caribbean were covered by Professor Enrique Dussel, then Director of CEHILA (Commission on Church History Studies in Latin America); the Pacific Region with Australia and New Zealand by Professor Ian Breward of Otago

University in New Zealand; and the Orthodox and Eastern Mediterranean Churches by Dr Otto Meinardus.

The African chapters were contributed by Dr Louise Pirouet, then teaching at the University of Nairobi, who took part in a number of Church History research projects both there and in Uganda and was later involved in work on behalf of refugees, first from the civil war in the Southern Sudan and then from Amin's Uganda. Dr Pirouet also gallantly undertook to act as co-ordinating editor for the book as a whole. Hers has been the difficult task of filling in some of the gaps and drawing together material from outside her own region of study, as well as creating a balance between the widely differing viewpoints of the various contributors and achieving a reasonably uniform level of language and perspective. She has also provided a short chapter on Western Europe and North America, not as a history of events there, on which plenty of introductory volumes are already available, but rather as a simple analysis of the changing ideas, attitudes and developments, both inside and outside the Church, which have chiefly influenced the modern missionary movement and growth of the Church world wide.

A big debt of gratitude is owed, not only to Dr Pirouet and to the other contributors, who at one stage or another have willingly given and received comments on each other's work, but also to the large number of individual consultants all around the world who have helped with advice and suggestions. In particular we must mention the late Bishop David A. Brown, Dr E. John Hamlin, Dr Victor E. W. Hayward, Bishop John V. Taylor, Dr Bernard Thorogood and Professor Andrew Walls.

Nicholas Beddow
Daphne Terry

The Plan and Use of this Book

As readers will notice at once, this book consists of material contributed by a number of different authors, each with their own individual
style and approach. Also, even though some general trends in people's
ideas and ways of life can be seen as common to every continent, the
actual political situation and shape of events since the year 1800 have
differed enormously as between one region of the world and another.

For these two reasons we have not attempted to arrange the chapters
in any specific order, nor to impose any one pattern or order of
contents, or cut-off date, within the chapters themselves. Some are
divided geographically and others according to dates or to the main
themes discussed, and the accounts are brought to an end in whichever
way or at whatever point in time seemed most appropriate for the
particular region.

The emphasis throughout is on the contribution made by local
Christians and missionaries to the development of the Church in each
area, as the work of missionary orders and societies as such is already
well-documented. There is one exception: the chapter on Western
Europe and North America is meant to provide a more detailed study
of the background information sketched out in the Introduction, and is
placed first for the benefit of readers who may wish to remind or inform
themselves of the factors which lay behind the 'sending' of missions, as
well as the need for 'mission' in the West itself. Other readers may wish
to skip the chapter altogether, or perhaps come back to it at the end.

STUDY SUGGESTIONS

Suggestions for further study appear at the end of each chapter, and
where appropriate are subdivided geographically. They are meant to
help readers to check their own progress and understand more clearly
what they have read, and to provide topics for individual consideration
or group discussion. They are of three main sorts:

1. *Words and Meanings.* These will help readers to check and deepen
their understanding of any technical or other terms used, including
some of the foreign words and phrases.

2. *Review of Content.* These revision questions are to help readers to
ensure that they have fully grasped and remembered the ideas discussed
and the facts presented. Students may find it useful to write down their
answers and then check them with the Key.

3. *Discussion Questions.* These will help readers to understand why
things happened as they did, to discern for themselves how the ideas
and events of the past have helped to shape the Church of today, and to

consider what the relationships are—or ought to be—between Churches in one region of the world and those in another.

These Study Suggestions are no more than suggestions. Some tutors may want to substitute questions more directly related to the situation in their own areas. Some readers may not want to use them at all.

The *Key* (p. 233) will enable students to check their own work of revision, but please note that the Key does not provide answers: it simply shows where in the text answers are to be found.

MAPS

The maps provided for each chapter/region are based on the present-day political situation. Exceptions are chapter 1 which is not really concerned with geography and therefore has no map provided, and the Africa chapters which are divided chronologically rather than regionally, and therefore show the situation at the end of the nineteenth century, at about 1950, and at present (late 1980s), respectively.

INDEX

The Index (p. 239) includes all the more important references to the people and places mentioned, and the main subjects dealt with.

FURTHER READING

Some of the source material for the period was produced within the various regions and may not be readily available elsewhere, and some may no longer be in print. The list of recommended further reading (p. 231) includes some of this material, but consists mainly of more general works. Students with access to a library, however, may well be able to track down those titles listed which relate to their own area, and probably others as well.

Introduction
The Background to Modern Missions

In the nineteenth and twentieth centuries Christianity made great advances. It has become a world-wide religion, and about a quarter of the world's population now identify themselves as Christians. The beginnings of this period of expansion were traced in Volume 3 of this TEF Guide to Church History. The present volume looks at some of the effects of that expansion through the eyes of Church Historians in different parts of the world. We start by noting briefly in this Introduction some of the developments in society and in Christian life in the West which made the expansion possible.

New Ideas of Political and Civil Liberty
In England, constitutional crises during the seventeenth century led to civil war, and eventually to the revolution of 1688, which limited royal power and made the monarch answerable to Parliament. In the eighteenth century the French revolution against the power of the monarchy and the aristocracy, and colonial revolutions in North America and in the Spanish American colonies, went much further. They spread new ideas about individual human rights and personal freedom, and about giving the people a voice in government.

In the nineteenth century, however, it began to be recognized that something seriously wrong was happening in North America. The same people who had fought to free themselves from domination by the English were themselves denying freedom to large numbers of black slaves. Members of the Society of Friends (Quakers) were the first to see this clearly, and were the first group of Christians to debar from worshipping with them anyone who bought and sold slaves. Earlier missionary work had been hindered by the growth of slavery, and by the failure of Christians to act against it, so this was a very important development. But it was not until the twentieth century that people in the West began to see that colonialism also violated human rights.

The Evangelical Awakening
The founding of Protestant missions in the eighteenth and nineteenth centuries resulted largely from a movement of spiritual renewal known as the 'Evangelical Awakening' which began in North America. The movement spread to Germany and Britain, and also to Scandinavia, and not only led to a new growth in personal Christian commitment, but also awakened people to the need for social reform. Christian philanthropists began to try to improve conditions in the prisons, to

1

support legislation to protect workers and children, and to put an end
to the slave-trade and to slavery. Quakers as well as Evangelicals were
active in this movement for reform. Some historians suggest that these
reforms had little to do with an awakened Christian social conscience.
They wish to explain everything in economic terms, and claim that
people had realized it was more profitable to use machines and properly
paid workers than to use slave labour. Better working conditions would
result in greater productivity, and there were so many slaves in the
United States already that there was no longer any need to import more
from Africa. The facts do not altogether support these economic
arguments. For instance, if the reason for abolishing the slave trade
was that it was no longer profitable, then why did it take so long to get
the trade abolished? And why did slave-traders still find it so profitable
to carry slaves, that for fifty years after abolition they continued to risk
all the dangers of trading illegally? Of course economics do affect the
course of history, but it is not sensible to try and explain everything in
economic terms. Certainly economic and technological developments
eventually made the abolition of the slave-trade easier for those whose
conscience had been awakened.

An equally important result of the Evangelical Awakening, and also
of the German Pietist movement that developed in the Lutheran
Church of the seventeenth and eighteenth centuries, was the new
impulse they gave to Christians to evangelize, both in their own
countries and in other parts of the world.

The Industrial Revolution

This too had important results for the spread of Christianity. The
invention of the steam-engine which revolutionized transport, and the
harnessing of steam-power to machines which revolutionized methods
of weaving cloth and other manufacturing processes, were matters of
fairly simple technology (today it would be called 'intermediate technology'). But this fairly simple technology, together with improvements
in agriculture, helped the West greatly to increase its wealth. More
people were able to afford education, and, in the Protestant countries
especially, the Churches took a lead in providing free education for
those who could not afford to pay. They did this in order to give people
a chance to 'improve themselves', as they put it, as well as to enable
them to read the Bible for themselves, something which was very
important to Protestants. Cheaper methods of printing and making
paper meant that many more people could afford Bibles. It also led to
the growth of newspapers, and these became a means of educating
people, who now learned, among other things, about parts of the world
their ancestors had not even known existed, and about people who had
never heard the Christian gospel. Missionary societies produced maga-

zines, and, in the days before radio and TV, these provided people with exciting reading, and stimulated them to contribute towards the work of the missions.

Such contributions were necessary, for the missions founded in the nineteenth and twentieth centuries did not receive money from governments in the way that earlier missions had done. They relied on voluntary contributions, and these came from a great many people, each of whom was a little better off than before. Cheap printing meant that the missions could obtain Bibles, missals and service books cheaply for those whom they converted, and the British and Foreign Bible Society helped to make these available in many languages. Missionaries took it for granted that they would teach their converts to read, and missions provided education just as the Churches in their home countries did. Safer and faster methods of travel too, enabled larger numbers of missionaries to work overseas.

Revolution in Scientific Thinking

Like the social change that resulted from the Industrial Revolution, the change in ways of thinking and of understanding brought about by new scientific discoveries had an important effect on the way Christians approached the task of evangelism. Among other things, science had taught people to think in terms of biological evolution. Human history, let alone the history of the universe, is now known to be much longer than was previously recognized, and scientists find that the universe is much emptier and vaster than our ancestors ever dreamed.

Christians, whose religion is based in history, became unsure of themselves when this new teaching first appeared. Some of the humbler and more sensitive among them hestitated to get involved in missionary evangelism, because it seemed too much like cultural aggression. Some of the ideas from biology were applied to human society, so that people came to think that society as a whole evolves over time in the same way that biological organisms do. People who live by hunting wild animals and gathering wild plants and fruit were regarded as 'primitive', and the more developed western-style democracies as 'evolved' and 'advanced'. From there it was only a short step towards believing that people who belong to less 'advanced' societies were inferior human beings, and towards thinking of religion too in evolutionary terms. Biological evolution is a genuinely scientific idea. But the idea that hunter-gatherers are inferior as human beings (or of less value to God than people belonging to modern industrialized societies) is *not* scientific. Advances in technology have nothing to do with people's moral and spiritual progress. However, such mistaken ideas became widespread in the nineteenth century. They were used to justify colonialism, and Western missionaries too became infected with them.

Important advances were also made in medicine, and some of these were of great importance for the missions. Two of the most important discoveries from the point of view of missions were that quinine could be used to combat malaria, and that vaccination could protect people from smallpox. These discoveries have been enormously important for people living in tropical countries, including missionaries, as indeed have many of the discoveries and new developments in tropical medicine—for example in the treatment and prevention of leprosy and yaws—which have resulted from the work of medical missions.

Voluntary Lay Organizations

During the nineteenth century groups of Protestants, including lay men and women, joined together in voluntary organizations outside the official Church structures, to undertake the work of evangelism. The missionary societies they established were a new sort of response to a new situation, reflecting the new ideas about the role of the individual in society. Lay people helped to formulate missionary policy and gave money to support missions. Both laymen and laywomen also became missionaries themselves. This had not happened before the nineteenth century. Some of the new missionary societies were formed within particular Protestant Churches, others included people from different Churches who felt they could work together. Although there was sometimes rivalry between missions, there was also co-operation, and a growing conviction that divisions among Christians were a hindrance to the gospel.

In the Roman Catholic Church a new beginning had to be made. By the end of the eighteenth century Roman Catholic missions had almost ceased to exist. In the nineteenth century, therefore, as a counterpart to the major Protestant missionary effort, new religious orders and societies of priests and sisters were formed by the Roman Catholic Church specifically to work in the missions. Lay people helped to support these, and in 1822 the Society for the Propagation of the Faith, an organization which collected vast sums of money to support the newly-founded missions, was started by a young Roman Catholic lay-woman. But only fairly recently have lay Catholics themselves been accepted as missionaries. The Popes have done much to encourage the spread of the faith through missions, and in the present century Ireland has produced the world's highest missionary force per head of population.

We must not assume, however, that these new missions were only concerned to send people from their own countries to evangelize other parts of the world. The nations of Western Europe were no longer Christian nations (though people often spoke as though they were). Most of them were secular states in which people were free to follow their own consciences in matters of religion. Spain and Portugal were exceptions to this: they remained officially Catholic states. But elsewhere freedom of conscience meant that people were allowed to belong to any branch of the Christian Church they liked, to practise any religion they chose, or to practise no religion at all. In the towns and cities of nineteenth-century Europe and America many people were completely indifferent to religion—as they are today. There were, therefore, 'home missions'. The Salvation Army is an example of a home mission which grew into a denomination, and now has overseas missions of its own. Almost all Churches ran home missions, since Europe and America needed to be evangelized afresh. In North America the population had to be reconverted to Christianity after emigration from Europe had weakened people's religious allegiances.

The Pentecostal movement which arose in the early 1900s also had its roots in North America, though it spread rapidly into Britain, Scandinavia and Latin America. Characterized by baptism in the Spirit and speaking in tongues, like the disciples on the day of Pentecost as described in Acts 2, and by charismatic preaching, Pentecostal missions have been active throughout the twentieth century. Their work in every continent is now carried on largely by indigenous missionaries. More recently, this movement of charismatic renewal has manifested itself in many of the mainline Churches of Europe and North America, in the form of ecstatic and prophetic prayer, tongues and healing. It may be stimulating a parallel renewal in evangelism—though in a quieter way than some of the militant evangelicalism prevalent in the USA, where its outreach is largely through television and radio.

Recurring Themes of this Book

In working through this volume readers will come to recognize certain themes which recur again and again as we trace the spread of Christianity in one region after another.

1. We shall notice that in Asia, Africa and elsewhere, newly-converted Christians quickly took up the work of evangelizing their own people. Missionaries from Europe and North America were not alone in the work of spreading the gospel. In this book we shall see how much the world-wide Church owes to thousands of indigenous catechists, teachers and evangelists in every land who became missionaries to their own people.

2. We shall notice that wherever the gospel has been preached, there is a concern to make the Church 'at home' in the local culture. By the nineteenth century Christianity had become so much at home in European culture that missionaries often found it difficult to distinguish between what was essentially Christian, and what was an

adaptation to European culture. Christians in Africa and Asia are still working to make Christianity more at home in their own cultures.

3. We shall see that the preaching of Christianity has sometimes resulted in a revival of traditional cultures and non-Christian religions. This Guide to Church History should really be read alongside the TEF Guide to Religions, or some other reliable book on world religions. Before reading about the Indian sub-continent, for instance, it would be helpful to look up Hinduism, Buddhism, Sikhism, and Islam.

4. Another recurring theme is that of nationalism. In many areas of the world there have been struggles for independence from colonial rule, and in some of the 'new' nations in Europe, like Germany and Italy, as well as those in other continents, there has been nationalist arrogance and 'empire-building'. So we shall see some of the dilemmas faced by Christians who had to fight in nationalist wars which they thought were wrong, or who sympathized with a nationalist cause but rejected the use of violence as a means of achieving the end. We shall discuss some of the disagreements within the Church on matters of nationalism and politics in nations where some Christians see nationalism, along with tribalism and racism, as divisive and harmful, while other Christians see nationalism, along with liberation and freedom from colonialism, as good.

People of different nationalities and who have lived and worked in different continents have contributed to the writing of this book. They have widely differing points of view about these issues. In putting their contributions together we have tried to present something of the differing opinions that Christians hold. The discussion questions at the end of each chapter may help readers to make up their minds about some of the issues raised, especially in so far as they affect the life of the Church in their own countries.

STUDY SUGGESTIONS

WORDS AND MEANINGS

1. (a) What was the 'Evangelical Awakening'?
   (b) What sorts of present-day Christians would you describe as (i) 'Evangelical' and (ii) Pentecostal?
   (c) What sort of present-day Christian activity would you describe as 'evangelizing'?
2. What is meant by a 'secular' society?
3. What do you understand by the term 'intermediate technology'?

REVIEW OF CONTENT

4. What effect did the Evangelical Awakening have on the advance of Christianity in the nineteenth century?
5. 'The Industrial revolution had important results for the spread of Christianity' (p. 2). What were some of those results, and in what ways did they help to promote the work of missions?
6. What effect did the nineteenth-century revolution in scientific thinking have on the attitude of Western missionaries towards the people of less developed societies?
7. In what ways did some of the nineteenth-century advances in medicine help the work of missionaries?
8. What was the chief difference between the ways in which both nineteenth and twentieth-century missions have been financed, and the way in which earlier missions had received money? What was the chief reason for the change?
9. What was the chief difference between the role of lay people in the work of Protestant missions during the nineteenth century, and their role in the work of Roman Catholic missions in that same period?

DISCUSSION

10. 'Earlier missionary work had been hindered by the growth of slavery' (p. 2). In what chief ways do you think the slave trade hindered missionary work?
11. (1) 'In the eighteenth century the French revolution ... and colonial revolutions in America spread new ideas about individual human rights and personal freedom ... Freedom of conscience meant people were allowed to practise any religion they chose' (p. 1).
    (2) 'In nineteenth-century Europe and America many people were completely indifferent to religion. . . . There were, therefore, 'home missions' (p. 5).
    What connection, if any, do you see between these two statements (1) and (2)? To what extent do people in your own country today have freedom of conscience? In your experience does such freedom make people more religious or less religious, and for what reasons?
12. What influence, if any, has colonialism had on the way people live in your country? What influence, if any, has colonialism had on people's religious belief and practice in your country? Do you regard it as a good or a bad influence, and why?
13. 'Some Christians see nationalism as divisive and harmful ... others see nationalism as good' (p. 6). What is your own opinion on the subject?

14. Which Christian denomination or denominations have been chiefly responsible for spreading the gospel in your country? What do you see as the main strengths and weaknesses of the missionary work of the following? (a) The Roman Catholic Church (b) The 'mainline' Protestant Churches (c) Evangelical and Pentecostal Churches (d) Indigenous Independent Churches.

15. Do the Churches in your country still depend on help from foreign missions, and if so, what sort of help? Do they undertake any missionary work themselves, either in your country or elsewhere? In your opinion is 'foreign' help a good thing for the Churches or a bad thing? Give your reasons.

1
Western Europe and North America
by Louise Pirouet

In this chapter we give only a brief account of Christianity in the West over the past two centuries. There are plenty of Church Histories available which concentrate almost entirely on what was happening in Europe or North America, in which this topic can be pursued further. In the Introduction to this volume we described in outline the background to the modern missionary movement. Here we simply look a little more closely at the developments in Western countries which seem most significant for that movement and for the Church worldwide.

BELIEF IN PROGRESS AND THE DECLINE OF FAITH

During the nineteenth century most people in Western Europe and North America believed that what they called 'progress' was inevitable. Science and technology were constantly opening up new possibilities, and it seemed as though every difficulty could be overcome. Railways and steamships made travel safer and faster, and machines speeded up production and made it possible to produce more goods more cheaply. People were healthier and lived longer because of improvements in hygiene, housing, and medicine; education became more widely available; and poverty was being overcome through the creation of vast new wealth. And at last slavery had been abolished. Europeans who went out to subdue foreign empires felt sure that they would bring enormous benefits to the people over whom they ruled. One of these benefits was Christianity, and many Christians thought that the progress the West had made was a mark of God's favour, and that theirs was a Christian civilization.

At the same time, the Churches were facing a huge task as a result of the Industrial Revolution. In the small towns and villages of pre-industrial Europe, religion—which meant Christianity—had been a community affair, with the Church at the centre of the community. People lived close to their relatives; they worked close to, or even in, their homes; and all the rituals of family life were celebrated by the Church. When people moved off the land and into big industrial cities, however, all this changed (and for those who emigrated to North America, the changes were even more pronounced). Families split up, church buildings were often at a distance from people's homes, or else there was no Christian community of the kind they had grown up with. People could no longer visit the graves of their ancestors in the local

9

churchyard. They had to do new kinds of work which were strange to them, and they felt uprooted. The Churches recognized the needs of such people living in the expanding cities, and they raised large sums of money to buy land and provide new church buildings. They also sent ministers to follow those of their members who had emigrated to North America and elsewhere. In spite of all these efforts, however, there was a gradual increase in the proportion of the population in Europe who had no Church affiliation. And in spite of the various revival movements, the growing number of people who had no time for religion were more willing to admit to the fact.

In the USA, on the contrary, people were being 're-converted', and by 1900 a far larger proportion of the population there were committed and practising Church members than was the case in much of Western Europe.

The rootlessness of the city dwellers in Europe was not the only reason for a decline in Church attendance. The growth of science and technology also played a part in the decline of Christianity. Or, to put it another way, the culture and intellectual attitudes of the West underwent a profound change, and Christianity is not even yet fully 'indigenized' in the new scientific and technological culture which has been emerging. Science developed so impressively that people began to turn to it rather than to religion for answers to their questions about life, and science rather than religion came to be regarded as the measure of truth. When there seemed to be a conflict between science and religion, people began to feel that it must be religion that was wrong. In particular people began to think that science contradicted the Bible, and the biblical account of creation. New knowledge about the age of the universe and the distance of the stars persuaded people that the universe could not have been created in six days just 6,000 years ago, and the application of evolutionary ideas in many fields of knowledge seemed to give a more credible account of the world at they saw it. There was a great deal of misunderstanding about the word 'myth'. Many people today use 'myth' to mean 'a story which is not true'. When scholars began to refer to the biblical accounts of creation as 'myths', people were shocked: surely the Bible did not tell lies? But biblical scholars and theologians mean something rather different by the word 'myth': not untrue stories, but stories which use picture-language to express truths which cannot be expressed in any other way. The truth which the Genesis creation stories express is that God made the world, and that God's creation was good until sin spoilt it. Theologians suggest that religious stories should be read for the sake of the religious truth they contain, and that we should not try to learn science from them. Most Christians are satisfied with this explanation when it is put clearly to them, but it is not always properly explained, and there are still people who do not fully understand what theologians and biblical scholars mean by 'myth' and 'religious truth', and who are perplexed because they fear that science contradicts the Bible.

The new scientific culture of the West also began to be applied to the study of the biblical texts. Archaeological discoveries shed new light on the political history of Israel and on the way people lived in OT and NT times, and these discoveries continued into the twentieth century. Historians and literary critics developed new ways of studying ancient texts, which they then applied to the study of the Pentateuch, the Gospels, and the rest of the Bible. Many people only half understood what the scholars were saying, and feared that they were undermining the faith by denying the 'truth' of Scripture. They found it disturbing that the Bible, a sacred book, should be examined in this way, and that the writers of Scripture should be treated as fallible human beings rather than as channels of divine truth. Once these questions had been asked they would not go away, and could not be ignored, but damage was done to the Christian Church because many people came to believe that the Scriptures could not be trusted. They misunderstood what the scholars were trying to say about different kinds of truth.

As a result of these controversies, some people who wanted to believe found it very difficult to do so. Others, however, found the new approach a great relief, because now they could voice their difficulties freely intead of having to pretend they did not exist. So what hindered some Christians, helped others. In Europe especially there were also many people who were glad to be rid of the necessity of believing at all. Religion seemed to them to curb their freedom, so they were glad to be rid of it. This 'modernism' affected Protestants much more than it affected Roman Catholics, who were forbidden to have anything to do with it. Catholic scholars knew what Protestant scholars were thinking, of course, but even if they agreed, they were forbidden to teach the new ideas. The First Vatican Council, which was held in 1869–70, strengthened the authority of the Pope and confirmed the Church's traditional teaching.

EVANGELISM AND SOCIAL ACTION

Nevertheless, in spite of a decline in church-going in Western Europe and the spread of doubt during the nineteenth century, there were still many deeply committed Christians. Those who went to church no longer did so simply by force of habit, but because of their personal commitment to the faith, and Christians were involved in all sorts of evangelistic and social activity. Thousands of missionaries from Western Europe and North America were at work, both in their own countries and overseas. The Churches were responsible for much of the spread of education which took place in this period, and the volume of Christian literature had never been greater. Christians worked to relieve poverty, reduce drunkenness, reform prisons, and care for orphaned children. Personal prayer and Bible-reading were widespread, and many families began and ended the day with family prayers and said grace before and after meals. One of the many purposes for which Christians gave their money was to subsidize Bibles for those who could not otherwise afford to buy them. There were renewal movements in both the Protestant and the Roman Catholic Churches. The less happy side of this picture was that some people's religious zeal was greater than their charity. There were deep divisions between the different denominations, and many Christians were both ignorant and intolerant, not only of other religions, but of Christians belonging to other denominations than their own.

One of the new movements which started in the nineteenth century was the Salvation Army, founded in England by William Booth and his wife Catherine. They and their helpers and converts were organized into the Salvation Army in the 1880s, and this movement was typical of one aspect of nineteenth-century Christianity. The Booths devised effective means of reaching poor people in the great cities who had lost touch with the Churches. The Salvation Army used popular music and brass bands which attracted attention on the streets, and their methods shocked more conventional Christians. But the Booths and their helpers won converts, helped some of the outcasts of society to rebuild their lives, and provided Christian fellowship for people who felt out of place in the other Churches. The uniforms worn by Salvation Army members helped to create a sense of belonging, and to overcome differences in income which were less noticeable when everyone was dressed alike.

In North America, besides the remarkably successful evangelistic campaigns in the new cities, 'camp meetings'—great weekend outdoor gatherings—had been held since the end of the eighteenth century. These brought together people from all kinds of different Church traditions who were pioneering on the frontier of white settlement as it moved westward, and who might otherwise have been lost to Christianity. The camp meetings were often noisy affairs, as people confessed their sins, cried aloud, and sang. The Spirit seemed to sweep throughout these gatherings, which were part of the process by which Americans were 'reconverted' to Christianity after leaving their European homelands and resettling in the New World.

TWO WORLD WARS

The events of the twentieth century, however, shattered nineteenth-century hopes of peaceful progress. We shall look at these events in turn, and then try to assess the position of Christianity in the mid-1970s.

The two World Wars of 1914–18 and 1939–45 and their aftermath, including the economic Depression that bedevilled the interwar years, changed the West fundamentally. They did not interrupt technological development, nor did they stop the general growth of wealth in the West, but they changed people's way of looking at themselves and the world. World War 1 destroyed the belief that progress was inevitable. The most technologically advanced part of the world fell apart in a conflict which resulted in millions of people killed or maimed, and which left the German people so demoralized by defeat and by the suffering which followed the war that they fell a prey to Adolf Hitler's aggressive nationalism and rabidly anti-semitic racism. The result was a Second World War at the end of which the West was appalled to discover that Germany, a 'civilized' nation and part of 'Christendom', had not only plunged half the world into war, but had also massacred six million Jewish people. Education and technological advancement had not taught people how to behave humanely, and Christians had been powerless to stop the horror. Roman Catholics were dismayed that the Pope did not act to save the Jews, though he was aware of what was going on. In Germany, only a small number of Christians resisted Hitler's Nazism. Most Christians on both sides during both World Wars thought that God was on their side, and prayed to Him to give them victory over their enemies.

There were exceptions to this, and at the end of World War II certain Christians stood out as having something to say which deserved attention. One was Bishop G.K.A. Bell of Chichester in England who, together with a group of other Christians, had somehow managed to keep in touch with those German Christians known as the 'Confessing Church', who had resisted Nazism. The best-known leader of the Confessing Church was Dietrich Bonhoeffer (1906–1945), who took considerable risks in serving this Church by continuing to train clergy for it after their seminary had been declared illegal. In 1939 he visited the USA, and was invited to stay there when it became clear that there was going to be war, but refused to save himself by doing so. He returned to Germany and was arrested in 1943. By mid-1944 some members of the Confessing Church decided that they could not remain inactive against Hitler any longer, and on 20 July that year they made an unsuccessful attempt to assassinate him. Bonhoeffer had been able to keep in touch with this group even though he was in prison, and he was executed for his part in the plot just weeks before the war ended. Bonhoeffer's writings have been very widely read. Among the books he wrote are *The Cost of Discipleship* (1937), and two which he wrote in prison, *Ethics*, which he was not able to finish, and *Letters and Papers from Prison*. These were published in 1949 and 1951. After Bonhoeffer learnt that the plot against Hitler had failed, and that his own involvement was known, he realized that he would be executed. He wrote a poem on his thoughts about his. Here is one verse of it:

> A change has come indeed. Your hands, so strong and active,
> are bound; in helplessness now you see your action
> is ended; you sigh in relief, your cause committing
> to stronger hands; so now you may rest contented.
> Only for one blissful moment could you draw near to touch
>   freedom;
> then, that it might be perfected in glory, you gave it to God.
> (*Letters and Papers from Prison*, Enlarged Edition (SCM Press 1971),
> p. 371)

After the war Bishop Bell worked to help the German Churches to move back into fellowship with other Christians again, and to recover from the Nazi ordeal. As a result, many Christians who had been on opposing sides during the war experienced repentance and forgiveness.

World War II finally ended with the dropping of atomic bombs on the two Japanese cities of Hiroshima and Nagasaki. By a terrible irony, these cities had the largest Christian populations of any cities in Japan. The devastation caused by these bombs appalled people. Nothing like it had ever been seen before, and quite new types of injury and sickness were experienced by the survivors. There is still no agreement in the West as to whether these attacks were necessary, and Christians are found on both sides of this disagreement. Some say that using atomic weapons was the only way to end the war, and that far more lives would have been lost had the war continued. Others say that the Japanese were about to surrender anyway, and that the British and Americans dropped the bombs because they wanted to test their effectiveness. Christians are also found on both sides of the argument as to whether it can ever be morally right to use atomic weapons, and whether they are really necessary for defence. Quakers believe all war is wrong, and they are prominent in the peace movements that have grown up since 1945, as are many other Christians as individuals, though by no means all. Nuclear weapons and their use (and indeed the development of nuclear power generally) are at the centre of one of the biggest ethical debates of the century, giving rise to peace and conservation movements on a regional and even global scale.

A further result of World War II was the eventual loss by the West of its former overseas empires. In the post-war years the countries of Western Europe needed to spend all their energies in rebuilding their own shattered economies, and few of them were prepared to try to hold on to their overseas possessions in the face of growing nationalism. We shall discuss this further below, in relation to the various regions of the world concerned.

MARXISM: SOCIETY AND THE INDIVIDUAL

Marxist teaching about the relationships between rich and poor, between individuals and society, and between Church and State concerns Christians in the West as well as those in Eastern Europe and elsewhere who live under Communist rule. The Russian Revolution which took place in 1917 was a turning point in modern history. Christians in the West were appalled by the propaganda against religion, and by the repression of religious activity which followed the Russian Revolution. The Vatican in particular was totally uncompromising in its denunciation of atheistic Communism, and in its defence of the Church's right to own property. The Vatican could not see how the Church could continue to function unless it had the right to own property without interference by the state. Christians in the West came to think of their countries as Christian countries by contrast with atheistic Communist nations, but, as we have seen, Christianity has been in decline in the West for a long time, and it becomes more and more difficult to define the West as Christian.

The Communist Party has had adherents in the West ever since its inception, and they are particularly numerous in France and Italy. Many of them believe that Communist rule need not be totalitarian as it is in the Soviet Union, and that freedom of conscience and of worship can be guaranteed even in a Communist state. Besides this, a great many people who are not Marxists at all accept some of Marx's insights into economics and the nature of society. Marxism has affected almost everyone's thinking on these topics, though not all of us recognize the fact.

People in the West find it difficult to counter Marxism effectively because the West no longer has a coherent philosophy of life or code of conduct to offer instead. Christianity has become a matter of private and individual choice rather than the religion of a whole people. The West refers to itself as 'the free world', but most people find it difficult to say what they mean by freedom, and by the 1960s freedom had largely degenerated into permissiveness on the one hand, and cutthroat business competition on the other. Even Christian parents have sometimes found it hard to know how to train and discipline their children, and what values to instil into them, because of their strong belief that everyone must at all costs be free to choose for themselves. The problem for the West today, in the absence of agreed values, is how to encourage responsibility and rebuild community. In this dilemma, some Christians see their task as trying to act as the light of the world and the salt of the earth through involving themselves in social and political life. The Roman Catholic Justice and Peace Commission is a good example of this kind of Christian concern for the world. Its members see their work as direct obedience to Jesus's teaching in Matthew 25.31–46. Others, however, consider that Christians should concentrate on individual evangelism, and not be 'side-tracked' into political and social affairs. Governments encourage such thinking whenever it seems that the Churches are calling their policies into question! By 1975 there were signs that some people were realizing that both sorts of Christian witness were needed. In 1968, for instance, the Evangelical Alliance in Britain had set up its own aid agency, TEAR Fund, and many Evangelicals who had previously stood somewhat aloof from aid agencies, preferring to help the Third World through giving to missionary societies, now welcomed TEAR Fund, and gave it their support.

We can see, then, that Marxism has helped to challenge Christians to take seriously questions about social justice and the needs of the poor, to recognize that development as well as charity and evangelism are needed, and to see that social systems as well as individuals need to be brought under the scrutiny of the gospel. But Marxism is not the only school of thought in the modern world that directs attention to people as members of society rather than as isolated individuals. Psychology and sociology also show how people's behaviour is affected by their upbringing, their relationships with the family, and their interaction with the community at large. The thinking of everyone in the West has been affected by this. Good teachers, for instance, do not simply punish children who are inattentive or disobedient in school: they also try to find out if there is some cause for this behaviour in the children's family circumstances or social background. Quarrelling parents, or poverty resulting from unemployment, may cause children to be frightened and badly behaved, or unable to attend in school. In the same way, causes are sought for adult crime; many people believe that circumstances are at least partly to blame for much of the crime in society. But if people's behaviour is largely the result of their circumstances, then they cannot be held responsible and blamed for their wrong-doing: their actions and behaviour are determined by forces which are largely outside their control. Some Christians find it difficult to reconcile this with the Church's teaching on sin, personal responsibility and judgement. Christianity teaches that people are responsible both for their own sins, and for their share in corporate wrong-doing. Theology has not yet formulated an adequate response to the problem of sin and evil in the modern world, nor defined the relationship between individual and corporate responsibility. Liberation theology, which has developed in

Latin America, and which we shall look at in more detail below, deals with one aspect of this problem, but provides only a partial answer.

ECUMENISM: REUNION AND DIVISION

The Ecumenical Movement began among Protestant denominations, but has since grown into something much wider. Two movements which were founded in the nineteenth century were important forerunners of the Ecumenical Movement: the Evangelical Alliance, founded in 1846, and the World Student Christian Federation, in 1895. Leaders from different Churches who later played an important part in the Ecumenical Movement first came to know and trust one another through working together in these earlier movements, and began to see the value of Christians working together.

The World Council of Churches (WCC) which was founded in 1948 brought together three strands of ecumenical activity. The first was the International Missionary Council (IMC) which had come into being in 1921 as the formally constituted 'continuation committee' to carry out the recommendations of the World Missionary Conference held in Edinburgh, Scotland, in 1910. This had been a meeting of representatives of almost all the major Protestant missionary societies. It was recognized that competition between missions was a waste of resources and a denial of the gospel, and that African and Asian Christians had no interest in the historical circumstances which had divided Churches in the West. The IMC held meetings every few years, and at the Jerusalem meeting of 1928 the expressions 'older' and 'younger' Churches were coined. A number of national missionary conferences were formed to continue the work of the IMC at a more local level.

The second strand was the 'Life and Work' movement which first met in 1925 to explore how Christians could relate their faith to the modern world, and to the new scientific culture which was emerging in the West. Those who were engaged in this discussion were mainly representatives of Western Protestantism, though the delegates from younger Churches to the 1937 meeting included such outstanding figures as Bishop V. S. Azariah of India, Y. Ichimura of Japan and Timothy Lew of China.

The third strand was 'Faith and Order' whose first meeting was held at Lausanne in Switzerland in 1927. This was formed to consider worship and teaching about the nature of the Church, and it had the most difficult task, for it was in these areas that the differences between the Churches had their roots. The Eastern Orthodox Churches were represented in this group, with full participation from 1961, and nine Roman Catholics were elected to the commission in 1968.

The first tangible results of this ecumenical activity were seen in 1925 when the United Church of Canada was formed, bringing together four different Churches. In England three separate groups of Methodists were reunited in 1932. Other Church unions have followed, and some will be mentioned in the following chapters, but these have been less important than the growth of friendliness and understanding which has developed among the major denominations, and the grass-roots understanding which has brought previously divided groups of Christians together in work and mission.

World War II delayed the formation of the WCC, and it was not inaugurated until 1948 in Amsterdam, three years after the end of the war in Europe. It was a triumph that Churches from countries which had recently fought one another were able to meet and overcome this division, as well as that parts of the Christian family which had been separated for centuries came together in friendship. In 1948 147 Churches from forty different countries took part. By the time of the fourth General Assembly of the WCC in 1968 the Orthodox Churches were strongly represented, and when the Assembly met in Nairobi, Kenya, in 1975 nearly 200 Churches from some ninety countries took part. (This number of Churches was actually *less* than in 1968 because of the various Church Unions which had taken place in the meantime.) There also was a strong group of official observers from the Roman Catholic Church at the Nairobi meeting, and the WCC was no longer dominated by the West.

But by 1975 there were signs that the West had begun to lose interest in ecumenism. Some Church union schemes had been successfully carried through, but others had foundered. The sticking points were seldom doctrinal: there were difficulties about the ownership of property, and people clung to old customs and did not want to change. In some places it became clear that the price of reunion would be a further division, as a section of a Church refused to join in and threatened to splinter off. The West was rapidly losing world dominance; Europeans felt uneasy and unsure of themselves, and were unwilling to take risks. Some groups of Americans, on the other hand, felt so sure of themselves that they could see no reason for making concessions.

Although the Roman Catholic Church does not belong to the WCC, it too has become involved in ecumenism. The Second Vatican Council (Vatican II), called by Pope John XXIII, which met in Rome from 1962 to 1965, inaugurated a new era in relations between Roman Catholics and other Christians. It made co-operation possible in many kinds of Christian activity from social work to Bible study and translation, and opened the way for some non-sacramental worship to take place jointly with other Christians. In a number of places, church buildings are shared, and talks on doctrine, worship and ministry are in progress between Roman Catholics and several other Churches.

Despite the 19th-century decline in churchgoing, thousands in Europe and N. America offered for missionary service. The Basel Mission in Switzerland trained men of all professions, like these young farmers and craftsmen, who kept up their practical skills while on their seminary course in the 1890s.

Below The Ecumenical Movement began among Protestant Churches, but soon became something much wider. When the General Assembly of the WCC met in Nairobi in 1975 the Orthodox Churches were strongly represented, and the Roman Catholic Church sent official observers.

Although there has been increased co-operation between those Churches whose roots are in the Reformation, new divisions have appeared. The sharpest divide is now between those Christians who are sometimes described as 'ecumenical' Christians, and those Christians who are ultra-conservative, or fundamentalist in theology, and who may be right-wing in politics as well. A number of such groups will have nothing to do with the WCC, and may even look upon it as the work of the devil. Such Christians are particularly numerous in the USA and West Germany, and are sending increasing numbers of missionaries to Asia, Africa and Latin America just at the time when the older missions have handed over responsibility to nationals. A part of the missionary motivation of many of these new conservative groups is to stop the spread of Communism, and some take action to support right-wing political parties, though they do not always realize that their support is political. It seems to them to be simply essential Christian action.

Some of these fundamentalist Christians are found in what is known as the 'house-church' movement. They reject what they describe as the 'institutionalized' and 'purely nominal' Christianity of the older Churches; but they are inevitably developing institutions of their own, and are often rigidly controlled by leaders whom they believe to be specially guided by the Spirit. When disagreements occur, new groupings form, and this quite often happens. In a world where change is taking place at a frightening speed, and where the old certainties have disappeared, they seek security and assurance in belonging to closely-knit groups of like-minded people who use the same forms of words to describe the same kinds of religious experience. They have a particularly conservative approach to the Bible which they try to interpret literally. Their greatest strength is that they take very seriously the call to personal evangelism, but they are much less often involved in other forms of Christian witness. Most of them totally reject the greater respect which most 'ecumenical' Christians now show towards other religions: this they consider to be a betrayal of the truth. The division between fundamentalist and ecumenical Christians threatens to become just as serious as the disagreements which have divided Christians in the past, and fundamentalists and ecumenicals each find it equally difficult to understand the other, or to recognize the other form of Christianity as true to the gospel. So while some barriers to Christian unity have melted away, new ones have arisen.

RENEWAL IN THE ROMAN CATHOLIC CHURCH

Vatican II not only opened up contacts between Roman Catholics and other Christians; it brought about widespread renewal within the

Catholic Church. One of the key words of the Council was '*aggiorna-mento*', or 'bringing up to date'. Those who met in council tried to see where the Spirit was leading the Roman Catholic Church in the modern world. One aspect of *aggiornamento* was liturgical renewal, and a cornerstone of this was the recognition that people need to be able to worship in their own languages. Although it had long been Catholic practice for parts of the liturgy (readings from the Bible; the sermon) to be in the vernacular language of the worshippers, much of the service had continued to be in Latin. Now the whole of the liturgy was simplified and translated. Not all Catholics were happy to lose the old and loved Latin forms (just as some Anglicans find it difficult to accept modern versions of the Book of Common Prayer). But many felt liberated, and were able to join more fully in worship than they had ever done in the past.

Another very important result of Vatican II was the encouragement of Bible reading and study, not only by the clergy, but by lay people as well.

STUDY SUGGESTIONS

WORDS AND MEANINGS

1. What is the meaning of each of the following terms, used to describe the standpoint regarding belief or practice of differing groups of Christians?
   (a) Evangelical (b) Ecumenical (c) Fundamentalist (d) Pentecostalist

2. There was misunderstanding about the word 'myth' (p. 10). Many people use it to mean 'a story which is not true'—which is the *secondary* meaning of the word given in most English dictionaries today. Look up the *primary* meaning of the word as given in a dictionary (or, if you can, in several). Then:
   (a) Think of any 'myth' relating to the traditional history or religion of your own country, and say how far you think the dictionary definition is appropriate to it.
   (b) Say how you would answer the question: 'If the account of the creation of the world as given in the OT is a myth, why should I believe any part of the accounts of Jesus's life and death in the NT to be historically true?'

REVIEW OF CONTENT

3. What were some of the changes brought about by nineteenth-century developments in science and technology, which affected the way Western people lived, and their attitude to religion in general and to Christianity in particular?

4. In what specific ways did these new ideas and attitudes undermine some Christians' faith in the truth of the Bible and its teaching?

5. (a) Give examples of some of the 'evangelistic and social activity' with which Christians in Europe and North America concerned themselves in the nineteenth century.
(b) What 'less happy' aspects of the Churches' activity appeared alongside the movements of renewal?

6. (a) What were some of the ways in which World War I changed people's ideas about themselves and the world in general?
(b) What were some of the ways in which World War II changed the political relationship between the countries of the West and the rest of the world?

7. Who was Dietrich Bonhoeffer, and in what way did his influence— and that of the 'Confessing Church'—act as a reconciling force after World War II?

8. (a) In what chief way does Marxist doctrine conflict with Christian belief?
(b) What has been the relationship between the Churches and government in Communist-ruled countries?

9. Name two Christian organizations set up to provide help and support to the needy and oppressed.

10. (a) What two movements founded in the nineteenth century can be seen as forerunners of the ecumenical movement, and why?
(b) Describe, briefly, with dates, the contribution of each of the following to the early development of the ecumenical movement, which led to the foundation of the World Council of Churches.
(1) The International Missionary Council (2) Life and Work (3) Faith and Order
(c) In what two particularly important ways have recent WCC assemblies differed from the inaugural meeting in 1948?
(d) Which Christian groups have continued to remain aloof from the WCC, and for what reasons?

11. What are some of the ways in which 'aggiornamento'—'up-dating', or renewal—has been taking place in the Roman Catholic Church since the Second Vatican Council in the 1960s?

DISCUSSION

12. 'In pre-industrial Europe religion had been a community affair with the Church at the centre' (p. 9). This is still true of some rural areas of Europe and North America. How far is it true of your own country? In what ways if any is the situation changing, or do you think it is likely to change, and with what effect on the Church?

13. In 1939 Dietrich Bonhoeffer refused to save himself by staying in the USA, but returned to Germany to serve the Confessing Church

and resist Nazism. In the fourth century St Athanasius caused some controversy when he wrote (in the light of Matt. 10.23): 'We should flee when persecuted, and hide'—though he also wrote: 'We should be ready to contend for the truth, even unto death.' What was the chief difference between Bonhoeffer's situation and his actions and that of the Christians suffering persecution in the fourth century? How do you think Christians suffering persecution today can decide whether to 'flee and hide' or to 'contend' or actively resist?

14. 'There is a strong belief in the West that everyone should be free . . . but people find it difficult to say what they mean by freedom' (p. 15). What do *you* mean by 'freedom'? How far do you think it is possible to achieve such freedom?

15. 'The problem for the West in the absence of agreed values is how to encourage responsibility and rebuild community' (p. 15). Some Christians favour involvement in social and political action; others believe in concentrating on individual evangelism. What is your opinion?

16. Psychologists teach that people's behaviour is the result of their circumstances, so they should not be blamed for wrong-doing. This conflicts with Christian teaching about sin, personal responsibility, and judgement. What is your opinion? How far is it reasonable to expect 'Christian' standards of behaviour from people who do not claim to be Christians, have probably never been taught what those standards are, and have no proper knowledge of what Christianity is really about?

17. By 1975 there were signs that the West had begun to lose interest in ecumenism, and some Fundamentalist Christian groups will have nothing to do with the WCC. Some others have left the mainstream Churches for the 'house-church' movement. What is the situation with regard to ecumenism in your country generally?—in your Church? What do you see as the strengths and weaknesses of (a) fundamentalist Christianity, (b) ecumenical Christianity? Which of the two do you see as truer to the gospel—as expressed perhaps in such passages as Matt. 10.16; John 13.34–35; and 1 Cor. 9.19–23?

2
North-East Asia
from material contributed by Chang Sik Lee, with V. E. W.
Hayward (on China) H. D. Beeby (Taiwan) and T. Hawthorn
(Hong Kong)

Our first area of study is North-East Asia, that is, China with Hong Kong and Taiwan, Japan, and Korea. (Readers possessing Volume 3 of this TEF Church History Guide may find it helpful to look again at pp. 132–137, describing the Roman Catholic missions to China and Japan between 1500 and 1800.) In the seventeenth century the emperor of Japan banned all foreign traders and missionaries after a serious uprising in which Christians were involved. Christians were fiercely persecuted, and Christianity in Japan seemed to have disappeared altogether. In China there were about 250,000 Christians at the beginning of the nineteenth century. Roman Catholic missionaries had worked in China since the fifteenth century, but the Church had suffered severe persecution and was still small. There were about eighty Chinese priests and a few foreign missionaries to minister to these Christians. There were no Protestants at all. During the nineteenth century both Roman Catholic and Protestant missionaries grew in number, as did the Chinese Christians, but throughout the century there were periods of persecution.

CHINA IN THE NINETEENTH CENTURY

1807–1844: A Time of Great Difficulty

Early in the nineteenth century the British and Foreign Bible Society became greatly concerned that there was no Protestant witness to the many millions of people who spoke Chinese, one of the world's most widely-used languages. The London Missionary Society (LMS) responded to the Bible Society's concern, and set out to recruit a missionary who would be able to translate the Scriptures into Chinese. The man appointed by LMS was Robert Morrison (1782–1834), and his arrival in China marks the beginning of the modern development of the Church there.

Morrison prepared himself for missionary work by learning medicine as well as theology, by starting to learn Chinese, and by copying out a dictionary of Chinese and a Roman Catholic version of most of the New Testament. He lived and worked in Canton which was the only port in China then open to foreign trade, and succeeded in finding two

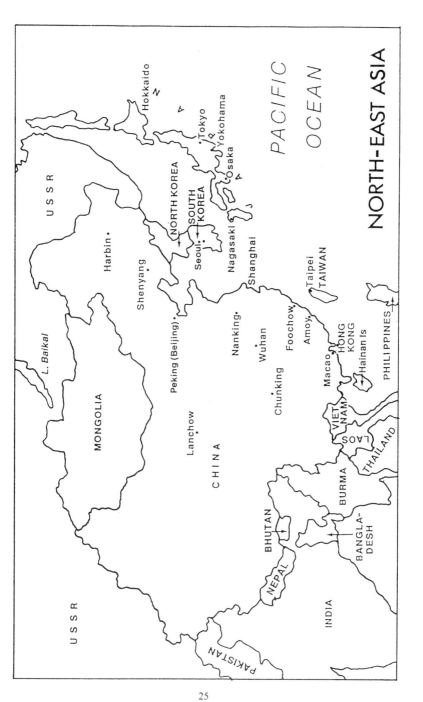

NORTH-EAST ASIA

Roman Catholic Christians who helped him to continue his study of the language. By 1819 he had made his own dictionary of the Chinese language and a first translation of the whole Bible. He and other Protestant missionaries used the Roman alphabet (the sort of letters used for English and most European languages) to write the Chinese language. The Chinese themselves wrote their language in beautiful but very complicated ideographs which took so long to master that relatively few people learnt to read. The missionaries wanted as many people as possible to be able to read the Bible, but Chinese scholars despised the Christians for not using the traditional Chinese method of writing. Chinese people today use a very much simplified version of the ancient script, because the government wants to encourage widespread literacy.

Morrison's first convert, named Tsae A-Ko, was baptized in 1814. After thirty years of Protestant missionary work there were still fewer than 100 Chinese converts, but one of them was a printer named Liang A-Fan (1789–1855). He worked secretly for Robert Morrison, and helped him to print the Chinese Bible. He was baptized in 1816 and ordained in 1823 as a Congregational minister, the first Chinese Protestant clergyman. Fifteen of the early Protestant converts had been educated at the Anglo-Chinese College which Morrison founded at Malacca. From the beginning Protestants were keen on education, and wrote and distributed booklets about the Christian faith. One of these was called *Good Words Exhorting the Age*. It consisted of passages of Scripture with explanations and comments, and was the work of Liang A-Fan.

The T'ai P'ing Movement

A Chinese named Hung Hsin-Ch'uan read Liang A-Fan's booklet and became very interested in what he found. He had received some Christian instruction, but had not been baptized. Hung started a movement to rid China of the corrupt Manchu rulers, to stop the smoking of opium which was doing great harm, and to teach the worship of one God. In this movement, which they called T-ai P-ing, meaning 'Great Peace', Hung and his followers practised baptism, kept Sunday, and adopted much Christian ethical teaching. They also kept many Chinese customs, including polygamy. The Roman Catholics opposed the movement, but some Protestants at first hoped that it would do great things for the spread of the gospel. One of Hung's praise songs went like this:

Praise God, the holy and heavenly Father;
Praise Jesus, the holy Lord and Saviour of the world;
Praise the Holy Spirit, the sacred spiritual force;

26

Praise the three persons who, united, constitute one true Lord! (quoted in S. C. Neill, *A History of Christian Missions*, 1970, p. 287.)

This is perfectly orthodox Christianity. But the T'ai P'ing movement turned into a revolutionary movement, and Hung hoped to make himself emperor. During the 1850s huge areas of the country were devastated by fighting, and as many as twenty million people are thought to have died. Roman Catholics were massacred because they would not accept the T'ai P'ing movement as Christian. Hung's followers were well-disciplined, and the Chinese government only brought the revolution to an end with British help. Scholars are still divided between those who think that T'ai P'ing was basically Christian, and those who think it was thoroughly evil. The Communist Revolution has been much more radical in its rejection of aspects of Chinese culture, and has also been willing to use violence to achieve its aims.

1844–1900: Treaties and Unrest

The Chinese did not want contact with the outside world, and in particular they wanted to prevent the import of opium from India. Treaties were made with foreign nations and then broken. In the end Western nations and Japan forced China to accept trade, and went to war with her to ensure that the treaties were kept. Between 1844 and 1862 a series of treaties gave the West certain trading rights and privileges in five Chinese ports, and in Hong Kong, which the British annexed. Both Roman Catholic and Protestant missionaries took advantage of these treaties, and France protected Catholic missionaries in China. Because of this, Christianity has often been associated with imperialism, and was therefore resented. French tactlessness resulted in the destruction of buildings and the murder of Chinese Catholic Christians and missionaries in a terrible massacre in Tientsin in 1870. Riots against all foreigners occurred from time to time during the remainder of the nineteenth century. Propaganda against the Christians was written and distributed. One anti-Christian tract ended with the words, 'Alas! If the doctrines of Jesus drive out the teaching of Confucius, what sort of world will it become? Let each of us draw the sword for vengeance' (quoted in C. Carey-Elwes, *China and the Cross*, 1957, p. 202).

From 1896 onwards Chinese hatred of foreigners increased. Parts of China had been seized by foreign powers, and Japan and Germany were especially feared. By this time, however, there were numbers of Chinese who thought that reform was urgently needed, and that Western-type education could help China. The Chinese people were

27

therefore divided. But the most powerful section of the population were the reactionaries led by the Dowager Empress. The uprising against foreigners which they led is known as the Boxer Rising. Resentment was focused on the missionaries and their converts. In 1900, 30,000 Chinese Roman Catholics and nearly fifty Roman Catholic missionaries were killed, as well as 2,000 Chinese Protestants and 200 Protestant missionaries. The rising was fiercely repressed by the Western powers and Japan, and China was ordered to pay for damage done to foreign-owned property. One missionary leader, however, refused to ask for or accept any money in compensation. He was James Hudson Taylor (1832–1905), founder of the China Inland Mission (CIM), the largest Protestant society in China.

Hudson Taylor and the China Inland Mission

Hudson Taylor had worked as a missionary in China for some years before he founded the China Inland Mission in 1865. This mission did not open schools or try to build up the Church. Its aim was to spread the gospel and make conversions as widely as possible throughout China. When a Christian community had developed, CIM missionaries would move on to start another. Taylor did not demand high standards of education of all his missionaries, though some of them became expert in the Chinese language and culture. They wore Chinese clothes and followed Chinese customs as far as possible. (The only other missionaries who as a group adopted Chinese dress were the Jesuits.) CIM missionaries were not much interested in spreading Western culture: Hudson Taylor clearly understood Chinese resentment of foreign customs being forced on them. Other missions sometimes criticized the CIM for not giving people enough Christian instruction, and thought they should have run schools and colleges as the other missions did. A further characteristic of the CIM was that it was interdenominational. Its missionaries came from many Protestant Churches, and in China they were grouped according to the Churches they came from.

CHINA IN THE TWENTIETH CENTURY

Political Events from 1900 to 1950

By the end of the nineteenth century there were about 40,000 Chinese Protestant Christians, and 750,000 Roman Catholics with over 500 Chinese Catholic priests. There was also a group of Orthodox Christians around Peking who had been converted by Russian Orthodox missionaries. In spite of civil war and invasions, the number of Christians grew greatly in the first half of the twentieth century.

Immediately after the Boxer Rising many Chinese realized that they must come to terms with the new situation, and they decided to acquire modern education. The examinations in Confucian learning by which a person qualified for the civil service were abolished in 1905 as being unsuitable in the modern world. The government of the Manchu rulers was weak and corrupt, and their rule was ended in 1911 when Sun Yat-Sen seized power. Sun Yat-Sen had been educated in a mission school, and wanted to reform his country with the help of Western ideas. But he proved unable to control or unite China, and there was increasing chaos as rival war-lords took power over different areas. A strong Anti-Christianity League grew up in opposition to his policies. In 1924 Russian Communists helped to organize the Nationalist Party, called in Chinese the 'Kuomintang'. In 1926 Chiang Kai-Shek succeeded Sun Yat-Sen as ruler, and the following year he attacked the Communists, who were forced to retreat to a northerly part of China where they remained confined for some years. In 1930 Chiang Kai-Shek was baptized as a Christian, and he encouraged the missions, especially in the work of education.

But there was still no peace. From 1931 onwards Japan tried to seize power over China, and in 1937 the Japanese invasion started. The Kuomintang was unable to defeat the invaders, and the Japanese were only defeated in 1946 at the end of World War II. Chiang Kai-Shek's government was accused of corruption and inefficiency, and in 1949 the Communists were able to seize power after sweeping through the whole country and getting rid of all who opposed them. Only in the island territory of Taiwan (Formosa), to which Chiang Kai-Shek withdrew along with some two million mainland Chinese, did Nationalist control continue (see pp. 37–39).

The Growth of the Church from 1900 to 1950

The first developments in the twentieth century were among the Protestants. The first National Christian Conference was held in 1907, the centenary of the beginning of Protestant missions in China. As we have seen, this had been a troubled and difficult hundred years, and the Protestant community was still small. There were no Chinese Christians at this conference, only missionaries, but it was followed by a movement which aimed to make the Church in China self-propagating, self-governing, and self-supporting (see p. 130). John R. Mott, a prominent leader of the Ecumenical Movement, visited China in 1912 and encouraged co-operation among Protestants. In 1922 a National Christian Council was formed, and within five years its leadership was firmly in Chinese hands. Its purpose was to 'foster and express the fellowship and unity of the Christian Churches in China'. One of the Chinese leaders was Dr Timothy T. Lew (1890–1947), who had studied at St John's University in Shanghai before going overseas to the USA for further study. He was ordained as a minister of the Congregational Church, and played an important part at the meeting in 1922 when the National Christian Council was formed. 'We must agree to differ, but resolve to love', he told the meeting. Dr Lew went on to become Chairman of the Religious Education Fellowship, and he founded and edited three theological journals. Dr Lew was Chairman of the Union Committee which, in 1936, produced a new hymnbook called *Chinese Hymns of Universal Praise*. He died of tuberculosis in the USA in 1947.

A second prominent Chinese Christian leader of this period was Dr Cheng Ching-Yi (1881–1939). He came from a Christian family, and his father was a Congregational minister. Cheng Ching-Yi followed his father's example and was ordained as a Congregational minister. Like Dr Lew he studied abroad, and while he was in England in 1903 he helped to translate the New Testament into Mandarin, one of the main forms of the Chinese language. In 1910 Cheng Ching-Yi attended the Edinburgh Conference (see p. 17), and surprised the delegates by telling them that Chinese Christians were not interested in the sort of differences which had divided the Churches in Europe. His career showed his strong commitment to ecumenism. For ten years, from 1924 to 1934, he was Secretary of the National Christian Council, and then became founder of the Church of Christ in China, which brought together several small Christian denominations. In 1918 he helped to organize an interdenominational missionary society to enable Chinese Christians to evangelize their own people. From 1928 to 1938 he was one of the Vice-Presidents of the International Missionary Council (see p. 17).

From 1910 onwards Chinese Christians began to form Churches which would be free from mission control. These usually laid great emphasis on the Holy Spirit and His gifts. One of them was the Jesus Family, which was founded in 1922, and was organized on Chinese lines. Its members practised strict poverty, and were energetic evangelists.

The number of Christians continued to grow until 1949. In 1900 there were some 750,000 Roman Catholics; by 1912 there were nearly twice as many (1,300,000), and about 800 Chinese priests. One of the missionaries, Fr Vincent Lebbe (1877–1940), urged Catholics to adopt new missionary methods, saying they should abandon the old methods of attracting people by charitable works or gifts, and of trying to civilize 'backward' peoples. Instead they should approach the Chinese as equals, and win them to Christ by demonstrating the love of Christ in their own lives. Fr Lebbe also insisted that the Church should become less foreign—'it must be Chinese or perish,' he said. As a result of Fr Lebbe's work, the Roman Catholic Church became much more involved in education, and ran hundreds of secondary schools and several universities. Greater efforts were made to train Chinese priests, and missionaries began to hand over responsibility to them. In the next twenty years the number of priests doubled, and many women became nuns. In 1939 the Roman Catholic Church made it possible for the first time for Chinese Catholics to join the civil service. Previously they had been forbidden to do so because all civil servants had to pay respect to the great Chinese sage and philosopher, Confucius. Now the Vatican recognized that these rituals were not worship, which should be given to God alone, but simply a mark of respect and honour in which Christians might join. (The public veneration of Confucius has since been abolished by the Communists.)

In 1946 the Vatican gave the Roman Catholic community in China full status as a Church, with its own bishops and archbishops. Cardinal Tien was the first Chinese to be honoured with a cardinal's hat.

The Protestant Churches had greater difficulty in training clergy. They did not demand such high standards of education, and this meant that educated Chinese did not always respect Protestant clergy. Churches had to co-operate to run theological colleges, as some were too small to run one on their own.

The Anti-Christian League and Opposition to Imperialism

While these developments were taking place, however, resentment against the unequal treaties and Western imperialism was growing. The Anti-Christian League, which had been formed in protest at Sun Yat-Sen's policies, became a nation-wide organization. Its members resented mission control of Western-type education, wanting all education to be controlled by Chinese, and they won the support of cultural societies and political parties. In 1925 British soldiers fired on a group of students who were demonstrating against the unequal treaties, and this increased hatred. The National Christian Council and student Christian organizations sympathized with the Nationalists, and in 1927 the National Conference of Christian Students decided to oppose Western imperialism and the unequal treaties. Many students, including Christians, became Communist, feeling that this was the only way to oppose imperialism.

The Japanese Invasion and World War II

During the Japanese invasion and occupation of China, missionaries from European countries at war with Japan were imprisoned by the Japanese. (In World War II Japan was on the side of Germany and Italy. Many of the missionaries were British, French, and American, to whom Japan was thus opposed.) In spite of the enmity between the Chinese and the Japanese occupying forces, when Chinese and Japanese Christians met they sometimes became friends because of their shared faith. Chinese Nationalists objected to this. On the other hand, Christians won the approval of many for the way in which they worked to relieve suffering during the war. After the war ended, many missionaries returned to China, and conversions to Christianity increased. Chinese missionary societies were founded, and Chinese Christians took responsibility for evangelizing their own people. But peace did not last long. As already noted, in 1949 the Nationalist government of Chiang Kai-Shek fell to the Communists. At first many Christians welcomed this, believing that only the Communists could free the country from imperialism. Also, the new government promised freedom of worship.

CHINA UNDER COMMUNIST RULE

The First Period of Communist Rule: 1949–1966

Under Communist rule Christians soon found themselves divided and in great difficulty. The Roman Catholic Church was totally opposed to Communism, and was the first to suffer. In the years immediately before the Communists gained control of the whole country, thousands of Chinese Catholics and many missionaries were killed in the fighting, and in the areas taken over by the Communists. Fr Lebbe was spared, but seven Catholics who were with him acting as stretcher-bearers were buried alive by the Communists.

Once the Communists were in power, they told the Churches to purge themselves of all imperialism, and Christian socialists were appointed to lead and control them. Y. T. Wu, a leader of the YMCA, worked with forty other Chinese Christians to produce 'A Christian Manifesto'. In this they called on the Churches to support the Communist government, to get rid of all imperialist influences, especially American imperialism, to work for peace, and try to unite all groups of Christians. The Communists called on everyone to purge society of all 'incorrect' attitudes, and, as part of this process, people were encouraged to accuse themselves and one another of faults. Compulsory meetings were held at which accusations were made, and the Communist government refused to recognize the right of the Church to exist unless the Churches held such meetings. So Christians got caught up in the process: a daughter accused her father, and Chinese Christians accused missionaries. In October 1951 the Seventh Day Adventists met and condemned three of their leaders to death. As a result, the Church was recognized and allowed to continue. Y. T. Wu described this as 'forceful demonstration'. The China Inland Mission, however, and many other missionary societies, withdrew all their missionaries from

China, because their presence seemed to be a danger and embarrassment to the Chinese Church. At first the Roman Catholic Church decided to do the same, but then changed its policy and ordered the missionaries to stay. The Communist government tried to persuade the Catholics to set up a Church which would be independent of Rome and of the Pope, but they refused to break their ties with the rest of the Church. By its nature the Church is universal—that is what the word 'Catholic' means. A great many missionaries and Chinese Christians were killed because of this refusal.

It was at this point that Chinese Christians launched the 'Three-Self Movement', to achieve self-propagation, self-government, and self-support for their Churches, and a similar movement was set up within the Roman Catholic Church. Missions in China and elsewhere in the world had worked for years to plant indigenous Churches which would be all these things, but their efforts sometimes lacked urgency, and converts found it tempting to go on accepting dependency for the sake of gaining material support. Now, however, the achievement of self-government, self-propagation and self-support became a matter of life and death. Unless the Chinese Churches could work together to prove themselves truly Chinese and independent of foreign imperialisms, they could not continue to exist. Richard Deutsch, a theologian who taught for a number of years at Chung Chi College in Hong Kong and revisited China in 1984, reported that the Chinese Christians felt they had achieved more than mere survival: 'They would claim that the Marxist take-over made them experience "Liberation" from dependence on outside sources for money, personnel, and strategy. Now they feel they can become "themselves", which means, of course, "Chinese"'. Deutsch goes on to say:

> The Three-Self Movement had from the outset in 1950 the task of educating individuals and groups to accept each other. They are still working at it. In many places some groups will do everything together although they still remember their former identities as Methodist, Baptist, Anglican/Episcopalian, Presbyterian, Lutheran. Yet they can work together. Others still insist on separate services at least occasionally: Little Flock and Adventists among others ... Administration, finance and personnel are being shared, otherwise no single group would stand a chance.

In 1954 the National Christian Council met and was renamed the National Christian Conference (see pp. 29, 30). By 1960 when it met again some 500,000 of the 600,000 Protestants known to exist in China at that time had joined it. It was unable to meet again until 1980.

During all this period it was difficult for those outside China to discover what was going on in the Chinese Church. On the one hand Bishop K. H. Ting visited Britain in 1956 and reported that the Church was strong and growing, and some people who were able to visit China made similar reports. On the other hand there was news that some pastors and lay people had been imprisoned and forced to accept Communist teaching against their will. Roman Catholic priests who had refused to break their ties with Rome remained in prison. In 1957 the Reverend Marcus Cheng, who had been a leader of the Three-Self Movement, spoke out before the Chinese People's Political Consultative Conference in Peking, saying that Churches were not allowed to hold services, and that church buildings and furniture had been confiscated by government. He said that freedom of religion did not really exist, and that the Communists reviled the Christian God. For a short time Mao Tse-Tung allowed people to voice their criticisms of the government. In May 1957 he declared, 'Let a hundred flowers bloom and let a hundred schools of thought contend.' But this period of freedom of expression was short-lived. Those who did speak out were accused of being reactionary, and a campaign was launched against them. The government closed many churches and tried to force others to amalgamate. In several regions this was achieved.

The Cultural Revolution (1966–1976) and its Aftermath

By far the worst period for Christians, and for members of all religions, in China, was the era of the Cultural Revolution, when all cultural activity came to a halt, educational standards fell disastrously, Muslims were fiercely oppressed, not a single Christian or Buddhist place of worship remained open, sacred books were burnt, and even the tomb of Confucius was vandalized. The Cultural Revolution did not stop there: 'Everything which gave colour, variety and amusement to life was summarily forbidden so that the Chinese people should have no distraction from "making revolution"' (Philip Short, *The Dragon and the Bear*, 1982, p. 188). This appallingly destructive episode in China's history came to an end when Mao Tse-Tung died in September 1976, and a reversal of the policies of the previous ten years got under way.

Since then it has become apparent that in spite of the persecution of the Cultural Revolutionary years in particular, Christianity has survived in China, though it is not easy to get a full picture of the strength and state of the Church there. The Roman Catholic Church is not able to maintain links with Rome as Catholics do in the rest of the world, and some priests have remained in prison because of their continuing loyalty to the Pope. Some Protestants have been able to visit Churches in other countries and receive visitations. Many church buildings have been reopened for worship by congregations who for years had to meet secretly in people's homes or out of doors. Bibles may be printed again,

Robert Morrison, LMS missionary and Bible translator, working with Chinese colleagues.

Today a young Chinese priest distributes Holy Communion during Christmas celebrations at Nantang Church (*young* Chinese priests are still extremely rare).

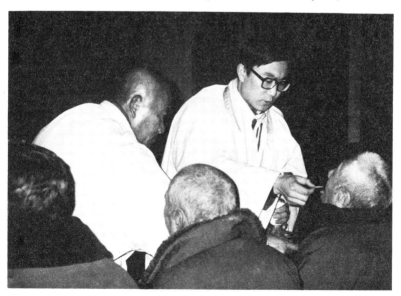

and training for the ministry has been restarted. It is clear that the Chinese Church survived the difficult years since 1949, and has even been spiritually strengthened, though its members are still only a tiny proportion of the total population, less than half of one per cent.

TAIWAN

The Nineteenth Century: New Beginnings

The first missionary to Taiwan was a Dutch Reformed minister who landed in 1627. The Dutch Mission of which he was part—one of the earliest of all Protestant missions—ended with the expulsion of the Dutch in 1661. A gap of almost 200 years followed, until Spanish Dominican Catholic priests arrived in the middle of the nineteenth century. They were followed by English Presbyterians in 1865, who crossed the Formosa Straits from their mission field in South Fukien and began work in South Taiwan. In 1872 the first Canadian Presbyterian missionary arrived, and agreed to concentrate his work on the north of the island. 'Comity' agreements amongst Protestant missions not to compete with each other ensured that other denominations did not enter Taiwan, thus leaving the island to Spanish Dominicans and Presbyterians until almost the middle of the twentieth century.

Beginning in villages of mixed race—Chinese and 'aboriginal'—the Presbyterian Church developed slowly but firmly. Early in its existence it added to the original medical and evangelistic work, by setting up schools, theological colleges and facilities for printing in both Chinese and the Romanized script of the Taiwanese dialect which had originated in South Fukien.

Since 1661, Taiwan had been ruled without much concern or enthusiasm by the Manchu dynasty in China. In 1895 this ended with the island's cession to Japan, when it became part of the Japanese Empire. This example of Asian colonialism paralleled its Western counterparts and brought both good and bad effects. One of the good effects was the opportunity given to the Church to benefit from Japanese theological education and religious publishing, both of which were much further advanced than in China. With the beginning of World War II the Presbyterian missionaries were obliged to leave. But because of good theological training, a long tradition of local clergy and a largely literate Church, the two synods of North and South were not weakened by the loss. They were actually strengthened, as they had been brought to a stage when they could benefit by standing alone. The Church came of age during the War.

Taiwan Since World War II

After the War the missionaries were invited back. On their return, despite the hardships of war, they discovered a mature Church on the plains, and the beginnings of a totally new Church amongst the mountain aborigines. This latter expanded rapidly and before very long a majority of the quarter million aborigines had joined with either a Roman Catholic or a Protestant Church.

The defeat of Japan meant that the islanders exchanged one form of Asian colonialism for another, for the allies invited the Nationalist Government of China to be the occupying power. The occupation rapidly turned into a takeover, and from being a part of the Japanese Empire Taiwan became a province of China. In 1949, with the defeat of the Nationalists by the Chinese Communists, the island became the only province of China under Nationalist control. These political changes were accompanied by great changes in the fortunes of the Church. Many Christians from the mainland came over with the government and its military forces. They quickly established Mandarin-speaking Churches, in some cases taking over the buildings which had been occupied by Japanese Christians. Even more significant was the great number of 'refugee' missionaries from China who flocked to Taiwan. A small Roman Catholic and a small Presbyterian Church were soon joined by priests, nuns, ministers and evangelists from almost every order and type of Christian Church. There was much confusion as unheard-of forms of Christianity and unfamiliar doctrines threatened the peaceful scene. But with the confusion there was great growth. Churches of every kind, new schools, new hospitals, even new universities proliferated. In two decades the picture had changed almost beyond recognition. Though still a small minority, Christians had become increasingly articulate and influential, with a significance in society much greater than might be expected from their numbers, which amount to no more than five per cent of the total population.

The coming of many new denominations and movements in the post-war years resulted in much misunderstanding and tension. Unwelcome teachings, cultural differences between aborigines, Taiwanese and mainlanders, as well as a suspicion of ecumenicity in general, made co-operation difficult. An additional problem was the division along language lines which separated those who worshipped in the languages of the island from those who used Mandarin Chinese. This division corresponded to a difference of opinion on political matters, and on the direction that government policies ought to take. The Nationalist claim to be the government of China was supported by most Mandarin speakers, while native Christians held other views. All, however, were united in the determination that Taiwan should not become part of the Chinese State, nor be governed from Peking.

An attempt in 1971 by a representative ecumenical group to speak on behalf of the majority of Taiwan's inhabitants was foiled, and finally it was the Presbyterians alone who issued a statement in 1972 demanding self-determination by the people and increasing democratization. This was followed by further statements in 1975 and 1977, the latter speaking openly of an independent Taiwan. This activity meant that the security forces paid special attention to the Presbyterian Church, and finally in 1979 the General Secretary, Dr C. M. Kao, and several others were arrested and imprisoned. This increasing involvement in social and political matters has been similar to movements in many parts of the world; the closest parallels being with contemporary events in South Korea and the Philippines.

A period of rapid growth in all the Churches during the fifties and sixties levelled off during the seventies. The reasons, no doubt, were numerous, but the slowing down coincided with the phenomenal growth in industrial development and prosperity. Have the 'western disease' and the acids of modernity begun to affect this very recent member of the 'rich man's club'?

Taiwan's Christianity: Special Features

Parallels with other Churches have already been noted. Taiwan's Christianity is not unique, but it has its own special features:

1. A Scottish respect for education in the early missionaries and a love of religious scholarship, combined with the Japanese connection, produced a theologically mature Church and a well-trained ministry, competent, assured and confident. The gospel was received joyously as Asian good news to an Asian situation. Western missionaries were welcome heralds and not a cultural threat.

2. Absence of the xenophobia (fear of foreigners) and anti-Western feeling shown by China and Japan. This is partly due to Taiwan's unusual history, which the islanders see as one of 'Asian colonialism'. First they were ruled by the Manchus, then by the Japanese, followed by the Nationalist Chinese, with more recently the threat of absorption by the Chinese Communists. This colonial past has much to do with the growth and strength of the Church in Taiwan.

3. Many factors, including the youth and frailty of the Christian cause amongst Chinese, had contributed to Churches on the mainland and amongst overseas Chinese in South-East Asia being unresponsive to social, political and national affairs. On the whole, pietism of various forms was the rule. The pattern was broken in Taiwan in the early 1970s when, like neighbouring Protestants in that other victim of Asian imperialism—Korea—they affirmed the Lordship of Christ over the whole of life by speaking on behalf of the whole nation of Taiwan.

4. The political protest and the related 'new theologies' have, with few exceptions, been soundly based in Scripture and little affected by

political ideologies of right or left. This has resulted in social and political concern which in no manner threatens the fundamentals of the historic faith. It has been firm adherence to the latter which has prompted the former, and which continues to be its inspiration and critique. This balance of sound theology, evangelical fervour, and intense concern with public affairs provides an example that many other regions could do well to follow.

HONG KONG

We have already seen that for a time Macao was the base for Christian missionary work in China (Vol. 3, p. 132). From the middle of the nineteenth century Hong Kong replaced Macao in this role. Ceded by China to the British in 1842, with a fine natural harbour, Hong Kong became an international trading, commercial, financial and industrial centre. The island and nearby coastal region, though small in area even with the 'New Territories' leased to Hong Kong by China in 1898, together form a densely populated city state.

Under British Rule the Chinese inhabitants soon became increasingly involved in all aspects of the life of Hong Kong except that of government. Great Chinese enterprises, as well as foreign ones, were built up. Though captured by the Japanese in World War II, Hong Kong quickly recovered afterwards. The flexibility, ingenuity and drive of its people is well illustrated by the levelling of hills to build the airport out into the harbour.

The People's Republic of China has recognized the importance of Hong Kong as a trading centre and outlet to the rest of the world. An Agreement made with the British promised that Hong Kong's activities and way of life should continue unchanged until 1997, when the lease granted in 1898 will come to an end, and Hong Kong, with the coastal territories, will be returned to China.

Nineteenth-Century Developments

From the beginning, Christian institutions had been built up in the Colony on British lines, including the Church of England as part of the 'establishment'. The first English bishop in China, appointed in 1849, was George Smith of Hong Kong, who set up St Paul's College for Christian boys for the work of the Church.

The Roman Catholic Church also arrived in the Colony early on, and so did the London Missionary Society, which though interdenominational was supported largely by Congregationalists. The Roman Catholics started a seminary for training boys for the priesthood, and sisters came to staff schools and welfare organizations. Church buildings were put up, and eventually a cathedral. The LMS similarly offered training in schools, and initiated medical work. Congregations were gathered, and some of the church buildings are now long past their centenaries. The LMS printing press produced Scriptures (aided by the British and Foreign Bible Society) and other Christian literature and school textbooks.

As time passed, Churches founded by missions from many lands made their witness in Hong Kong, and cared for the needy. In the nineteenth and early twentieth centuries emigrants from mainland China passed through Hong Kong on their way to the rest of the world, and in times of difficulty there were many refugees. All these strained both Hong Kong's economy and its living space. So there came to be a great contrast between the life-style of the people enjoying great riches and the poverty and overcrowding suffered by families living in slums on land or in small boats permanently moored. Following the Communist 'Liberation' in China in 1949 people crossed the border in such numbers that the government of the Colony housed them first in simple camps, and then in great tower-blocks of flats, even creating new towns in the New Territories. At all stages the Churches tried to provide a ministry for the changing population. There are parishes of 40,000 people all living in high-rise buildings, and Church workers have many stairs to climb! Some of the Church school buildings are shared by two schools in shifts, and clinics are run on the ground floors of apartment blocks. The colonial government and the Churches have traditionally co-operated in educational, medical and social work, and in training at all levels.

The early introduction of training led to the ordination of the first Chinese Protestant minister in 1818, followed by many others, worthy and faithful, both ordained and lay. The story of the Roman Catholic Church in Hong Kong is the same. As on the mainland, Chinese Christians have been influential out of proportion to their numbers. As we saw, Sun Yat-Sen, the great leader of the nation, became a Christian in Hong Kong in 1884.

In the second half of the nineteenth century Roman Catholic sisters staffed orphanages, saving castaway girl babies from death, and the Churches generally pioneered the education of girls and the training of women as teachers and nurses, thus contributing to the emancipation of Chinese women.

The temptation for Christian missionaries to adhere to the culture, structures and methods of their homelands was sometimes too strong. Though English is now an international language, its use as the medium of teaching did exclude many young people from the schools and colleges, and institutions based on Western models and with foreign leadership also hindered the emergence of Chinese responsibility and indigenous development. On the other hand, by the turn of the century Hong Kong's wealth was already encouraging Church self-support, and the influx of trained Christians following the Communist 'Liberation' on the mainland strengthened the trend to self-government.

New Trends in the Twentieth Century

The great variety of Protestant Church life which developed in the nineteenth century continued in the twentieth, but new trends also began to emerge. The YMCA and YWCA cut across the denominations, and union Churches appeared. As elsewhere, the Churches not only worked together, they also sought ways of ecumenical advance. There are opportunities too, in Hong Kong, for Christians to have dialogue with people of other faiths, especially with Buddhists. On a hill in the New Territories there is To Fung Shan, a Christian centre for the study of Chinese religion and culture, to which visitors come from all around the world.

The Church in Hong Kong has occasionally broken out from the colonial situation. During World War II, when priests were unable to reach certain Anglican congregations, Bishop R. O. Hall ordained a Chinese woman Church worker so that they might not be deprived of the sacraments, and thus raised for the Anglican Communion the question of the ordination of women. The United Christian Hospital in Hong Kong has an internal organization of all staff, porters and cleaners as well as doctors and nurses, with joint responsibility for the work of the hospital. And all staff are trained, while serving the local community in their various callings, to be links in two-way communication. The old pyramid of power has been replaced by neighbourly fellowship. When the Colony returns to the government of the mainland its Churches will play their part in life and witness, and bring in their experience of contact with the Church worldwide.

JAPAN

After foreigners were banned from Japan in the seventeenth century, the country remained closed to missionaries and traders until the mid-nineteenth century. Then the rulers of Japan decided that their country could not remain isolated from the rest of the world any longer. They feared that if they refused to allow the West to trade, force might be used against them, and they also wanted the benefits of Western science and technology. They recognized that trade could be profitable to them, so they entered into treaties with America and other Western countries. The American Ambassador at the time, Townsend Harris, was a devout Christian, and he worked hard to get permission for foreigners to be allowed to live in certain ports, and to have freedom to practise their religion there. However, missionaries were not permitted to enter the rest of the country, and Japanese were forbidden by law to become Christians.

The 'Hidden Christians'

By 1856 Roman Catholic missionaries had already begun work on the Riu Kiu Islands to the south of Japan. As soon as possible they returned to Nagasaki, scene of their earlier missions, and built a church. In November 1856 the missionary priest there, Fr Petitjean, was greatly surprised when fifteen Japanese came to Mass. He soon learnt that there were many other Christians in the area. The persecutions of the seventeenth century had not, after all, destroyed the Japanese Church. Many of its members had secretly continued to practise their religion, and had handed it on to their descendants. Several thousand 'hidden Christians' lived in the hills and islands around Nagasaki. About 10,000 of them rejoined the Roman Catholic Church now that it was once more present in Japan, but a still larger number decided not to do so. Over the centuries they had developed their own way of life and worship, and they did not want to change.

The law still forbade Japanese to become Christians, and the Japanese government was shaken to discover that, in spite of persecution and government decrees, thousands of Japanese had retained their faith throughout the years. For the next few years they gave these hidden Christians a hard time, and about 3,000 of them were exiled to other parts of Japan. However, in 1873 all the laws restricting Christianity were abolished. The rulers of Japan wanted to make new trade agreements with America and the West, and they were willing to risk missionaries and Christian influence rather than lose any of the advantages which they hoped to gain through these treaties. We should note here that Japan never came under colonial rule. Trade and change were freely accepted, and not forced on the country by colonial powers.

Nihon Kirisuto Kokwai

By this time there was already a Japanese Church in existence as a result of modern missionary work, besides the hidden Christians. Some Japanese living in the treaty ports where foreigners were allowed had become Christians, and in 1872 they had established the Nihon Kirisuto Kokwai, or 'Japanese Church of Christ'. A missionary was its first pastor, but the idea of the Japanese founders was that this Church would be for all Japanese who became Christians, so that Japan might avoid the divisions which separated Christians in the West from one another. In 1878 this Church founded the Evangelical Society of Japan through which Japanese Christians would take the gospel to their own people. But Nihon Kirisuto Kokwai did not succeed in saving Japan from the divisions of Western Christianity. By the end of the nineteenth century missions from various Protestant Churches were at work, and had made converts to their own denominations.

Education and Church Growth

The Japanese had a written culture and a highly developed educational system of their own, but when missionaries introduced Western-style education it proved extremely popular because of the desire of the Japanese to learn technological skills. The rulers of Japan came from the *samurai* or warrior class, and *samurai* families sent their children to be educated at mission schools. The result was that some of the first converts were from the *samurai*. Although Protestant missionaries in particular presented the gospel as a way of attaining individual salvation, many of the converts were more interested in the ethical teaching of the Gospels, and saw Christianity as a possible way of national and social renewal. Western technology would change people's ways of living and working; new ideals and beliefs would be needed if the changes were not to destroy Japan. They did not want to give up Japanese culture, but they saw that it needed renewing.

Some of the schools and colleges founded by the missions and Churches in the nineteenth century later became Japan's leading modern universities. The oldest university in Japan, however, was founded, not by a missionary, but by a Japanese Christian. J. H. Neesima (1843–1890) came from a *samurai* family, and in 1864, while the law still forbade Japanese to become Christians, he succeeded in getting to America, where he went to college and then to a theological seminary. In 1874 he returned to Japan and founded several Christian congregations and a school in the country's ancient capital city of Kyoto. This school, Doshisha, became Doshisha University.

The Imperial University in Tokyo, Japan's modern capital, also had a Christian foundation, having developed from a school founded by an American missionary, G. H. F. Verbeck, a gifted man who was trusted by court officials who came to him for advice on drafting modernizing legislation. Sophia University, also in Tokyo, is a Roman Catholic foundation which developed into a university in 1913.

These Christian schools and colleges became very important for the growth of the Church, and in the early days the Church had more student members than adult members. Christian literature also developed rapidly. Books written in the West were translated by Japanese scholars, and soon Japanese Christians were producing literature of their own. Theological schools and seminaries trained Church leaders, and soon reached a high standard.

The fastest period of Church growth was in the 1880s. In 1883

Doshisha University School of Theology, Japan

Taipei Theological Seminary, Taiwan

Anglican Theological College, Seoul, Korea

Chung Chi College, Chinese University of Hong Kong

Japanese theological schools founded in the 19th century soon reached a high standard, and the work of colleges like those above (all shown as they were in the 1960s) was further developed with help from the WCC's Theological Education Fund (p. 172).

Protestant missionaries held a missionary conference at which Japanese Christians were present. Later the same year the Japanese Church held its own national Christian conference, attended by many ordinary Christians as well as official delegates. A spirit of revival was first seen at the missionaries' conference, and was even more marked at the national Christian conference which followed. People re-dedicated themselves to service and to evangelism, and the results of this were soon apparent among groups of Protestant Christians. The new spirit swept through Doshisha campus, for instance. Huge meetings were held in schools, in public halls, and even out of doors, and the gospel was preached to many who were outside the Church.

Between 1882 and 1888 the number of Protestant Christians increased fivefold, from 5,000 to over 25,000, faster than ever before or since. The average Church congregation grew from forty-two members to 106, and many congregations became self-supporting. New schools were also established during these years.

In the 1890s Church growth slowed somewhat, and some of the enthusiasm for Western education died away as Japanese took a renewed interest in their own culture. But steady growth continued, and by 1914 there were about a quarter of a million Christians altogether (103,000 Protestants, 70,000 Roman Catholics, and 32,000 Orthodox).

The Orthodox Church in Japan was started by Fr (later Archbishop) Nikolai Kasatkin (died 1912), a chaplain to the Russian Consulate, who also worked as a missionary. The Orthodox Church never had many missionaries in Japan: it quickly trained Japanese priests. One of the first converts was a man who came to see Fr Nikolai intending to kill him because the *samurai* thought he had come to enslave the people. Instead of killing Fr Nikolai, the man was converted, and became one of the first Japanese priests. The Orthodox suffered a setback in 1904 and 1905 when Russia and Japan were at war, but Fr Nikolai told the Japanese to be loyal to their own country, and he was able to remain at work. By 1914 only one Russian was left: Fr Nikolai himself, by then an archbishop. Under him were thirty-five Japanese priests, assisted by 106 catechists, to serve 266 congregations, with eighty-two students studying for the priesthood. The years after Fr Nikolai's death were difficult for the Orthodox Church in Japan, as the Russian Church was unable to support the mission. By the mid-1970s the Orthodox Church had 25,000 members in 108 congregations, organized into three dioceses linked with the Orthodox Church in Moscow.

Japanese Independent Christian Movements

Mukyokai, the 'No-Church Church', was started by a Japanese Christian named Uchimura Kanzo (1861–1930). He was converted when a student at Sapporo Agricultural School, and started Mukyokai after deciding to leave the government school where he was a teacher, in order to give all his time to Bible teaching. Mukyokai was not a Church: it had no organization or sacraments. It was a wholly Japanese movement which placed great emphasis on Bible study. Uchimura Kanzo's writings were frequently reprinted, and they spread widely.

One of Japan's best known Christian leaders was Toyohiko Kagawa (1888–1960). He came from a wealthy family, but his parents died when he was young and he had an unhappy childhood. He was sent to a mission school where he received the affection he lacked at home, and became a Christian. While still a theological student in Kobe he decided to make his home in the slums and try to help the very poor. Kagawa believed that rapid industrialization was the cause of the poverty he found in the slums, and tried to apply his Christian faith to the reform of society. He helped people to form trade unions and co-operative movements, and he supported social settlements. He wanted to bring about necessary change through love and by non-violent means. Kagawa earned his living by writing novels and poems, as well as books on social conditions and meditations on the Scriptures. In several cities he worked with the authorities to clear away the slums. He was also a great preacher and evangelist, and became the leader of the Christian social movement known as the Kingdom of God Movement.

World War II brought a difficult time for Japanese Christians. Many missionaries were interned, and the government imposed controls on the Churches and forced them to unite, preferring to have only one Christian organization to deal with. The body that came into being was called the United Church of Christ. After the war the Anglicans, Baptists, Lutherans and Salvation Army broke away from the United Church, but it still remained the largest Protestant Church in Japan, with 200,000 members in 1970. The Roman Catholic Church was centred around the city of Nagasaki on the southern island of Kyushu, one of the two Japanese cities that were the targets of atomic bombs at the end of the War. In spite of this appalling setback, the Catholic Church has continued to grow. By 1960 there were 227,500 Roman Catholics served by 416 Japanese priests and 3,359 religious sisters, and fifteen years later the number of Catholics had risen to 650,000.

Although the number of Japanese Christians is small, a much larger number of Japanese are interested in Christianity and read the Scriptures than are actually members of Churches. A Buddhist leader who attended a Roman Catholic conference stated, 'Whether I shall ever be baptized is not for me to say, but one thing is certain: in my own mind I am already an anonymous Christian' (quoted in D. Barrett, *World Christian Encyclopaedia*, OUP 1982, p. 420). He is typical of a number of Japanese who are interested in the teachings of Christianity though not in the organized Churches. Many students report an interest in Christian teachings.

Japan has become known since World War II for an enormous growth of new religious movements as well as for its industrial success. These new religious movements draw on Buddhism and Shinto, which are the traditional religions of Japan, and some also on Christianity. They are an indication of the way in which modern Japanese are seeking for answers to life and for a faith to live by. The Christian Churches are active in evangelism, and Roman Catholics and Protestants are increasingly seeking ways of working and witnessing together.

KOREA

The earliest Christian contacts with Korea go back to the sixteenth century, when invading Japanese armies included some Christians who made a few Korean converts. In the late eighteenth century a group of Koreans made an official visit to Peking in China. One of them, Lee Sung Hoon, was converted through the Jesuit mission at the emperor's court, and was baptized. When he returned to Korea in 1784 he began to spread the faith. Ten years later a Chinese missionary priest, Fr James Choo Moon Mo, entered Korea, and found some 4,000 Korean Christians awaiting him. These Roman Catholic Christians existed under great difficulties, and there were periodic outbreaks of persecution in which more than a hundred people were martyred. By 1865 the Catholic Church had almost been wiped out. In 1882 Korea signed a treaty with the USA, and American Protestant missionaries entered the country. Within a few years there was a ready response, though they met with some official opposition. By 1910 there were some 30,000 members of the Presbyterian and Methodist Churches. From the beginning the Korean Christians were encouraged to know the Bible thoroughly, to witness to Christ among their neighbours and work-mates, to support an indigenous ministry, to be responsible for building their own churches in their own architectural style, and to develop a Church which did not rely on missionary help from outside. In the years up to 1950 Protestants were responsible for most of the missionary work in Korea, and the Presbyterian and Methodist Churches were predominant. After 1950 Catholic work was strengthened, and since then the Roman Catholic Church has greatly increased in numbers, though it remains much smaller than the total of the Protestant Churches.

A Land of Divisions in Church and State

In 1910 Korea again came under Japanese rule, and as Christians would not acknowledge the Japanese emperor by joining in Shinto worship, they had a difficult time. They suffered severely for taking part in a nationalist uprising in 1919. During World War II they suffered more severe repression. At the end of the war the country was divided between Soviet and American occupying forces, and the division has continued ever since. Many Christians fled from the Communist-ruled North Korea, and Christianity no longer officially exists there, though groups of hidden Christian are known to have survived. In South Korea missionaries were welcomed back and the churches were full. They continued to grow in spite of the havoc of the further three years of war which followed the invasion of South Korea by the North. By 1975 a quarter of the population of South Korea was Christian, and a high proportion of those who claimed to be Christians practised their faith.

Although Christians are numerous in South Korea, and the numbers continue to grow, the Churches are very divided. Presbyterians and Methodists have suffered from internal schisms, as a result of which the Roman Catholic Church is the largest single Christian body, though Presbyterians are more numerous, and had the largest seminary in Asia with over 800 students by 1975.

A number of independent Churches have also appeared, most of which are fairly small, but two of which deserve mention here. The Holy Spirit Association for Unification of World Christianity (the Unification Church), founded in 1954 by the Rev. Sun Myung Moon, has small groups of members in many other countries, and controls a vast network of industries both in Korea and in the USA. It began as a Christian Church, but by 1975 had moved a long way from orthodox Christianity, and saw Sun Myung Moon as a new Messiah. The Olive Tree Church was founded in 1955 by Elder Pak T'ae-son, who claims to be the olive tree of Rev. 11.4. It too manages huge industrial and urban complexes, and considers its founder to be possessed of almost divine powers.

Since the late 1960s the government of Korea has become increasingly dictatorial, and Christians have found themselves in opposition to the state on a number of issues, especially since the imposition of martial law in 1972, and the introduction of a new constitution which gave the President almost unlimited powers. Both Roman Catholic and Protestant leaders spoke out against the misuse of state powers, and violations of human rights. In 1971 the Roman Catholic bishops issued a joint letter entitled 'Let's defeat today's injustice', in which they spoke out against corruption and injustice practised by the government. Both

Catholics and Protestants have been arrested and detained without trial, and long-term sentences have been passed against others. In 1975 the Catholic poet Kim Chi Ha openly criticized the government for executing a number of political prisoners, and was himself imprisoned and given a life sentence for doing so.

About a third of Korean Christians belong to Protestant Churches which are members of the National Christian Council. There is also a National Association of Evangelicals, a fundamentalist body to which thirteen Churches belong. Co-operation between Roman Catholics and Protestants in the social sphere is well-established.

In spite of its relatively short life, the Church in Korea has a wealth of experience, and throughout most of its history has had to witness in situations of great difficulty.

STUDY SUGGESTIONS

China

WORDS AND MEANINGS

1. Who or what was or is each of the following, and what do the Chinese names in (b) and (c) mean in English?
   (a) Manchu (b) T'ai P'ing (c) Kuomintang (d) Confucius
   (e) Mandarin

REVIEW OF CONTENT

2. (a) What was the general attitude of the Chinese people to the rest of the world in the nineteenth century, and what was its effect on Christian missions?
   (b) What was their attitude to foreign trade at that time?
3. Who was the first Protestant missionary to China, by whom was he sent, and what were some of his most important achievements?
4. (a) Who started the T'ai P'ing movement, and what were his chief aims?
   (b) What was his attitude to Christianity?
   (c) What effect did the movement actually have on the position of the Church?
5. Briefly describe the causes and effects of the following, and give their dates: (a) the Tientsin massacre; (b) the Boxer Rising.
6. Who founded the China Inland Mission, and when; and what were its chief aims and characteristics?
7. What were some of the changes which took place in the late nineteenth and early twentieth centuries:
   (a) in the general attitude of the Chinese people?
   (b) in the political situation in China?

(c) in the organization of the Church in China?

8. Two of China's twentieth-century leaders were Christians. Who were they, and how far did this help or hinder the work of the Churches?

9. What were the two important events in the development of the Church in China which took place in (a) 1907 (b) 1922?

10. Give a brief description of the work and particular importance to the Church of the following:
(a) Dr Timothy Lew (b) Dr Cheng Ching-Yi (c) Fr Vincent Lebbe

11. When and for what reason did it become possible for Chinese Catholics to join the Civil Service?

12. What was the general effect on the life of the Churches in China of each of the following, and how did the Churches respond in each case?
(a) World War II (b) The first period of Communist rule, 1949–64 (c) The Cultural Revolution

13. What are the aims of the 'Three-Self Movement', and in what ways does it seek to achieve them?

DISCUSSION

14. In what ways do you think the spread of the gospel is helped or hindered when Christian missionaries adopt the dress and customs of the countries to which they go?

15. In what ways, if any, do you think it is helpful for missionaries to be 'protected' by the governments of their home countries?

16. 'Chiang Kai Shek encouraged the missions, especially in the work of education' (p. 29). 'As a result of Fr Lebbe's work the Roman Catholic Church became much more involved in education' (p. 30). 'The Protestant Churches did not develop high standards in education ... and educated Christians did not always respect Protestant clergy' (p. 31). To what extent are the Churches in your country involved in education? What do you see as the advantages and disadvantages of such involvement?

17. 'In 1927 the National Conference of Christian Students in China decided to oppose Western imperialism. Many students including Christians became Communists as the only way of doing this' (p. 31). In what circumstances, if any, do you consider that Christians are justified in becoming Communists in order to achieve political 'liberation' for their country?

Taiwan

WORDS AND MEANINGS

1. Explain what is meant by each of the following as used in the chapter:

(a) Comity agreements (b) Asian colonialism (c) Xenophobia (d) Aboriginals

REVIEW OF CONTENT

2. What is meant by the statement that 'the Church came of age during the War' (p. 36)?
3. What changes in the position of the Churches accompanied the political changes in Taiwan in the years following World War II?
4. Which two Christian denominations were at work in Taiwan, to the exclusion of others, until the mid-twentieth century?
5. (a) In what ways did the Church benefit or otherwise from the cession of Taiwan to Japan in 1895?
   (b) In what way was the Church in Taiwan strengthened when Presbyterian missionaries were forced to leave at the beginning of World War II?
   (c) What were the chief changes affecting the Church, when the Chinese National Government under Chiang Kai-Shek was set up in Taiwan after World War II?
6. What *four* special features have distinguished the development of the Church in Taiwan, as compared with the situation in other countries?

DISCUSSION

7. 'The Presbyterians issued a statement in 1972 demanding self-determination by the people and increasing democratization ... finally the General Secretary and others were arrested and imprisoned' (p. 38). Some Christians say that the Church should not become involved in secular politics. What is your opinion? In what circumstances, if any, do you think such involvement is right?
8. 'The coming of many new denominations and movements resulted in much misunderstanding and tension' (p. 37)—but it also resulted in great growth. In what particular ways do you think that tension, rather than 'peace' can sometimes contribute to Church growth?

Hong Kong

REVIEW OF CONTENT

1. (a) In what ways does the political history of Taiwan in the nineteenth century (i) resemble, and (ii) differ from that of Hong Kong?
   (b) What particular effect has Hong Kong's colonial status had on the development of the Church there?
2. (a) For what chief reasons is Hong Kong important to the People's Republic of China?

(b) What important changes will occur in Hong Kong's political status in 1997, and what effect could this have on the life of the Church?

3. What factors have chiefly contributed to the density of population in Hong Kong, and what advantages and disadvantages have these brought for the work of the Church?

4. Which British missionary society was particularly active in Hong Kong in the nineteenth century?

5. Give the dates of the following events:
(a) Appointment of the first English bishop in China
(b) Ordination of first Chinese Protestant minister
(c) Baptism of the Chinese political leader Sun Yat-Sen

6. What are some of the chief strengths of the Church in Hong Kong, and what have been the reasons for them?

7. In what ways has the role of Christian women in Hong Kong been especially important?

DISCUSSION

8. 'The government and the Churches have co-operated in education, medicine and social work and in training' (p. 40). Some governments—and some Christians—say the Church should only involve itself in social and educational work where governments *fail* to provide such services. What is your opinion?

9. 'There are opportunities in Hong Kong for Christians to have dialogue with people of other faiths' (p. 41). What are the chief benefits to Christians, of such dialogue? What if any are the dangers?

10. 'Bishop Hall ordained a Chinese woman' (p. 41). Is the ordination of women customary in your own Church? What do you see as the chief arguments for and against the ordination of women? What is your own view-point on the subject?

Japan

WORDS AND MEANINGS

1. Who or what are or were the following?
(a) Nihon Kirisuto Kokwai (b) Samurai (c) Mukyokai (d) Doshisha

REVIEW OF CONTENT

2. Who were the 'hidden Christians'? Why had they hidden? What made it possible for them to come out of hiding, and when?

3. What were the particular aims of the Nihon Kirisuto Kokwai, and how successful was it in achieving them?

4. What was the attitude of the Samurai to the work of Christian missions and the development of the Japanese Church?
5. At what period was the Church in Japan growing the fastest, and by how many did the number of Protestant Christians increase at that period?
6. (a) Describe very briefly the development of the Orthodox Church in Japan.
   (b) Describe very briefly how the United Church of Christ came into being in Japan, and how it has developed.
7. (a) What were the chief characteristics and aims of Uchimura Kanzo's 'No-Church Church'?
   (b) What were the chief ideas and aims of Toyohiko Kagawa?
8. Whereabouts in Japan was the Roman Catholic Church chiefly centred, and what 'appalling setback' did it suffer as a result?

DISCUSSION

9. What do you think is the reason why many more Japanese are interested in Christianity and read the Scriptures than actually join the Churches?
10. 'Japan has become known for an enormous growth of new religious movements' (p. 47). What, in your opinion, has been the cause of this growth? What effect is it likely to have on the work and growth of the 'mainline' Churches?

Korea

REVIEW OF CONTENT

1. Describe briefly, with dates, the part played by each of the following in the history of Christianity in Korea:
   (a) Lee Sung Hoon (b) James Choo Moon Mo (c) Sun Myung Moon (d) Kim Chi Ha
2. (a) What event opened the way for Protestant missions to enter Korea, and at what date?
   (b) Which two Protestant denominations have been predominant in Korea?
3. (a) What political changes in the early nineteenth century resulted in a period of difficulty and repression for Christians in Korea?
   (b) What proportion of the population of South Korea was estimated to be Christian by the mid-1970s?
4. 'Presbyterians and Methodists have suffered from schisms' (p. 48). In what way has this affected the Roman Catholic Church in Korea?
5. What particular similarities do you see between the two Indepen-

dent Churches described in the chapter: the Unification Church and the Olive Tree Church?

6. What similarities and differences do you see between the relationship of Church and State in Korea in recent years, and that of Church and State in Taiwan?

DISCUSSION

7. 'Presbyterians and Methodists have suffered from schisms' (p. 48). Find out what have been some of the chief causes of internal disagreement which have caused parts of some Churches to separate themselves from the 'parent' Church in the present century. In what circumstances, if any, do you think that 'schism' is a satisfactory way for Christians to resolve their differences?

8. Both the Unification Church and the Olive Tree Church in Korea are described as having control of very large industrial interests and urban properties. Do you think it is right for Churches to have such financial (and social) interests and responsibilities? What are some of the consequences—and some of the dangers?

3

The Indian Sub-Continent, Sri Lanka and Nepal
from material contributed by T. V. Philip

Until 1947 the whole Indian sub-continent formed one country known as India. We shall therefore use the name 'India' to refer to the whole sub-continent when dealing with events before 1947. At the time of Independence this area was partitioned between India (mainly Hindu) and Pakistan (mainly Muslim). East Pakistan was separated from West Pakistan in 1971 and became Bangladesh. Sri Lanka used to be called Ceylon.

INDIA: THE MISSIONARY ERA

The Church in India Before 1800

For the earlier history of Christianity in India, readers may find it helpful to look at Volume 1, ch. 8 of this TEF Church History Guide, and Vol. 3, ch. 10. Here we may recall that, according to Indian tradition, St Thomas the Apostle brought Christianity to India in the first century AD, and that this tradition may well be true. The ancient Church whose members are found in South India was for many centuries linked with the Syrian Church of the East (see p. 225 below). They are sometimes called Thomas Christians and sometimes Syrian Christians.

When the Portuguese came to India in the sixteenth century, most of the Thomas Christians lived in Kerala in south-west India. During the Portuguese period, Jesuit Roman Catholic missionaries made converts in Goa and along the coast to the south, and they brought the Thomas Christians into obedience to Rome. In the seventeenth century, however, many of the Thomas Christians broke away from Rome again because they disliked being subjected to the Portuguese and the Jesuits. They were unable to get help from the Church of the East, so they linked themselves with the Syrian Jacobite Church in Antioch (see pp. 226, 227). At the beginning of the nineteenth century, therefore, we find three groups of Christians in India: (1) Roman Catholics, using the Latin rite in the mass, and mostly living in Goa and on the Fisher Coast; (2) Eastern Rite Catholics, mostly in Kerala, whose ancestors had been Thomas Christians; and (3) Thomas Christians, linked with the Patriarch of Antioch, also mostly in Kerala. In the early nineteenth century the Eastern Rite Catholics were struggling to prevent their Church from being forced to conform to the Latin rite. There were also some Protestants, mainly the result of Danish missionary work.

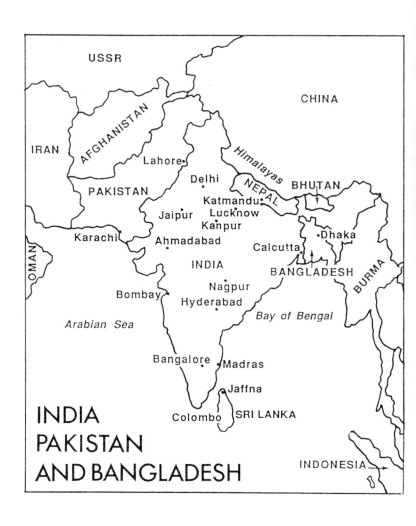

INDIA
PAKISTAN
AND BANGLADESH

Early in the nineteenth century Anglican missionaries came to South India, and this led to yet further division. Some of the Thomas Christians became Anglicans, and others set up a reformed but independent Church called Mar Thoma, which sought to test all teaching and worship by the Bible. Since then, some of the Thomas Christians have again formed links with the Church of the East, and have broken away from the group linked with the Patriarch of Antioch. The whole group of Churches is now vigorous and growing, and many reforms have been carried out, but it is also deeply divided.

Christianity and Colonialism

During the Portuguese period, the progress of Christianity in India was closely connected with Portuguese rule. The Portuguese came to India to look for spices and to make Christians, and their soldiers felt they were fighting for the King of Heaven as well as for the King of Portugal. The Portuguese used the Catholic Church to strengthen their rule.

In the eighteenth century India was in a state of decline. For centuries the majority of the people, who followed the Hindu religion, had been ruled by Muslim Mogul rulers. As a result, they were defensive about their religion and culture. The Mogul Empire finally collapsed in the middle of the nineteenth century. By this time, both the British and the French, as well as the Portuguese, had acquired possessions in India. The British now defeated the French, and proclaimed imperial rule over the whole sub-continent. The Portuguese retained some small possessions, including Goa.

British domination was at first exercised through the British East India Company, which was mainly concerned with trade. In the eighteenth century the Company had opposed the work of missions, because they did not want missionaries upsetting or antagonizing the people with whom they were trading. The first British missionaries such as the pioneer Baptist missionary, William Carey, and early missionaries of the Church Missionary Society and the London Missionary Society were therefore confined to areas where Europeans lived. It was not until 1833 that the British East India Company agreed to lift restrictions on missions. In 1857 Company rule ended, and direct British rule began. In South India the Indian Christians welcomed this because they wanted to be protected against their Hindu neighbours.

The British, like the Portuguese, used Christianity to support their rule, and this has sometimes led to too close an identification between imperialism and Christian missionary work. It did, however, make it easier for the missions to gain converts during the colonial period. K. M. Panikkar, an Indian historian, has written:

With the exception of the Syrian Christians, the Indian Christians are the product of European rule in India. . . . Therefore, after giving up Hinduism, they leaned heavily on the European rulers for protection, which made them suspect in the eyes of the Hindus. They are now trying to disarm their suspicion by being too yielding. (Introduction to K. N. Subramanyam, *The Catholic Community in India*, Madras, 1970, p. v)

The Numerical Growth of Christianity

From the late eighteenth century onwards, Protestant and Roman Catholic missionaries came to India in growing numbers. At first, most Protestant missionaries tried to convert individuals from among the educated Indians of the higher castes. They hoped that if a good number of these became Christians, it would be easy for the rest of the population to follow. But it was very difficult for a high-caste Hindu to become a Christian, because he had too much to lose. To become a Christian meant cutting himself off from his family and friends, and from his former privileged position. A few high-caste Hindus did become Christians, but the missionaries came to realize that they could not hope to evangelize India by this means.

At the bottom of Hindu society there were large groups of people called 'outcastes' because they had no place in Indian caste society. They were considered 'untouchables'. They owned no land, and they did work which other people thought too low or degrading to do themselves. They were very poor and despised by the rest of society. They formed about one-sixth of the total population. Between 1870 and 1920 India suffered from a series of severe famines and epidemics, and naturally the people who suffered most were the very poor. The Christian Churches organized relief for them. In 1877 a group of 200 outcastes came to Dr John Clough, an American missionary, and asked to be baptized. They had been converted, not by a European missionary but by one of their own number, Yerraguntla Periah, who had heard something about Christ and had gone home and told his friends and relatives. Dr Clough did not really want to baptize them; they knew very little, they had had no education, and he wondered if they were properly converted. However, at last he agreed, and within the next thirty years half a million people from these depressed classes became Christians.

The same sort of thing happened in the Punjab. A small lame man called Ditt started a movement through which many thousands of people became Christians, and there were not enough missionaries to care for them all properly. In the years that followed there were many such 'mass movements', but not all missionaries welcomed them. Some thought that many of the poor only joined the Church so as to get famine relief and aid, and had no real desire to follow the Christian faith; and they feared that if the churches were filled with 'untouchables', no one else would want to join them. They also believed that people should be converted as individuals—they did not understand the Indian social system in which people were more accustomed to acting as groups rather than as individuals. Other missionaries saw things differently. They thought the Spirit of God was showing the way by which India would be won for Christ.

So when the outcastes came to church on Sundays, the missions were uncertain what to do. The question of caste was discussed by the Vatican Council of the Roman Catholic Church in 1870, and the delegates agreed that caste distinctions were un-Christian. But if a parish priest had tried to make people of different castes sit together in church, nearly all the high caste people would have walked out. Sometimes two different services were held; sometimes different parts of the building were reserved for people of different castes. Protestants faced the same difficulties as Roman Catholics. Many Christian schools made it a condition of entry that no caste distinctions should be observed in the classrooms, but some boarding schools permitted pupils of different castes to eat and sleep separately from one another.

The caste system had already been challenged both by Islam and by the Sikh religion. Now because Christian missions agreed to baptize 'untouchables' and taught that caste distinctions must be abolished, the conscience of the Hindus was stirred. Mahatma Gandhi, the best-known of Indian nationalist leaders, who had seen the destructiveness of racist divisions in South Africa, campaigned against the divisiveness of caste when he returned to India. At Independence in 1947 'untouchability' was abolished by law, and the 'untouchables' were renamed 'scheduled castes', but it takes a long time to change old attitudes, and even today the battle is not yet fully won.

The missions have been equally successful among the Adivasis, or tribal people. These are the descendants of the indigenous people of India, who were pushed into the forests and hills by later invaders, and were not part of the Hindu socio-religious system. K. N. Subramanyan says they

> keep to traditions and beliefs of their own. In the general Indian set-up, their social and economic status is very low and theoretically all the so-called advanced people of India are contributing to the development of these people. . . . In real practice they are among the most oppressed and were, until recently, the least educated in India. (*The Catholic Community in India*, Madras, 1970, p. 51)

In 1885 Fr Constant Lievens, a Jesuit missionary from Belgium, went to work among a group of these people called the Nagas. He found them oppressed by money-lenders and landlords. He helped them to bring court cases, and agitated for a change in the law. By 1921 175,000 of them had become Roman Catholics. Today more than half the Nagas are Christians, and the same sort of mass turning to Christianity has occurred among other Adivasi groups. The Christian gospel has the same appeal for the Adivasis as for the scheduled castes, and for many of the same reasons.

Far fewer converts have been made from among the Muslims of India, but some have become Christians, mostly from among the very poor. If a Muslim became a Christian, his family was likely to disown him, so the Churches had special funds to help such converts. The missions had rather more success among the Sikhs, a much smaller religious group, living mainly in the Punjab. Here, too, mass movements took place among the depressed classes.

By the 1970s nearly fourteen and a quarter million people, or about 2.8 per cent of the population of the Indian sub-continent had become Christian, half them being Roman Catholics. The relative strengths of the main denominations are shown in the diagram below:

1 7 million Roman Catholics (including Eastern Rite Catholics)
2 2 million Thomas Christians
3 1,500,000 Church of South India (uniting Congregationalists, Presbyterians, Anglicans and Methodists)
4 750,000 Lutherans
5 600,000 Methodists
6 500,000 Church of North India (uniting Baptists, Brethren, Disciples of Christ, Methodists and Anglicans)
7 1,600,000 other Protestants

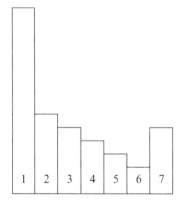

The Churches and Social Action

In the early nineteenth century the missionaries wanted to bring about big changes in Indian society. As we saw, Christian attitudes to caste caused Hindus to question this aspect of their society and eventually to pass laws abolishing 'untouchability'. A nineteenth-century missionary, Alexander Duff, called the caste sytem 'the cement which held Hindu society together', and thought that if the caste system could be destroyed, the Hindu religion would be brought to an end. Today we find that most Hindus themselves look forward, at least in theory, to an ideal 'casteless society'.

In 1829 a British governor, Lord William Bentinck, risked Hindu anger by forbidding the practice whereby Hindu widows were burnt on the funeral pyres of their husbands. There was far less anger than he had feared. The missions had particularly hated this practice, and also deplored the killing of unwanted children, child marriage, and the debased position of women in both Hindu and Muslim society.

After the uprising against the British of 1857, the British government discouraged missionaries from 'interfering' in social questions in case they caused trouble. By this time the missionaries were in any case turning their attention elsewhere, and for a number of reasons. (1) Large numbers of 'outcastes' and Adivasis had become Christians, and the missions needed to spend time in helping them. (2) Missionaries were becoming less sure about the rightness of attacking social customs. Perhaps this should be done by Indian Christians. (3) They knew they would no longer get government support if, in trying to change customs, they antagonized people. So the Churches concentrated on other kinds of social action, setting up schools, orphanages, hospitals and leper colonies, and running agricultural and other kinds of training schemes. They turned their attention to the masses who had become Christians, and tried to instruct them in the faith and lift them out of their extreme poverty.

But the missionaries also continued to try to win converts from among the higher castes. Fr William Wallace, a Protestant who became a Roman Catholic and a Jesuit priest, pleaded for missionaries to study Hinduism, and it was largely because of his work that Hinduism was taught in the seminaries that trained Indian priests.

The missions' work in general education was partly aimed at winning converts among the higher castes. Protestant missions were the first to become involved in higher education. Before 1833 they had concentrated on primary education in the main Indian languages. From 1833 onwards they concentrated on running secondary schools and colleges with instruction in English. They hoped these would attract high caste pupils and students, and that pupils studying Western literature and science would be more easily converted to Christianity. The government gave grants-in-aid to help run these schools. Christian schools and colleges were also established in mainly Muslim areas, though fewer people took advantage of them there. Many of the educational institutions founded at this time have played a leading role in Indian education. The government gave less money to the missons after 1857 when it began to establish its own schools. However, the missions continued to found schools and colleges for girls, for whom they felt a special responsibility.

Two great missionaries to India: *Left* Pioneer Baptist William Carey,
Right Alexander Duff, first overseas missionary of the Church of Scotland.
Below Pandita Ramabai taking orphans to *Mukti* in the 1895/6 famine.
Bottom Mar Chrysostom addresses the Church of South India Synod.

The Roman Catholics began to expand their educational work later than the Protestants. The Portuguese created difficulties in territory which they ruled because they claimed that the *padroado* (Spanish: *patronato*) Agreement gave them the sole right to evangelize in India, and to appoint bishops there. This 'patronage' Agreement had been made in 1493, when Spain and Portugal were the only two nations engaged in overseas mission, and the Pope divided responsibility for world evangelism between them. By the eighteenth century they were no longer able to fulfil their responsibilities. (See TEF Church History Guide Vol. 3, pp. 81, 87.)

During the 1850s and 1860s the Vatican took action to free Roman Catholic missions from Portuguese interference. Since the Portuguese would not accept non-Portuguese bishops and could not provide enough themselves, the Pope appointed Vicars-Apostolic, with episcopal powers, to take charge of mission areas, and Catholic work grew greatly from this time on. The first Catholic university college was opened in 1868, and by 1958 there were twenty-nine such colleges for men and thirty for women, with 28,000 students in them, more than half of whom were non-Catholics. The Roman Catholic missions also ran hundreds of secondary schools. But only a small number of non-Christian pupils and students became Christians as a result of Western education.

The Churches still continue to take an important part in medical work in India. During the past 100 years they have started colleges for training doctors, and institutions for training nurses. The Vellore Medical College, the Medical School at Ludhiana, and St John's Medical College at Bangalore are three outstanding Christian medical schools. In 1940 ninety per cent of all nurses in India were Christians, and eighty per cent of all nurses had been trained in Christian institutions. In 1964 the Roman Catholic Church alone ran 205 hospitals. Christians are willing to perform services for patients which others have been unwilling to do, and even today many Muslims and Hindus prefer to go to a Christian hospital rather than a government one. The Churches run special hospitals for tuberculosis, leprosy, and psychiatric illnesses. Most Christians now recognize that healing is itself a Christian activity; Christian hospitals are not simply a means of making converts.

The most famous home for widows and orphans was founded and run by an Indian Christian woman, Pandita Ramabai (1858–1922), who came from a Brahman (high-caste) family and was well-educated in Hindu philosophy and religion. She was converted through Fr Nehemiah Goreh, himself a converted Brahman, and when her husband died, in 1882, she travelled to England with her young daughter. There she was greatly helped by Anglican nuns of the

Community of St Mary the Virgin at Wantage, and was baptized. She returned to India and opened a home for child-widows which she called *Mukti*, meaning 'deliverance'. In 1895–6 there was a severe famine, and she began to accept orphaned children into Mukti. Gradually a large community developed there including schools, a dairy farm, a rope-making industry, and so on. Pandita Ramabai remained as head of this institution until she died in 1922.

The missions set up a number of different training schemes to try and improve the position of the poor. The Basel Mission, for instance, had tile-making and textile industries on the west coast of India, and at other places missions taught carpentry and furniture-making. The YMCA, the Student Christian Movement, and the National Mission-ary Society (an entirely Indian organization) did important work in the rural areas. These schemes fitted in very well with Mahatma Gandhi's call for the improvement of rural life.

CHRISTIANITY AND THE INDIAN CULTURAL RENAISSANCE

In this section we shall look briefly at the history of ideas, always a difficult topic, but a very important one for the history of modern India.

During the nineteenth century Indian religious leaders, writers and scholars began to be interested in Christ and His teachings. Not many of them became Christians—some in fact actively opposed missionary teaching—but all of them, in one way or another, were deeply influenced by what they learnt about Christ.

First, there were those who made use of Christian missionary education in order to attack Christianity. Muhammed Mohar Ali, a Bangladeshi historian, has written:

> The Hindus even utilized the gifts of English education in opposing missionaries. . . . In so far as the [missionaries] furthered the cause of education, they sharpened the weapon of which they themselves were to feel the edge.

One of the leaders of the Hindu opposition to Christianity was Dayanand Sarasvati. Born in 1824 into a wealthy high-caste family, he studied the Hindu religion deeply, and his religious teacher told him he should take up the task of reforming Hinduism. Dayanand turned to the *Vedas*, the most ancient Indian religious writings, dating from more than a thousand years before Christ, and he rejected all later develop-ments in Hinduism, especially the practice of using images in worship. The Vedas, he said, were the source of all knowledge, and Egypt and Greece were sunk in ignorance until they learnt wisdom from India.

(We may note that the Rig-Veda is the oldest written text in any Indo-European language, and some scholars think that the Greek philosophers were influenced by Hindu thought.) Dayanand was merciless in his criticism of Christianity and of the sort of Hinduism which most people practised. In 1875 he established the Arya Samaj to carry on his work. He was unusual in attacking Jesus himself; most Hindus have a deep reverence for Jesus even though they reject institutionalized Christianity.

Secondly there were some Hindus who thought that Hinduism should be reformed in the light of Christ and of His ethical teaching. One of the earliest of these was Ram Mohun Roy. Born in 1774 he too belonged to a high-caste family. He first learnt Sanskrit, the language of the ancient Hindu scriptures, which he studied deeply; and then Arabic and Persian, and came to know a lot about Islam. Later still he learnt Hebrew so that he could read the Old Testament, and he knew some Greek as well. Like Dayanand Sarasvati, he also rejected the polytheism which he saw in popular Hinduism. He turned to the Upanishads for inspiration. The Upanishads are also Hindu scriptures, but not as old as the Vedas, having probably been written between 800 and 500 BC. They are concerned with the mystery of being, with questions of life and death, and with the unity of all existence, and are among the world's greatest writings. From 1800 onwards, Ram Mohun Roy began to study the New Testament, and in 1820 he wrote a book with the title *The Precepts of Jesus the Guide to Peace and Happiness*. Here and elsewhere he wrote of his beliefs that the teachings of Jesus are the best guide to living:

> The consequences of my long and interrupted researches into religious truth has been that I have found the doctrines of Christ more conducive to moral principles, and better adapted to the use of rational beings, than any others which have come to my knowledge. (Quoted in S. C. Neill, *The Christian Church in India and Pakistan*, 1970, p. 121.)

But Ram Mohun Roy never became a Christian.

Keshub Chandra Sen, born in 1838, came from a deeply pious Hindu home, but was sent to an English-language school. He joined the reform movement started by Ram Mohun Roy, and eventually reached the conclusion that God is one, but can be reached by many different ways.

> God never Himself becomes man by putting on a human body. His divinity dwells in every man, and is displayed more vividly in some. Moses, Jesus Christ, Muhammad, Nanak, Caitanya, and other great teachers, appeared at special times, and conferred great benefits on

the world. They are entitled to universal gratitude and love. (Quoted in S. C. Neill, *The Christian Church in India and Pakistan*, 1970, p. 121.)

We must also mention Swami Vivekananda, who lived from 1863 to 1902. He spoke of 'the Lord who is in every religion . . . the Brahma of the Hindus, the Ahura Mazda of the Zoroastrians, the Buddha of the Buddhists, the Jehovah of the Jews, the Father in Heaven of the Christians'. Both Keshub Chandra Sen and Swami Vivekananda are very typical of one aspect of Hinduism, for the Hindu religion is able to absorb many ideas, and to find a place for all within it.

We should note that Hindus who admire Jesus Christ admire Him as a person and as a teacher. They have a profound respect for His teachings in the Gospels. Christians think of Jesus as the only Saviour and Lord as well as a teacher. Not many Hindus have been interested in the Christian gospel of forgiveness and salvation from sin.

In 1897 Swami Vivekananda founded the Ramakrishna Mission, which does educational and social work in India, as part of the renewal of Hinduism which these thinkers were working for. Recently the mission has become active in America and Britain and elsewhere, and is winning converts to Hinduism from Western societies which have lost sight of spiritual values.

Thirdly there were Christians who wanted to see Christianity freed from Western cultural trappings, and thus able to make its way among Indians. They were able to think constructively about this because of the rediscovery of India's past heritage which had resulted from the Indian renaissance. Both Western and Indian scholars contributed to this rediscovery of India's past, and Christians as well as Hindus shared in it.

J. N. Farquhar wrote a book entitled *The Crown of Hinduism* whose theme is that, for Hindus, Christianity should be understood as the fulfilment of Hinduism. V. Chakkarai, an Indian who developed the same theme, said:

> We are proud that in our veins flows the blood of our fathers to whom the world owes some of the richest things in the domain of religion. Our fathers are not Athanasius and Augustine, Luther and Wesley, Chrysostom and Calvin (though we do not disclaim these); they are Vysa and Vasishata, Kabir and Kamban, Manicavasagar and Markandeyan. (Slightly simplified. Vysa, Vasishata, etc., are Indian religious thinkers.)

Some Christians suggested that, instead of reading the Old Testament, Indian Christians should read the Hindu scriptures. Others thought such syncretism, or mixing of religions, was dangerous because it diluted the uniqueness of Christianity.

So far we have considered Hinduism. What about Islam? The Indian renaissance of the nineteenth century affected Hindus far more than it did Muslims. Hindus have sometimes spoken slightingly of Muslims as mere newcomers, because the Hindu religion is so much older than Islam. But Christian teaching did have an effect on Islam, and Muslims defended themselves against it. They were more reluctant than Hindus to send their children to mission schools, for instance, and one reaction to Christian missions was the Ahmadiyya Mission, a parallel to the Ramakrishna Mission. The Ahmadiyya are a group of Muslims whom other Muslims consider unorthodox, even 'non-Muslim'. But they are themselves ardent missionaries, and have adopted some of the methods used by Christian missionaries. They will even translate the Qur'an, which orthodox Muslims refuse to do. They are not acceptable now in Pakistan, where they originated, but their missions have had considerable success in Africa.

These efforts for reform in religion and society in nineteenth-century India led to political movements, to which Indian Christians reacted in varying ways.

The Christian Community and the Nationalist Movements

In 1885 the Indian National Congress was formed, partly as a result of the self-assurance which the cultural renaissance had given to the Indian people. In its early days a number of Christians supported Congress, the most respected of these being Kali Charan Banerjee. When Congress began to agitate for full political freedom, the British government became hostile to it. After this, many Indian Christians were for a while reluctant to uphold Congress because their Churches still depended on mission support, and they feared losing government protection. Some Christians feared the possibility of India becoming independent under a Hindu government. In the twentieth century the National Christian Council, which co-ordinates Protestant activity, felt unable to take a definite stand on the struggle for political freedom.

Some Christians, though, saw things differently. K. T. Paul, a layman from South India, recognized that Christians could not always rely on British protection, and warned them of the dangers of doing so. But George Joseph of the Syrian Christians—a Church that was not mission-dominated—was almost the only Christian to support Gandhi's first non-co-operation movement. In the 1930s and 1940s, however, the Christians of Kerala, most of whom are members of the Syrian or Mar Thoma Churches, led the way in supporting the nationalist movement in their state. In 1945 the creation of a League of Minorities was proposed, to protect the rights of minority groups such as Christians, but by then opinion had changed greatly, and Christian leaders would not accept the idea. They also rejected the suggestion that there should be a separate electoral roll for Christians, believing that the Church should dedicate itself to the good of everyone, not fight for advantages only for its own members.

TOWARDS AN INDIGENOUS CHURCH

As already mentioned, the Christian Church as introduced by the missions seemed foreign to most Indians, and so the idea of 'indigenizing' the Church began to take hold. All over the world today Christians are engaged in making the Church at home in their own cultures. We have already seen that there were aspects of Hindu culture which Christians could not accept, the most notable being the state of 'untouchability'. The modern government of India is also dedicated to getting rid of caste distinctions, but is finding that it is easier to pass a law than to change people's ways of thinking. On the one hand Christianity must be indigenized; on the other hand, society must be Christianized.

Authority and Leadership

Already in the nineteenth century some Indian pastors, among them Lal Behari Dey, Golak Nath, and Kali Charan Chatterjee, protested against missionary domination, and demanded that Indians should take part in all Church discussions. Some missionary groups, including the Anglicans and Presbyterians, encouraged the Indian Church to become self-supporting, self-governing, and self-propagating. Others thought that missions should control the Churches so long as the Churches depended on mission money, and did not give sufficient encouragement to them to become financially independent. Progress towards handing over authority was extremely slow; but in the twentieth century the nationalist movement and the achievement of political independence speeded things up somewhat. World War II (1939–45) made it clear that colonial empires were coming to an end. Between 1940 and 1960 much was done to enable the Indian Churches to take responsibility for their own affairs, but even now the process is still incomplete.

Some statistics from the Roman Catholic Church will illustrate both the progress made and its incompleteness:

	Archbishops		Bishops		Priests	
	Foreign	Nationals	Foreign	Nationals	Foreign	Nationals
1935	7	2	19	15	?	3,025
1961	2	13	29	33	1,100	4,500

By 1961, 1,500 religious brothers and 19,800 religious sisters were nationals. In India, as in other traditional societies, life in a religious order has often proved particularly attractive to women. It offers them an alternative to their traditional role as mother and housewife, closely tied to the homestead. A sister is respected by society although she is not married; almost all religious orders arrange for their members to have a good education; and able women are usually encouraged to have a professional training. In India and elsewhere women and girls have fewer opportunities of education than men and boys. Membership of a religious order also offers some security to an unmarried woman, an ordered way of life, and one in which she can serve God and serve the community.

Since Independence in 1947, Pakistan has become a Muslim state, with Islam as the state religion. India and Bangladesh are both secular states which guarantee freedom of religion. But many Hindus regard Hinduism as rightfully the religion and culture of India, and there has been a strong movement to reduce the number of missionaries of other religions entering the country, as is also the case in Pakistan. Christian missionaries have sometimes been denounced as imperialist agents. This climate of opinion has probably made Christians on the sub-continent too timid.

The fiercest denunciation of such anti-missionary propaganda comes from the Hindu writer, K. N. Subramanyan. In his book, *The Catholic Community in India*, published in Madras in 1970, he denounces such propaganda as hypocrisy. He is greatly impressed by the social, educational and medical work done by the Churches and missions, and says that many of those who denounce Christian missions send their children to Church schools, and go to Church-run hospitals for medical treatment. He challenges Christians to come out of their ghettoes and not to be timid about their religion, since they have so much to offer.

Handing over authority cannot of itself make the Church at home. There is also a need to find indigenous ways of worship and living the Christian life. Reverence, joy, thanksgiving, and fellowship are expressed differently in different cultures. Two examples of the way in which individuals have contributed to this 'indigenization' in India were: (1) Narayan Vaman Tilak (1862–1919) who became a Christian in 1893 through reading the New Testament. He taught, lectured and wrote, and was eventually ordained as a Presbyterian minister, though he had no regular Church ministry. His greatest contributions to the Indian Church were, perhaps, the hymns he wrote in the Marathi language: most of the Marathi hymn book was written by him. Today Indian musical instruments and tunes are increasingly used in Christian worship. (2) Sadhu Sundar Singh (1889–1929) who expressed his Christian faith through a pattern of living strange to many Westerners but traditional in India. He was born into a wealthy Sikh family, and was converted from violent opposition to Christianity to fervent faith. He started to study theology, but left to become a *sadhu*, a wandering preacher in the Indian tradition, whose ministry eventually extended beyond India to Europe. His saintliness impressed all who met him. In 1922 he departed on a journey to Tibet, and was never seen again.

Another pattern of Indian religious life is the ancient institution known as an *ashram*, or settlement where people live together to meditate and pray and serve others. Those who join an ashram live very simply. Indians expect a holy person to live a simple and disciplined life, and riches are considered a hindrance to holiness. In 1912 K. T. Paul suggested that there might be Christian as well as Hindu ashrams. A number of people have taken up this idea, and there are Christian ashrams scattered throughout India, but no large-scale movement. The Roman Catholic Church and Anglican religious orders have attracted far more people.

An Indian Theology

The development of an Indian way of understanding the gospel is perhaps more important still. Theology must grow out of people's experience of Jesus Christ in their own society. V. Chakkarai has said, 'Life must form its own body, and the water of life must cut its own channel.'

When Indians first began to write theology, they thought in terms of translating Western theology, or else restating Western theology so that Indians could understand it more easily. Then they began to turn to the Hindu religious tradition for inspiration. Some, like Dayanand Saravasti, turned to the Vedas, and thought that for Hindus they should replace the Old Testament. We have noticed that some people thought this a dangerous idea which would lead to syncretism. Bishop A. J. Appasamy turned to the Hindu *Bhakti* tradition as the basis for his theology. Bhakti means loving devotion to a particular deity. The *Bhagavad Gita* (the Lord's Song), the most famous of the Hindu scriptures, expresses Bhakti to the Lord Krishna. Bishop Appasamy saw Christianity as Bhakti to the Lord Jesus Christ.

One of the most important twentieth-century Indian theologians was P. Chenchiah of Madras who reinterpreted the teaching of St Paul on the 'new creation' in a way which was meaningful to Indian Christians. More recently M. M. Thomas and others at the Christian Institute for the Study of Religion and Society in Madras have been developing an Indian theology of social witness.

A world-famous example of Christian social witness is the work of Mother Teresa and her sisters in Calcutta. Mother Teresa is a Roman Catholic nun born in Yugoslavia, so not an Indian, though most of the sisters in her congregation are Indians, but she has become a symbol of Christian selfless caring, and we cannot omit her from any account of the Church in India. She works among the very poor of Calcutta, and from there her work has spread throughout the world. There are many people in Calcutta so poor that they have no home at all. Even when ill or dying, they have nowhere to lie but the streets. Mother Teresa and her sisters see them as people in whom Christ lives, and who should be cared for with a love like Christ's love. So they collect the dying off the streets and give them a chance to die with dignity and with someone caring for them. The sisters also help lepers and orphan children. The sisters receive a long and thorough education and training—nothing but the best is good enough for the destitute of Calcutta.

Christian Co-operation and Church Union Movements

During the nineteenth century Protestant missionaries of different denominations worked together in various ways, for example in running schools and hospitals. But they began to see that co-operation needed to go further than this. The differences of belief and practice which divided the missionaries meant nothing to Indian Christians, who protested against 'imported' divisions. This led to discussions on Church unity.

In 1887 a group of Indian Christians, led by Kali Charan Banerjee, left the mission Churches and founded the Calcutta Christo Samaj. Their purpose was to spread the Christian faith and to encourage unity. They hoped all Indian Christians would join the Christo Samaj and so become free from missionary divisions and paternalism. Banerjee said that the Indian Church should be 'one, not divided; native, not foreign'. The essentials of the faith were contained in the Apostles' Creed and could never be changed, but matters like Church organization were non-essentials, and could and should be changed. Another group of people formed the National Church with somewhat the same purpose. Those who joined such movements were mostly the better-off; the majority of Indian Christians were poor and relied on the missions for help. But such movements were important nevertheless, as the Danish missionary theologian, Kaj Baago, observes:

> It has often been pointed out that it was first and foremost the situation in the mission fields in Asia and Africa which gave rise to the ecumenical movement. . . . Denominational differences suddenly seemed not only absent but harmful. Generally the missionaries have been given the credit for seeing this and having started the discussion which led to the ecumenical movement. It is a question, however, whether the credit should not go to the Indian, Chinese and Japanese Christians, who started the protest movement against western denominationalism.

The efforts of the nineteenth century began to produce results in the twentieth century. First some small Church unions took place, between Congregationalists and Presbyterians in South India, for example, who belonged to different branches of the Reformed Church tradition. Then more important unions took place. In 1947 the Church of South India brought into unity the one and a half million members of the Anglican, Reformed and Methodist traditions, and later, in North India, Baptists, Church of the Brethren, Disciples of Christ, Methodists and Anglicans joined together to form the United Church of North India. These union movements had an enormous effect on ecumenical thinking, and led to new developments in Church organization and in liturgy.

They did not, however, create an *Indian* Church, nor did they deal with *Indian* divisions, but only the European divisions which had been imported into India. Indian Christians point out that there are other causes of division which are more important to them. The things which divide India are language, religion, culture, and caste. Divisions in language, religion and culture led to the separation of India and Pakistan in 1947, and to the uprooting of millions of people. These are the divisions which Indian Christians need to overcome.

More recently, since the Second Vatican Council of the Roman Catholic Church, Catholics, Orthodox and Protestants have come closer together, and are beginning to find ways in which *all* Christians can co-operate and bear witness to the reconciling power of Christ.

PARTITION—INDIA, PAKISTAN AND BANGLADESH

So far we have been mainly concerned with the period before 1947, and with the Indian sub-continent as a whole, We must now look briefly at the more recent period.

Before partition, Muslims were the majority of the population in two main areas. The first was the north-west of the sub-continent, the second was around the Ganges Delta. These two areas were separated from one another by over a thousand miles, but in spite of this they elected to form the one nation of Pakistan when the sub-continent became independent of British rule. The remainder of the sub-continent became the mainly Hindu nation of India. Hindus living in areas that were to become Pakistan, and Muslims in areas that were to become India feared to remain in a nation where they would be in a religious and cultural minority, and many thousands fled to the nation where their religion and culture would predominate. Many Sikhs from West Pakistan and some Christians from East Pakistan also decided to move into India. The first few weeks after Independence were marked by terror and massacre. The problem of resettling millions of refugees remained for much longer. In both countries minorities remained, who have sometimes felt extremely insecure.

The Christians in Pakistan were less than one per cent of the population at the time of partition, mostly the result of mass movements in the late nineteenth and early twentieth centuries. Most of the converts came from the rural areas of the Punjab, and from the poorest sections of society. They have benefited from education, and moved to many parts of the country. Since Independence evangelism has been undertaken, especially among the non-Muslim section of the population, and the number of Christians has risen significantly. The standard of clergy education has also risen, and three institutes for the study of Islam have been founded. The National Council of Churches of Pakistan has grown out of the Punjab Christian Council, begun in 1923.

At the same time, Pakistan has increased its commitment to Islam. In 1956 Islam was made the official religion, and since 1970 all racial and religious minorities have come under the Ministry for Minority Affairs. In 1974 the term 'Muslim' was legally defined so as to exclude the two million strong Ahmadiyya sect from being considered as an Islamic group. Christian missionaries have suffered some restrictions, but freedom of religion is still guaranteed in the constitution. Christians in Pakistan have found it necessary to be entirely independent of Christians across the border in India, so could not become part of the Church union scheme which created the Church of North India. The Church of Pakistan, founded in 1970, unites Anglicans, Methodists, Lutherans and Presbyterians. There is also an Evangelical Fellowship of Pakistan uniting more conservative Christians.

Pakistan has suffered a series of political crises, and in 1971 India intervened in East Pakistan. As a result this area became the independent nation of Bangladesh. The proportion of Christians in Bangladesh is even smaller than in Pakistan, and the Churches lack well-trained leaders. Some of the better-educated Christian leaders left in 1947 to live in India. D. A. K. Mondal, a leading Christian from Bangladesh, has said:

The idea of self-support has been in the air for long, but nothing significant has happened. Heavy dependence on foreign funds is one of the major weaknesses of the Church in Bangladesh. Other areas of weakness are: lack of creative national leadership, tension between evangelical and liberal Churches, inadequate facilities for theological education. These weaknesses, coupled with the minority character of the Christian community, have hampered the mission of the Church in Bangladesh.

And yet Mondal goes on to say that the Churches are now beginning to show a new awareness of their responsibility towards society. They have established a Christian Commission for Development, and a Christian Health Care Project. The first of these is concerned with developing the fishing industry, weaving, and agriculture. The second has started a rural health care organization. Health workers of the National Christian Council work closely with the government of Bangladesh in caring for mothers and children.

Bangladesh faces enormous problems: too little land, a rapidly expanding population, extreme poverty, and floods and typhoons which strike the country almost every year. The action of the National Christian Council is a brave effort by the tiny Christian minority to show Christian caring for the whole community.

SRI LANKA

The population of Sri Lanka is mostly Buddhist, but there are Hindu, Muslim and Christian minorities. There were once Thomas Christians in Sri Lanka, but by modern times they had disappeared, and some ninety per cent of Christians there today are Roman Catholics. Roman Catholic missionary work dates from the sixteenth century. During a period of Dutch rule in the seventeenth century, no Catholic priests were allowed in the country, and Catholics were under pressure to renounce their faith. Some reverted to Hinduism or Islam; others became Protestants, but returned to the Roman Catholic Church as soon as Dutch rule ended. This happened in 1796, when the British expelled the Dutch and declared religious liberty. Roman Catholic missions were at a low ebb in the late eighteenth century, and it was not until 1834 that a Vicariate Apostolic of Ceylon was created, and the Catholic community began to expand again. In spite of this setback the proportion of Christians to the total population (eight per cent) is higher than anywhere else in the region. Until 1955 Roman Catholic priests for the whole of the Indian sub-continent and Sri Lanka were trained at the Pontifical Seminary in Kandy, but it was then transferred to India, and the buildings at Kandy now house a regional seminary.

Protestant missionary work began in 1812, and the British government gave more encouragement to missions in Sri Lanka than in India. In particular they encouraged education in the English language. Many of the schools were run by the missions. One result of the educational policy was that the rate of literacy was comparatively high in Sri Lanka. A second result was that Christians who benefited from mission education became prosperous under British rule, and formed a Western-educated elite. Sri Lanka became independent in 1948, and in the changed situation it was a disadvantage rather than an advantage to be

In Sri Lanka Protestant work began in 1812, and this Wesleyan mission house and chapel, Colombo (first Methodist chapel in Asia), date from 1816.

Below National Christian Councils in both Pakistan and Bangladesh encourage better standards of leadership and train Church members for evangelism and community care. In this women's class Bible teaching is followed by lessons in child welfare and agriculture.

a Christian. This became even more so after 1956 when Sinhala became the official language. In 1960 a national education system was introduced, and almost all the mission schools were taken over.

We have seen that in India Christian teaching led to a reform movement within Hinduism. In Sri Lanka it led to a revival of Buddhism in the second half of the nineteenth century. When Sri Lanka became independent, Buddhists started a movement to restore their religion to its former position, and to recover privileges which they felt they had lost. Lynn A. de Silva, the Director of the Ecumenical Centre for the Study of Society and Religion, notes that Christian preaching was often seen as part of foreign aggression. The Buddhist movement is both religious and nationalist, and although it has been aimed primarily at Christians, other minorities also feel threatened. There were riots when Sinhala was made the national language, and Tamil speakers, who include most of the Hindus in Sri Lanka, have recently demanded to be treated as a separate community because they felt threatened by militant Buddhism.

In the changed political and cultural situation since 1948 there are signs of new movements in the Church. As in so many places, there has been a growing concern for indigenization. Selva Ratnam, head of a Christian ashram, Bishop Kulundran, and D. T. Niles of the Methodist Church have been the leaders in this, and it has affected the training of clergy and other aspects of Church life. D. T. Niles is perhaps the best-known Sri Lankan Christian. He was for a time General Secretary of the Christian Conference of Asia, and later its Chairman. He was a man of outstanding Christian leadership whose great contribution to the ecumenical movement is well known.

Christians have also become more aware of their political and social responsibilities. The Christian Workers' Fellowship in Colombo is concerned with social justice in society. The Centre for the Study of Society and Religion is engaged in the study of Buddhism and in dialogue with Buddhists. This centre publishes a journal called *Dialogue*. These are hopeful signs for the Church in Sri Lanka.

NEPAL

Nepal is a small mountainous kingdom on the north-east border of India, which by the mid-1970s had a population of some fourteen million. The majority are Hindus, but there are also Muslims and Buddhists. Jesuit missionaries started work there in the late seventeenth century, but in 1767 they and their converts were expelled to northern India, where their descendants can still be found. No more missionaries were allowed into the country until 1951, and by the mid-1970s the people of Nepal were still not permitted to change their religion.

However, missions had long worked close to the border of Nepal, and already by 1900 the Bible had been translated into the language of Nepal, and a few converts were made, but had had to live outside the country.

In 1951, following a change of government, missions were allowed into Nepal to do social work but not to evangelize. The Roman Catholic Church, Protestant groups, and some Mar Thoma Christians entered the country on these terms. They are running schools and public health programmes, and also training people in agriculture. The Roman Catholics opened a hospital in Kathmandu in 1953. Nepalese who had become Christians but were living outside the country were permitted to return home and practise their religion.

By the mid-1970s there were about 500 Christians in Nepal, 125 of whom were nationals. Christian parents were allowed to have their children baptized, but Nepalese who were not Christians were still forbidden to change their religion. The Christians were scattered, but formed small, autonomous congregations, and built two churches. The Nepalese Christian Fellowship has brought them all together once a year.

STUDY SUGGESTIONS

WORDS AND MEANINGS

1. Match each of the following words (a)–(h) with its appropriate description in the list (i)–(p) below.
   (a) Moguls; (b) Adivasis; (c) Mukti; (d) Ramakrishna Mission;
   (e) Ahmadiyya; (f) Sadhu; (g) Brahman; (h) Bhakti
   (i) Tribal descendants of the indigenous Indian people.
   (j) A wandering preacher.
   (k) A group of missionary but unorthodox Muslims.
   (l) A Hindu educational and social mission.
   (m) Loving devotion to a deity.
   (n) Muslim rulers of North India for several centuries.
   (o) A community established to care for child-widows and orphans.
   (p) The highest rank in the Indian caste system.
2. What does the word 'Untouchable' mean in the Indian caste system?

REVIEW OF CONTENT

3. (a) Which three groups of Christians were working in the Indian sub-continent at the beginning of the nineteenth century?

(b) What changes in the political and commercial situation in India in the nineteenth century led to the arrival of a further group of Christians?

(c) Who were the new arrivals at that time, and what was the effect of their coming?

4. In what chief way was the relationship between Church and government under British rule similar to that under the earlier Portuguese rule?

5. (a) Give a brief description of the Indian caste system. In what chief ways does it differ from the class system still prevailing in many Western societies?

(b) Why did Protestant missions start by trying to convert Indians of the higher Brahman caste, and why did they find it difficult to do so?

(c) From which caste did the majority of new Christians come in the nineteenth century? What chiefly persuaded them to join the Church? What were some of the factors which led to their 'conversion', and what were some of its effects on everyday Church practice?

6. By what means did the Churches chiefly hope to attract Muslims in the nineteenth century?

7. What was the so-called 'patronage' system, and what effect did it have on Roman Catholic missionary work in India?

8. Describe very briefly the contribution made by each of the following in the development of the Church in the Indian sub-continent: (a) Yerraguntla Periah; (b) Constant Lievens; (c) Alexander Duff; (d) William Wallace; (e) V. Chakkarai; (f) Narayan Vaman Tilak; (g) D. T. Niles

9. (a) Name two of the leaders of Hindu opposition to Christianity, and briefly summarize the teaching of each of them.

(b) For what particular qualities do some Hindu thinkers admire and respect Jesus, while denying His divinity?

10. (a) What are some of the similarities between the Ramakrishna Mission and the Ahmadiyya movement?

(b) What is the chief difference between them?

11. (a) What, if any, are the similarities between the Arya Samaj and the Christo Samaj?

(b) When was each founded, and by whom?

(c) What is the chief difference between them?

12. Give details of four Church union movements which have taken place in India in the twentieth century.

13. (a) Compare and contrast the work of Pandita Ramabai, starting in the nineteenth century, with that of Mother Teresa since World War II.

(b) What particular advantage does membership of religious orders offer to Indian Christian women?

14. Describe very briefly the political history of Pakistan and Bangladesh since 1947.

15. (a) In what chief ways has the Church in Pakistan developed since 1947, and what chief difficulties does it have to face?
    (b) What special problems does the Church in Bangladesh have to face today? What are some of its weaknesses, according to D. A. K. Mondal, and in what ways has it been developing?

16. (a) What 'setback' did Roman Catholic work in Sri Lanka suffer at the end of the eighteenth century, and when did it start to expand again?
    (b) At what date did Protestant missionary work begin in Sri Lanka, and in what ways did Independence in 1948 prove to be a disadvantage rather than an advantage to the Church there?

17. (a) What setbacks have chiefly hindered the development of the Church in Nepal?
    (b) On what terms were Christian missionaries allowed to re-enter Nepal in the twentieth century, and which denominations did so?
    (c) What has been the situation of the Church there since then?

DISCUSSION

18. (a) In the past new Indian Christians leaned on the European rulers for protection, which made them suspect to Hindus; now they are trying to disarm suspicion by being too yielding (see p. 58). How does this compare with any changing relationships between Church and traditional religion(s) during and after any period of colonial rule or other form of state control in your own country?
    (b) Since Independence, Pakistan has Islam as the state religion. India and Bangladesh, both secular states, officially guarantee freedom of religion. In what ways and in what circumstances can government protection—or control—help or hinder the growth and health of the Church?

19. In 1870 the Vatican Council agreed that caste distinctions were un-Christian, but high caste people still would not sit with low caste people in church. Later, Mahatma Gandhi campaigned against the divisiveness of caste, comparing it to racist divisiveness in South Africa (pp. 59, 183). What division(s), if any, exist in the Church(es) in your country today? What, if anything, is being done to overcome them? What more do you think could be done?

20. The diagram on p. 60 compares the relative strength of the many Christian denominations in India. Find out if you can the strengths of different Churches in your country, and make a similar diagram

to compare them. What conclusions, if any, do you draw from the comparison?

21. Indian Churches continue to take an important part in medical work. Most Christians now see healing itself as a Christian activity, not merely a means of making converts (see p. 63). What are the chief advantages and disadvantages to a Church of running its own hospitals and medical training? What are some other ways in which Christians can exercise a healing ministry?

22. Some Christians have said that for Hindus, Christianity should be understood as the fulfilment of Hinduism, and so they should read the Hindu scriptures instead of the Old Testament. Others think that such a mixture of religions is dangerous (see p. 66). What is your opinion?

23. 'Roman Catholics, Orthodox and Protestants are beginning to find ways in which *all* Christians can co-operate' (p. 72). 'The Churches' (in Bangladesh—and also Sri Lanka) 'are beginning to show a new awareness of their responsibility towards society' (p. 74). What connection, if any, can you see between these two statements? To what extent are such trends occurring in your own country, and how do you think they are likely to develop?

4
South-East Asia
from material contributed by John Roxborogh

From Colonialism to Independence

The Churches, like the nations, of South-East Asia have achieved independence out of a long history of colonialism and the development of a sense of national identity. Today they face the questions of how to be true both to their own cultures and to the Christian gospel. The story of the last two centuries is vital for an understanding of who they are and where they are going. We are not just talking about history, but about identity and mission.

There are common factors as well as very individual situations in the Churches of the region. Thailand is unique in having successfully avoided colonial rule, yet it shares with 'Indo-China' generally the influence of French Catholicism. The Philippines remain largely Roman Catholic, reflecting the years of Spanish influence before the coming of the Americans at the start of this century. In 1824 the British and the Dutch created the divisions which are seen in the present borders of Malaysia, Singapore and Indonesia. The legacy of missionaries is evident, and the influence of worldwide movements within Christianity is felt here as everywhere else, but by the mid-1970s at least the Churches in each country were under the direction of their own leadership.

In the past the presence of Christianity was brought into South-East Asia by trade, conquest, and migration as well as by the straightforward desire to spread the gospel wherever there was opportunity. We shall briefly trace the story of that process in this chapter. But today 'partnership' is the word we should use to describe the relationship with the older 'sending' Churches, because that story truly brings us to a new era in the history of the Church.

THAILAND

Thailand has long maintained political independence and a large measure of religious freedom. Christians have been welcomed for their social contribution through education and medicine, and have enjoyed generally friendly relationships with the government. Yet there is a sense of frustration that their impact has not been greater. In 1980 Christians were about one per cent among a society that remains over ninety per cent Buddhist.

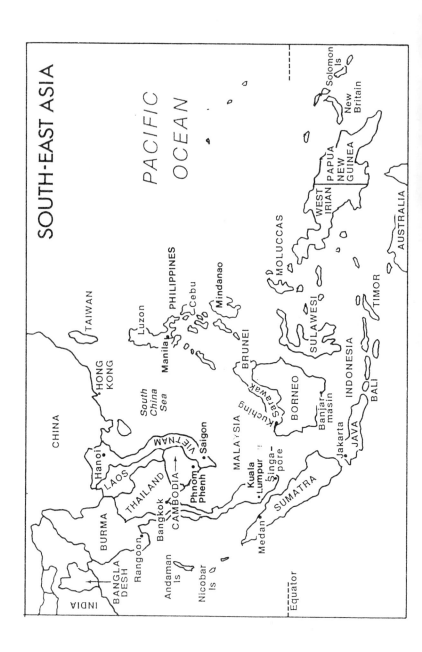

SOUTH-EAST ASIA

PACIFIC OCEAN

Solomon Is

New Britain

PAPUA NEW GUINEA

WEST IRIAN

AUSTRALIA

MOLUCCAS

TAIWAN

PHILIPPINES

Cebu

Mindanao

Luzon

Manila

SULAWESI

TIMOR

HONG KONG

BRUNEI

South China Sea

INDONESIA

BALI

CHINA

Saigon

Sarawak

Kuching

BORNEO

Banjar-masin

Jakarta

JAVA

Hanoi

VIETNAM

LAOS

Phnom Penh

MALAYSIA

Kuala Lumpur

Singa-pore

SUMATRA

THAILAND

CAMBODIA

Bangkok

Medan

BURMA

Rangoon

Andaman Is

Nicobar Is

BANGLA DESH

Equator

INDIA

After periods of repression in the seventeenth and eighteenth centuries, Roman Catholic missions were slow to recover. Protestant work began in 1828. A Buddhist monk, later to be King Mongut (Rama IV), developed a deep friendship with the Catholic Vicar-Apostolic, Bishop Pallegoix (1841–1861), and also had good relationships with the American Protestant Dr D. B. Bradley who arrived in 1835. The medical work of Bradley and the production of a Thai-Latin-French-English dictionary by the Bishop showed that the Church's role was socially useful and appreciated, yet its evangelism was ineffective. Twenty years passed before Protestants saw their first Thai convert.

In 1930 the Siam National Christian Council was formed, and in 1934 the Church of Christ in Thailand (CCT). Mission influence remained considerable, but leadership was more firmly in Thai hands from 1957. The first Thai Roman Catholic bishop was consecrated in 1945, and two archbishops in 1956. The CCT has drawn together many of the Protestant missions, most of them American—Presbyterians, Disciples of Christ, Baptists; but also German Lutherans; Japanese and Filipino United Church of Christ; Korean Presbyterians; and the Church of South India. Others such as the Christian and Missionary Alliance (in Thailand from 1929) and the Overseas Missionary Fellowship (from 1951) have become associated with the Evangelical Fellowship of Thailand, founded in 1974.

Missionaries have long sought to explain why their success has been so very largely limited to groups whose sense of religious and national identity is not very strong: Chinese and Vietnamese in Bangkok, tribespeople in the north, Malay speakers in the south. Administrative weaknesses and the chaos of Protestant fragmentation account for particular missions' failure more than for the Churches' general lack of impact. Christians generally seem to have underestimated both the strength of State Buddhism combined with Thai nationalism, and the capacity of Buddhism to be fundamentally unyielding even though tolerant on the surface. However, a Catholic monastery founded in 1970 has tried to be explicitly Thai in character and open to contacts with Buddhist monasteries. A Thai Church historian writes of the situation among Protestants:

The missionary has done much of his 'apologetical missionary proclamation' to Thai Buddhists through Christian service. This, of course, is not outside the framework of Christ's ministry. But it can be said that this type of proclamation has touched the 'Thai Buddhist feeling' more than the 'Thai Buddhist mind'. . . . One of the factors behind this weakness is probably the inadequacy of philosophical training for the missionary and lack of interest in other religions in

American seminaries. (M. Pongudom, *Apologetic and missionary proclamation*, PhD thesis, University of Otago 1979, p. 396f.)

Without underestimating the value of its social mission, the Church in Thailand, like many others in countries with a strong culturally and politically established religion, is still discovering how it can be true to its context and faithful to all aspects of its calling. It is being helped in this by a clear determination to become aware of its own history, and a marked willingness to be critical as well as appreciative of its particular origins.

BURMA

Roman Catholic efforts to evangelize Burma from Thailand had only resulted in martyrdom. The pioneer Protestant missionary was the American Baptist, Adoniram Judson (1788–1850), who arrived in 1813. Like those who followed him, despite a strong commitment to the Burmese he found his greatest response among the animistic hill tribes—the Karen, the Kachin and the Chin—among whom the greatest proportion of Christians are found today.

New openings were provided under the British, who extended their influence from India in a series of conflicts (1826, 1852 and 1886). Freedom from Britain came in 1948, and Burma has, from the early 1960s especially, maintained a remarkable non-alignment in world affairs coupled with a strong sense of national independence. For these reasons more than anything else, all missionaries were required to leave the country in 1966 and Church schools and hospitals were nationalized.

As in Thailand, Buddhism in Burma is strongly linked with national identity. While Christians are found in significant numbers among some of the hill tribe groups in rebellion against the central government, Christians in the main centres enjoy considerable freedom, and valued if limited contacts with the outside world. The Burma Baptist Convention and the Burma Council of Churches function as national bodies. The Churches are self-sufficient in theological education, and are noted for vigorous and capable leaders. Although their existence owed much to missionaries, and some groups of Christians have migrated from Assam in India and from the South of China, the main source of Church growth has always been their own members. The Anglican Archbishop Aung Hla would not be alone in explaining:

> It is mostly individual local Christians who have preached the Gospel; it has been done again and again around their fireplaces, hearths sunk in the floor of the house. They sat around the fire, drank tea and talked religion. (D. Morgan, *The restless ones*, SPG 1958, p. 52.)

VIETNAM

Success and tragedy have long been common features of the story of the Church in Vietnam. Energetic and fruitful evangelism in the seventeenth century had been followed by severe persecution in the eighteenth, and this pattern was repeated in the nineteenth, with periods of persecution in 1825, the 1840s and 1851. The last of these persecutions alone brought the death of 115 clergy and about 90,000 laity. Those who fled provided the core membership of Roman Catholic Churches in Kampuchea, Laos and Thailand.

A strength and a weakness of the Roman Catholic Church was its association with the French, whose government used the persecutions as a pretext for political involvement. By 1885, following the capture of Hanoi in 1883, the French had extended their influence from Cochin China in the South (1862–67) to Annam in the centre and Tonkin in the North. By the end of the century large numbers of French Roman Catholic missions were entering the country, with significant numbers of conversions following. However, as the Thai writer, Professor Kirti Buncha, has noted, 'this easy way of Evangelization gave the impression to the rest of the population that Christianity is the French religion . . . an instrument of the French for an easy and permanent dominion.' Although there had long been a fair proportion of Vietnamese priests, the first Vietnamese bishop was not consecrated until 1933, three years after Ho Chi Minh had founded his IndoChina Communist Party with the aim of getting rid of Western influences.

The French Government was reluctant to admit Protestants, and the Christian and Missionary Alliance was not able to begin work until 1911. World War II and the Japanese invasion gave the opportunity for a declaration of independence by Ho Chi Minh in August 1945. This resulted in a nine-year conflict subsequently extended into even more terrible tragedy following the division of the country into Communist North and Nationalist South, in 1954. American involvement in the civil war followed from 1964 to April 30 1975, when Saigon finally fell to the North.

At first the local Roman Catholic hierarchy supported the call for independence, but this was eroded by the French loyalty of many Catholics, and by mistrust and misdeeds on both sides. Future relations with the Communists were not helped when, in 1950, Pope Pius XII blessed the army of the French as defenders of 'Christian civilization in Vietnam'.

Following the 1954 Geneva agreement for partition, Roman Catholics were advised to take the opportunity to settle in the South. It is estimated that there were 1,400,000 laity and 1,100 priests in the North at this time, and that sixty per cent of the bishops, seventy per cent of the priests, and forty per cent of the laity (about sixty-five per cent of the total who migrated) took the advice and aid of the Americans and moved south of the demarcation line. Understandable as this may have been, it further compromised those in the North who were trying to be loyal to the Communist government. In the South it created a large community within the Church who were even less inclined to come to terms with the North at the stage of the Vietnam conflict when that was a serious possibility. Through no fault of their own, the migrants also aroused jealousy because of their access to aid funding and the privileges given them by the Nationalist regime under Ngo Dinh Diem, himself a Catholic.

The direct military involvement of America in the developing civil war from 1964 brought reconciliation between the Roman Catholic Church and the government in the North, where American bombing destroyed 500 churches and killed one bishop. The Northern Church, had earlier been denied international contacts, such as attendance at Vatican II, in case they might meet Roman Catholics from the South. Now they were able to play an active role in international peace efforts, especially from 1970 onwards.

In the South, Roman Catholics were in some ways in quite a strong position. They had more local priests than any other nation in the region, and were involved in a wide range of social, educational and welfare activity. Yet they were also associated with a doomed and corrupt regime and increasingly isolated from world Catholic opinion, which was now much more in favour of some sort of peace settlement. However, as the South collapsed at the end of April 1975 Church leaders accepted that their future lay in a reunited Vietnam rather than in further flight. In contrast to 1954, no bishop left his diocese. Just before Saigon fell Archbishop Paul Nguyen van Binh gave an indication as to how he intended to help the Church survive:

> Tell them in Rome that I will never betray the faith, the Church and the Pope. However I will be pliable where it is possible and collaborate with the government as long as it asks nothing of me which is contrary to my faith. (*Far Eastern Economic Review*, 1 November 1984, p. 42.)

Protestants were however in a more difficult situation, as the missions which had given birth to them were largely American, and some hundreds of pastors fled the country.

Since 1975 Christians have survived, but not without considerable difficulty. The government is suspicious of religions in general, and Catholics and Protestants have suffered along with Buddhists.

LAOS

Christian contact with Laos has mostly been from Thailand to the East or from Cambodia in the South. Several early nineteenth-century Roman Catholic efforts failed to establish a mission, but they were more successful when two priests from the Paris Foreign Missionary Society (MEP) began ransoming slaves in the 1880s. The resulting communities saw significant numbers of conversions. From an initial base among the Thai Lao of the plains, by the 1950s they were expanding with some success among tribespeople. Today Christians comprise some two per cent of the population of approximately three million.

The Swiss Brethren missionary Fritz Audetat began Protestant work when he arrived in the South in 1902. By 1932 he had translated the whole Bible into Lao. The Christian and Missionary Alliance have been active from 1929, encouraged and somewhat taken by surprise by a mass movement of more than a thousand tribespeople in 1950. The Overseas Missionary Fellowship was also a significant influence in the founding and supporting of Churches.

Laos suffered greatly from the disruption caused by war in the region. It was under the French from 1893, invaded by the Japanese, and rather more than on the sidelines during the conflicts in Vietnam and Cambodia from the time of its own independence (1953) to 1975. In 1976 the government restricted all religious activity, and among the refugees to Thailand were 450 Protestant families and their pastors.

In some ways the Church was in a good position to cope with this situation, but the Roman Catholics had only appointed their first Laotian priest in 1963 and bishop in 1974. More hope could be based on the numbers converting to Christianity of their own accord, and the important role of local catechists in building up the Church, especially among the mountain-dwelling tribespeople who comprise over one third of the Christian population. However the 'lessons of Laos' have included the dangers of over-concentration on institutional Christianity in an uncertain political environment, and the need to ensure that Christian literature is widely distributed.

KAMPUCHEA (CAMBODIA)

Although the Roman Catholic catechism was translated into Khmer, Cambodia's main language, by 1770, growth in the Church was slow (there were four churches and 222 members in 1842), and the membership was mainly Vietnamese, Chinese, and (after 1864) French. By 1969, nearly ninety per cent of the 62,000 baptized were Vietnamese, and there were only four Khmer priests in the country.

Left Church leaders in Burma are strong and capable, but according to Archbishop John U Aung Hla (here with his grandchild) the gospel is mostly spread by individual local Christians.

Below Christians are welcomed in Thailand for service to education and medicine. Nurse Soi, tending a small patient in Manoram Christian Hospital, is also a Church Elder.

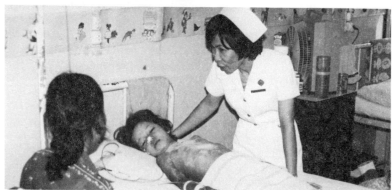

200 years of political upheaval and change have driven the Philippine Churches to find ways of relating the faith to social justice. Some do so through basic Christian communities—like these brave young members of a Christian non-violent resistance group against political oppression.

The French delayed Protestant missions until 1923, when the Christian and Missionary Alliance was able to start work. They were able to achieve a broader ethnic base, and a more obviously Cambodian Church resulted. American missionaries were obliged to leave in 1965, when the country's ruler Prince Sihanouk wanted to demonstrate Cambodia's neutrality in the Vietnam War. However, they returned after Sihanouk was ousted by his defence minister Lon Nol in 1970—at the very time when due to the anti-Vietnamese attitude of the new government Roman Catholics experienced severe persecution, with thousands killed and their membership reduced by two-thirds through death or flight.

The next five years saw an amazing revival in the Protestant Churches, and a ten-fold increase in membership. But in those years the country became the battleground for American bombers and South Vietnamese troops against Cambodia's growing Communist movement, the Khmer Rouge. In April 1975 the capital, Phnom Phenh, fell to the Communists under their leader, Pol Pot, and in the chaos that followed evacuation of the city, Catholics and Protestants suffered alike. With the massacre of all who had education or foreign contacts and the destruction of the economy, banks were blown up, money was used for making bags, and up to 1,000,000 people were killed.

The Vietnamese invaders drove the Pol Pot regime to the fringes of the country in 1978, but it is difficult to discover what remains of Christian faith and practice in Kampuchea.

THE PHILIPPINES

Christianity had been brought to the Philippines in the sixteenth century by the Spanish conquerors. Their missionary work, carried out at first by Friars of the Augustinian religious order, followed by Franciscans, Dominicans, and later some Jesuits and others, was immensely successful (see TEF Church History Guide Vol. 3, pp. 88, 131, 132). Today the Roman Catholic Church is the strongest institution in what was the first, and remains the only, 'Christian' nation in Asia. However since the turn of the century America has been the dominant power, and Protestants have been allowed to share in missionary work. Today among a great variety of Churches, and with a significant Muslim minority in the South, eighty per cent of the population are Roman Catholic, and about ten per cent Philippine Independent Church.

In the nineteenth century growing Philippine nationalism led to opposition to the Catholic Friars, who represented both Spain and the Church. There was no doubt that Catholicism was the Church of the people, but there was widespread resentment at the Friars' failure to train and appoint Filipino clergy, and the amount of power and property concentrated in the hands of the religious orders. Within the Church there was also conflict over the bishops' rights of visitation in their dioceses, and varying attitudes to new ideas of liberty. The Catholic leaders in Manila, as in Rome, regarded all such notions as sacrilegious, and as deriving from the French Revolution.

Matters were brought to a head with the judicial murder of three Filipino priests, José Burgos, Jacinto Zamora and Mariano Gomez, on 28 February 1872, who were falsely accused of fomenting rebellion because they were known to be sympathetic to those who were critical of the Friars. Among those convinced of the injustice of their execution was the reformer José Rizal (1862–1896), whose writings were to be important in moulding Filipino and world-wide opposition to the Spanish regime.

Throughout the nineteenth century the greatest agitation had been *against* the Friars (though it was not necessarily anti-Catholic), and *for* equality with citizens of Spain—which was promised and withdrawn on several occasions. As time went on the demands changed to a call for political independence. Insurrection was breaking out when Spain and America went to war over Cuba, and the Americans destroyed the Spanish fleet in Manila Bay. The Treaty of Paris in 1898 transferred sovereignty to the United States. Although there was strong debate in America, the Filipinos were denied their independence, resulting in further war until 1902. Political independence was not to come until after the Second World War, on 4 July 1946.

In this situation the Roman Catholic Church was faced with a change of government from one where there had been the closest possible alliance between Church and State to one whose policies called for complete separation between them. In practice agreement between the Vatican and the American Government in Washington was not long in forthcoming. The Spanish clergy were replaced with new foreigners, including American bishops acceptable to the American President. The United States Government paid $7,000,000 compensation for lands previously occupied by Friars. The Pope issued some necessary reforms, and declared the end of the Spanish *patronato real*. The first Filipino bishop was appointed in 1905.

These turbulent years also saw the birth of the Philippine Independent Church (PIC). It began as a indigenous takeover of Roman Catholic churches by Filipino clergy. Under the leadership of Gregorio Aglipay (1860–1940) and Isabelo de los Reyes (1864–1938), and fuelled by nationalism and hatred of the Friars, it was initially very successful. But its occupation of church buildings was challenged in the courts, and property had to be returned to the Catholic hierarchy. This severely damaged the movement. It was also weakened by differences between the republican and Unitarian ideas of its leaders, and the more staunchly Catholic views of ordinary Church members. (Unitarians reject the doctrine of the Trinity, and believe in God in One Person only, not Three.) At one stage there was the surprising spectacle of a large Church which was 'Catholic in polity and liturgy, but Unitarian in theology'. After the death of the original leaders there was a return to orthodox teaching, and today there is a close relationship between the PIC and the Protestant Episcopal Church in America.

The element of protest which brought the PIC to birth was not enough to sustain it, but the call for indigenous leadership and autonomy continued in all denominations, and resulted in many schisms among Protestant groups as Filipinos complained of American dominance. At the same time as fragmentation occurred, there was at other levels a degree of warm co-operation. Comity agreements, begun with the formation of the Evangelical Union among a number of Protestant Churches in 1901, were relatively successful for several decades. Through a succession of changes shifting the emphasis from overseas mission to local Church, this became in 1969 the National Council of Churches in the Philippines. However, despite a number of successful unions, the overall situation is more marked by fragmentation.

Since the 1960s both Catholics and Protestants have had to come to terms with the relationship of their faith to social justice, and also with the fact that the traditional Jesuit missionary policy of building on rather than supplanting pre-Christian beliefs did not go far enough in determining what is distinctively Christian. Considering Evangelical separatism and suspicion of 'liberal' social activism on the one hand, and the persistent conservatism of the Catholic hierarchy on the other, the degree of Church support which aided the overthrow of the Marcos dictatorship in 1986 showed what a revolution had taken place in the thinking and action of many Christians. The influence of Latin American Liberation Theology has been perhaps more that of an inspiration than a model. But the basic Christian communities—small groups of Christians working at parish level to live out their faith together—have provided a means by which faith and action can be welded together in a potent force for personal and social transformation.

MALAYSIA AND SINGAPORE

British influence in the area provided the umbrella for a new phase of Christian influence following that of the Roman Catholic Portuguese and the Protestant Dutch in Malacca from 1511 and 1641 respectively. This initially centred on the Straits Settlements of Penang (1786),

Malacca (1824) and Singapore (1819), and then followed the spread of British administration into the Federated Malay States, particularly Perak and Selangor, which resulted from the Treaty of Pangkor in 1874.

In the Federated States the British had agreed not to interfere with the religion or custom of the Malay peoples, and they permitted rather than encouraged missionary work among the Muslim Malays only in Singapore and Penang. Even here response was meagre, and today the few Malay-speaking congregations are likely to consist of 'Straits-born' Chinese, not Malays. Only in the East Malaysian states of Sabah and Sarawak is the Church primarily indigenous (among the tribespeople such as Iban, Kelabit and Kadazan). Elsewhere it is associated almost entirely with immigrant groups: Chinese, Indian and the Eurasian descendants of Portuguese or Dutch intermarriage.

Roman Catholic priests expelled from Thailand came to Penang via the Malay state of Kedah before the end of the eighteenth century, and soon founded the College General, which trained priests for the region for nearly 180 years. Although the East India Company was required by its charter to provide chaplains for the British settlements, it was slow to do so. The first missionaries were from the London Missionary Society, who came to the Malay Peninsula because they were unable to gain entry to China.

The Anglo-Chinese College at Malacca, founded by William Milne (1785–1822) in 1815 on the vision of the pioneer Protestant missionary to China, Robert Morrison (1782–1834), did serve as a meeting-place between cultures and as a base for other missionary work in the region, as well as providing a small nucleus for a local Church. However, the LMS abandoned their work in the Straits Settlements with the 'opening' of China after the Opium Wars of 1839–42 (see p. 27). It was only with the growth of Churches among the increasing numbers of Europeans that Presbyterians, Anglicans and Roman Catholics were significantly able to extend their work as missions. The greatest growth took place where Chinese and Indian immigrants were involved in the development of tin mining and rubber tapping. Migrants included a good proportion of Christians, and sometimes whole Christian communities, such as the Foochow-speaking Methodists in Sibu and Sitiawan and the Hakka-speaking Basel Mission converts in North Borneo. Despite an association with the government which occasionally worked to their advantage, as with the building of St George's, Penang, Anglicans were not able to obtain the money or the manpower to seize the new opportunities which existed from late in the nineteenth century. Methodists were able to do so, however, and benefited from their experience gained during thirty years' work in India. Their first missionary, William Oldham (1854–1937), was energetic and far-sighted, of considerable faith and vision, and was a Tamil-speaker brought up in India. With American funding and an international missionary force, Methodists were able to staff government schools and establish schools of their own throughout the country.

In East Malaysia the establishment of the Brooke dynasty from 1841 resulted in an interesting situation. James Brooke was English, but his rule was personal, and unlike others in the Straits Settlements he was firmly against the economic exploitation of the people he had come to rule. However he hoped that a Christian mission might hasten the suppression of headhunting, and in Francis Thomas (later Bishop) McDougall (1817–1886) he found a very able leader. Anglicanism in East Malaysia began as a missionary and not a chaplaincy Church, and for forty years had the field to itself. In 1881 the British North Borneo Company acquired what is today Sabah, and again the Anglicans were fortunate in their first missionary, though severely frustrated by a lack of adequate manpower or other resources.

The Japanese occupation in World War II, from late 1941 until 1945, profoundly changed the political and religious situation. Although British authority was restored after the war, independence was now foreseeable. It came in 1957 for Malaya, which was later joined by Sabah and Sarawak to form Malaysia in 1963. This initially included Singapore, which became independent from Malaysia in 1965.

Some Christians had recognized even before the war that the Churches were insular, expatriate, and failing in their duty to train local clergy and this now grew into conviction. The founding of Trinity Theological College in Singapore in 1948 was one sign of a new ecumenical and Asian commitment that had immense importance for the Churches of the whole region.

Ecumenical activity was not so easy to sustain in other ways. There had been co-operation in the past. Scottish Presbyterians had contributed to the Anglican Cathedral in Singapore and got it named after the Scottish patron saint (St Andrew), but were driven to build their own church when the 'High Church' influence of the Oxford Movement upon local Anglicans caused a breakdown in relationships. In Penang at the end of the century the Anglican Society for the Propagation of the Gospel (SPG) had a successful joint-venture with local Presbyterians for a mission among estate workers on the mainland. There had been sharing of church buildings when one or other was unfit for use after the war, and the occasional joint service. But proposals for union could not overcome the barriers of congregational suspicions and ethnic and language differences. Nevertheless Councils of Churches in Singapore and in West Malaysia in particular have been very important, and in 1986 a co-ordinating Christian body was formed in Malaysia which also incorporated Roman Catholics and the more independently-minded Evangelicals.

From 1948 to 1960 during the Malayan Emergency life in the country was disrupted by Communist guerrillas. As part of a campaign to isolate the guerrillas and gain the 'hearts and minds' of the people, thousands of rural Chinese were resettled. Missionaries and Church workers were invited to these 'New Villages', and many who had been forced to leave Communist China found a new sphere of service in Malaya.

By the mid-1970s Christians totalled some eight per cent of the population of Singapore, and six per cent in Malaysia, where Islam is the official religion. For Malaysia this figure disguises the very much greater proportion of Christians in the lesser overall population of East Malaysia. Church schools retain Church links but on a very much reduced scale. Many feel that the time has come for the more indigenous Churches of Sarawak and Sabah, with their strong base among tribespeople, to exercise a greater role in the leadership of the Church in the country as a whole.

INDONESIA

Christianity had come to the islands of Indonesia with the Portuguese in the sixteenth century, and with the Dutch from 1605 (see Vol. 3, pp. 89–90). The Dutch East India Company had little interest in evangelism, but by 1800 there were more than 50,000 local baptized Christians, about two per cent of whom were communicants. Today the population is largely Muslim, but about eleven per cent are Christian. Many of the Churches are based on ethnic groupings, with six per cent Protestant, three per cent Catholic and two per cent Indigenous. Indonesia has the largest Muslim population of any country in the world, one of the largest Christian populations in Asia, and one of the few in Asia where Protestants outnumber Catholics.

From 1799, with the bankruptcy of the East India Company, the occupation of Holland by France, and the rise of the Protestant Missionary Movement in Europe, the situation in Indonesia developed rapidly. Missionaries from Holland were welcomed during a short period of British rule from 1811 to 1816 under Raffles, later famous as the founder of Singapore. Roman Catholics were also allowed back into the country. However, the Dutch colonial administration maintained an extraordinarily tight control over the location of missions, and Roman Catholics in particular resented the restrictions which kept them out of large areas. Up till 1935, when some measure of autonomy was given, the Protestant Church of the Indies was under government direction to the extent that ministers and missionaries were state

Above Trinity College, Singapore is a united and co-educational theological school founded jointly in 1948 by Anglican, Lutheran, Methodist and Presbyterian Churches in Malaya.

Right and below Indonesian resettlement schemes have offered new opportunities for evangelism, as in Sumatra, where house-to-house distribution of Bible notes is backed up by a lending library of Christian teaching on cassettes.

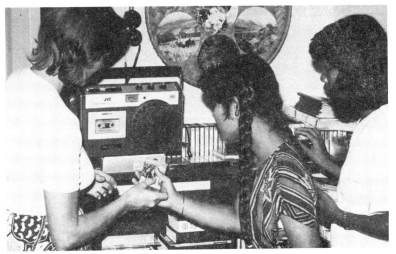

servants. They were paid for the baptisms they conducted, and their correspondence with the Church in Holland was vetted by the colonial administration.

With Indonesia's enormous number of islands spread over a huge area it is obvious that the story of the Church varied considerably from place to place. Earlier Dutch colonists had followed the Portuguese pattern, by beginning in the Moluccas and extending through Java from their base in Batavia (now Jakarta). Sumatra, the Celebes, Kalimantan (Borneo), Timor and other areas were gradually conquered. The Dutch regulated the growing of spices to avoid oversupply. Towards the end of the nineteenth century changes in Dutch economic policy led to a less exploitive if more paternalistic administration.

Mass movements have been a feature of Indonesian Church growth. In East Java the work of enthusiastic laymen, such as the planter F. L. Coolen (1770–1863) and the watchmaker J. Emde (1774–1859), resulted in numbers of conversions and the formation of Christian villages, although Coolen rather than Emde strove to encourage a 'Javanese Christianity' that did not simply mimic European forms. L. Nommensen (1834–1918) of the Rhenish Missionary Society was the first who systematically set out to establish an indigenous Church firmly related to village society and custom, and laid the foundations for the very successful Batak Church in Sumatra.

However, European dominance of the Church in Indonesia was first seriously questioned by the brilliant writer H. Kraemer (1888–1965) from 1927 onwards. He became one of a number of outstanding Dutch missiologists who formulated their ideas against the background of the mistakes and achievements of their nation's mission in the Dutch East Indies.

The degree of independence won by the Churches in Indonesia before World War II anticipated political developments. The Japanese presence from 1942 to 1945 hastened this process, and although Christian loyalties were occasionally stretched, to a notable extent the Churches supported and fought for the continuing independence of the nation when the Dutch tried to re-establish control after the war. But despite the slow acceptance of independence by the Netherlands government, once it was granted, Church links with Holland were again established.

The 1945 declaration of independence set forth the 'Pantja Sila' or 'five principles' which have provided the policy framework for religious activity ever since. Summed up as belief in one Supreme Being, humanitarianism, national unity and social justice, it has also been required, since 1965, that citizens belong to one of four recognized religions, Islam, Protestantism, Roman Catholicism, or 'Hindu-Buddhism'. There has been debate by both Islamic and Christian groups about accepting this as the basis of their respective organizations, but it has also served as an incentive to conversion. The failure of an attempted Communist coup in 1965, and the consequent upset, saw the start of a large mass movement in which all Churches grew, with over 2.5 million converts in five years.

The legacy of the Dutch in the Churches has been a certain standard of theological training and reflection, which has at times tended to become over-formalized. Economic independence was more difficult to achieve than freedom from the missionary organizations, and theological independence may be harder still. Much of the evangelism that has been behind the flow of conversions has been carried out by Indonesian Christians themselves. The (Reformed) Christian Churches of Mid-Java were not alone in taking the responsibility of sending missionaries elsewhere, in their case to South Sumatra. The Batak Church too has sent its missionaries; and government resettlement schemes have also provided opportunities for the Churches in new communities.

Providing enough clergy to care for the flow of converts of the late 1960s created some difficulties. And the Church in Indonesia, as elsewhere in South East Asia, is still learning what is the appropriate way of engaging with other ancient religions; and what its responsibility should be towards a state that is sensitive to criticism, demanding of loyalty, yet needs the critical and wise co-operation of the Christian members of society.

STUDY SUGGESTIONS

WORDS AND MEANINGS

1. What do you understand by the following terms as used in this chapter?
   (a) New Villages (b) *Pantja Sila* (Five Principles) (c) *Patronato real* (d) Basic Christian Communities (e) Straits Settlements

REVIEW OF CONTENT

2. (a) Which European countries have, in the past, had colonial interests in South-East Asia, and hence been involved in missionary work there?
   (b) In what ways has the history of Thailand been unique in this respect?
3. (a) Name two people whose good relationships with Thai people in the first half of the nineteenth century enabled the Church to play a socially useful role in Thailand.
   (b) Which two Christian organizations founded in the 1930s have

helped the development of indigenous leadership and the gradual reduction of missionary influence in the Thai Churches?

4. (a) Who was the pioneer Protestant missionary in Burma, when did he arrive there, and to which Church did he belong?

(b) Among which people in Burma are the greatest proportion of Christians found today?

(c) What has been the attitude of the Burmese government to the rest of the world since World War II, and why? What action of the Burmese government in 1966 has led to the development of a strong indigenous Church leadership there?

5. What are some of the reasons put forward for the fact that the Churches in both Thailand and Burma remain relatively small, and the impact of Christianity on the Thai and Burmese people at large has been fairly limited?

6. (a) 'In Vietnam fruitful seventeenth-century evangelism was followed by severe persecution (of Christians), and the pattern was repeated' (p. 85). At what periods did this persecution recur, and how did it affect Church growth in the neighbouring countries?

(b) Which Church predominated in Vietnam until the early twentieth century, and why?

7. (a) What has been the relationship between Church and state in Vietnam since World War II and Ho Chi Min's declaration of Independence?

(b) What decision taken by Roman Catholic Christians following partition of the country in 1954 affected the lives of a large number of Vietnamese clergy and lay Christians, and what effect did this have on relationships within the Church?

(c) What have been the chief similarities and differences between the role of the Churches in North Vietnam since Partition, and that of the Churches in the South?

8. (a) When did Roman Catholic missionary efforts in Laos begin, from which countries did they come, and with what effect?

(b) Which Protestant missionary agencies have been active in Laos during the twentieth century, and with what effect?

(c) What has been the situation of Laotian Christians, and their relationship with governments since Independence in 1953?

9. (a) Of what nationalities were most Christians in Cambodia (Kampuchea) during the nineteenth and early twentieth centuries?

(b) When did Protestant missions start work in Kampuchea, and with what results?

(c) What two events since 1969 have resulted in severe persecution of the Church in Kampuchea, and with what results?

10. (a) In what way does the history of the Church in the Philippines differ from that in any other Asian country?

(b) Give a brief outline of the political (colonial) background in the Philippines from the early nineteenth century to the coming of Independence after World War II.

11. (a) From its beginnings in the sixteenth century, Spanish missionary work in the Philippines was run by Friars of the various religious orders, who represented both the Roman Catholic Church and the ruling colonial power (p. 89). For what reasons did the Filipino people feel resentment against them, and what event in the 1870s brought opposition to the Spanish regime to a head?

(b) What important changes took place in the relationship between Church and state in the Philippines at the turn of the century, when sovereignty was transferred from Spain to the USA?

12. (a) Describe briefly how the Philippine Independent Church (PIC) came into being, and who were its first leaders.

(b) Describe briefly, with dates, the events leading up to the formation of the National Council of Churches in the Philippines.

13. (a) Which European countries had been involved in missionary work in Malaysia before the nineteenth century?

(b) Which country has been chiefly involved in missionary work there in the nineteenth and twentieth centuries, and what was the official attitude of government to missionary work?

(c) What events in other Asian countries contributed to Church growth in Malaysia in these centuries?

(d) In what way did the political and economic development in 'mainland' Malaysia affect Church growth, and how did this differ from the situation in East Malaysia (then Borneo) at that time?

14. To what Church or missionary society did each of the following belong, and for what particular activity or achievement in Malaysia/Singapore at what period is each remembered?
(a) William Milne (b) F. T. McDougall (c) William Oldham (d) James Brooke

15. (a) In what ways did events during and immediately following World War II change the political and economic situation in Malaysia/Singapore?

(b) Give some examples of co-operative and ecumenical action by the Churches in Malaysia/Singapore since World War II.

(c) In which areas of Malaysia/Singapore is the Church strongest?

16. (a) In what way has the effect of Indonesia's geography on the spread of Christianity been similar to that of the Philippines?

(b) What European country has been chiefly responsible for the growth of the Church in Indonesia over the past four centuries?

(c) What was the relationship between the colonial government of Indonesia and the Churches there during the nineteenth century and part of the twentieth, and what effect did it have on Church relations generally in the area?

17. (a) What special feature has distinguished Church growth in Indonesia from that in some other parts of South-East Asia?
(b) In what particular directions did the following help forward the development of the Church in Indonesia, and at what periods?
(i) F. L. Coolen (ii) J. Emde (iii) L. Nommensen (iv) H. Kraemer

18. (a) Describe briefly what is involved in the Pantja Sila (Five Principles) policy for religious activity and what has been its effect on the Indonesian Churches.
(b) What are some of the distinguishing features, strengths and difficulties being experienced in the Indonesian Churches today?

DISCUSSION

19. Christian missions in Thailand have sought to present the gospel to Buddhists through Christian service rather than theological debate (see p. 83). How does this compare with the Churches' approach to people of other religions in your own country? What factors in a situation do missions need to consider, in deciding what form their proclamation of the gospel should take?

20. 'In Burma the main source of Church growth has been through their own members ... individual local Christians who have preached the gospel ... sat around the fire, drank tea and talked religion' (p. 84). In what particular circumstances do you think individual Christians can be more effective in spreading the Gospel than organized 'missions', mass meetings, or radio and television, literature distribution etc.?

21. In Vietnam since 1975 the government has been suspicious of religion in general, and Catholics and Protestants have suffered along with Buddhists (p. 86). What effect to you think indiscriminate government opposition of this sort is likely to have on:
(a) the faith of individual Christians?
(b) relationships between Christians of different denominations?
(c) relationships between individual people of different religions?

22. In Laos the 'lessons' learnt by the Churches from a period when government had restricted all religious activity, have included 'the dangers of over-concentration on institutional Christianity in an uncertain political environment, and the need to ensure that Christian literature is widely distributed' (p. 87). In your opinion — or experience—what other dangers may Christians need to guard against in such a situation?

23. 'Since the 1960s both Catholics and Protestants' (in the Philippines) 'have had to come to terms with the relationship of their faith to social justice ... Church aid for the overthrow of the

Marcos dictatorship showed what a revolution had taken place in Christian thinking and action' (see p. 91). How far are Christians in your own country concerned with social justice? How far do you think Churches should aid political revolution?

24. In Malaysia (where Islam is the official religion) proposals for Church Union have failed to overcome barriers of congregational suspicion and ethnic and language differences (see p. 93). What other sorts of barrier may hinder achievement of union between Churches? What are some of the ways in which Christians can work to overcome such barriers?

25. (a) Until 1935 ministers and missionaries of the Protestant Church in Indonesia were state servants. What do you think would have been the advantages and disadvantages of that situation?
(b) 'Mass movements have been a feature of Indonesian Church growth ... the flow of converts in the late 1960s created some difficulties' (p. 96). What do you see as the sort of difficulties arising when large numbers of converts are seeking Church membership all at once, and in what ways might they be overcome?

26. In what ways does the end of the period studied in this chapter (mid-1970s) mark the end of an era in the history of the Church in South-East Asia?

27. Why is it sometimes difficult to be objective about the history of the Church in the past two centuries? What are some of the ways in which the present needs of your Church make it easy to either minimize or exaggerate the contribution from (or to) foreign missions in the past?

28. What do you understand by the word 'partnership', as applied to relationships between Churches in different countries? What effect do you think the increase in the number of independent nation states, and consequent strength of nationalist feeling, has had on such relationships—or is likely to have in the future?

5

Latin America and the Caribbean
from material contributed by Enrique Dussel

THE SPANISH COLONIAL PERIOD: 1492–1808

Beginning in 1492, Spain extended its rule over most of South and Central America and the south-western portion of what is today the United States. Brazil was conquered by Portugal, and there were small French and British colonies in the Caribbean area, but the Spanish influence was far the most important. In this chapter we study the whole of this area with the exception of those parts of North America which later became incorporated into the USA. A brief account of the Spanish and Portuguese conquest and the missions which led to the conversion of most of the indigenous people of Latin America can be found in the TEF Church History Guide, Vol. 3, Ch. 6. We start by recalling a few important points.

1. The conquerors were staunch Roman Catholics, who saw it as part of their duty to extend the faith. They saw the conquest of new lands as a way of achieving this. They destroyed non-Christian places of worship, attacked the indigenous cultures, and ordered Spaniards who had been allocated land, to give the people living on their estates instruction in the Christian faith, and to ensure that they were baptized. Missions received funding from the state, and the state used the missions to help subdue the conquered peoples. Today the vast majority of the population of Latin America is at least nominally Christian.

2. The Church in Spain and Portugal, and therefore in Latin America as well, was almost entirely under the control of the kings of those countries. This system was called the *patronato real*, or royal patronage. The Church received privileges and state aid, but it had little real freedom of action. The kings controlled the appointment of bishops, the creation of dioceses, the sending of missionaries, and many other aspects of Church life. Everyone had to pay tithe, a tax to the Church. This system remained in force until the nineteenth century.

3. The conquest was carried out with great cruelty, and the Amerindians (the name we shall use for the indigenous peoples of the area) were ruthlessly exploited. The existing cultures were wiped out, and many of the Amerindians were reduced to despair and to near-slavery. Individual Churchmen worked to defend the Amerindians, and laws were passed to protect their rights, but these laws could not be enforced. The best-known of these Churchmen were Bartolomeo de las

LATIN AMERICA
and
THE CARIBBEAN

Casas (1474-1566) and St Peter Claver (1580–1664). The former experienced a kind of conversion in 1514 which opened his eyes to the plight of the Amerindians, and he spent the rest of his life working on their behalf. St Peter Claver spent his life in the service of the black slaves who were imported in their thousands into Latin America. But the Christian conscience of these and others had only a limited success in curbing the selfish greed of the conquerors.

4. In the early years of the conquest almost all the clergy were Spanish born. Gradually they were joined by American-born clergy. But the Church was slow to accept *mestizos* (people of mixed descent) as clergy, and even slower to ordain Amerindians, so the shortage of clergy remained. There were many fine missionaries, but also many priests of poor education and morals. In many ways the Church reflected the economic and class divisions of society as a whole. Spaniards and others of European descent were at the top of the scale, and most of the wealth and power was in their hands. Below them came the *mestizos*, and at the bottom were the Amerindians and the black slaves. The Church tended to support the existing social system because of its privileged position within it, though there were always a few voices raised in defence of the poor and powerless.

5. In the 1760s the Jesuits were suppressed in France, Spain and Portugal, and expelled from Latin America (for the reason for this, see the TEF Church History Guide, Vol. 3, p. 124). This was a disaster for the missions in Latin America. Over 2,200 priests, the best of the Spanish American clergy, had to leave. Members of other religious orders tried to fill the gaps, but greedy landlords were able to move in to exploit the Amerindians whom the Jesuit missions had protected, but had not enabled to stand on their own feet and defend themselves against exploitation.

There are two contrasting ways of looking at the Spanish and Portuguese domination in America. One is according to the 'Black Legend', which emphasizes the negative side of the picture: the cruelties, the destruction of the indigenous cultures, the exploitation of the Amerindians and blacks, all carried out by people who called themselves Christians. The other is according to the 'Golden Legend', which sees only a tale of heroism and the spread of Spanish Christian civilization. If we are to evaluate events correctly we must take note of the heroic nature of the Church's evangelistic activity, and also of its mistakes, which brought about the later decline. The Spanish-American Church was well organized both as regards the clergy and as regards the schools, universities, presses, and hospitals which were founded. On the other hand there was much prejudice against ordaining Amerindians as priests, and this hindered the work of evangelization in depth.

Some people have claimed that the religion of the Amerindians and the *mestizos* was a mixture of Christianity and paganism, and have questioned whether the missionary effort ever really touched the group-consciousness of the Amerindian masses. To this question the answer must be 'Yes, it did'. The Amerindians did not simply adopt the Christian faith superficially or in appearance only; they were *beginning* to accept its very substance. The three centuries of colonial rule were an initiation into Christianity. The problems which arose were not so much the result of mixing Christianity with Amerindian culture, but rather of trying to combine Christianity and *Spanish* culture. This led to a permanent conflict between missionaries and colonizers, between bishops and representatives of the Spanish and Portuguese rulers.

How can we understand this matter of 'mixing' religions? As the Amerindians learnt the new faith, they used gestures and symbols of their old religion to express their new-found Christianity, but this does not imply a mixing of religions. Where the people were not fully evangelized, mixing occurred, but this disappeared as the process of evangelism continued. Where people were fully evangelized in the sixteenth century, they have remained Christians until the present. Many of the 'superstitions' which people have noticed are not pagan survivals, but grew up in the nineteenth century when the Inquisition no longer kept a watchful eye on lay catechists and missionaries. Where genuine pagan customs remain, we should understand it as a sign that the people have not yet been fully evangelized.

CHRISTIANITY IN CRISIS: 1808–1962

During the early nineteenth century most of Latin America won its independence, and the remaining countries were free of colonialism by the end of the century, though Cuba only became independent in 1898. The Latin American nations then had to face a series of complex problems. The people had to learn to think of themselves as members of these new nations, and to accept new responsibilities. They had to develop ways of governing themselves; they had to adapt to rapid social change, and sometimes they felt that religion could no longer provide a guide in the new situation. They also discovered that political independence did not always bring economic independence. The Church lost its way amidst all these conflicts. At first it tried to defend its ancient privileges, but when it became clear that these had gone forever, it began a vigorous renewal whose fruits can already be seen.

The achievement of independence meant the ending of the *patronato*. The Church came into direct relation with the Papacy in Rome, although the independent governments often tried to control the Church as closely as the Spanish (and Portuguese) kings had done.

Another important change concerned the relationship of the Church to society. Under Spanish rule, being a Christian was simply one aspect of being a member of society as a whole, and the nation itself was thought of as a Christian nation. When the countries of Latin America became free of Spanish rule, the situation changed. Christians found themselves living in secular societies where other religions too were permitted, and the Church could no longer look to the government to help it carry out its purposes. It had to act through its own institutions, and where necessary it had to create new institutions to meet new situations.

Two important movements, then, occurred during the nineteenth and early twentieth centuries in the Latin American Church. First there was the change from being in a Christian society to being in a secular, pluralist society. Secondly the Church had to create new institutions in order to evangelize the new society which had emerged. The nineteenth century has been described by some as the 'dark night' of the Latin American Church, a night from which it is emerging purified and renewed.

Crisis During the Wars of Independence 1808–1825

The parish priests and members of the religious orders played an important part in the independence movement in Latin America. Most of the bishops, however, resisted independence; they had been directly appointed by the colonial rulers, and were naturally inclined to remain loyal to them. Nevertheless there were some who supported the cause of self-determination. Among the many priests who not only joined the rebellion against Spain, but also inspired and led it, were Miguel Hidalgo and José Maria Morelos in Mexico, Gregorio Funes in Argentina, and José Maria Castilla in Guatemala. Spanish rule was at first replaced by conservative governments who tried to continue the patronage system, seeing themselves as successors of the Spanish crown. Even those more liberal governments who tried to introduce a secular state retained something of a colonial mentality, since they borrowed their ideas from French thinkers. In Argentina, for instance, between 1821 and 1827 Bernardino Rivadavia tried to reform the Church, basing his policy on ideas he had met when in Europe. He abolished tithes, curbed the religious orders, took control of Church property which was not actually used for worship, and abolished the privileges which the Church had acquired. Some of the clergy supported him, but others were violently opposed to these measures.

The wars of independence in Latin America led to complete disorganization in the Church. Bishops were not appointed, the parish system broke down, and seminary and university education was disrupted. In the conflicts of the time, the gospel seems to have been the biggest loser. Yet the new governments were not enemies of religion. In their constitutions most of them jealously guarded their right to 'defend the Catholic, Apostolic, and Roman Church as the only religion'. Nevertheless, countries such as Brazil and Argentina, which encouraged immigration, had to admit Protestants, and permitted them to practise their religion. Rome often found it difficult to know how to act, because of its close relations with the Spanish and Portuguese governments, who viewed the new Latin American states as rebels. As a result many countries were left without bishops for long periods.

The Crisis Deepens 1825–1850

In an encyclical of 1816, Pope Pius VII had referred to the revolutionaries fighting for independence in Latin America as 'promoters of sedition'. But this attitude slowly changed, partly as a result of the intervention of two Colombian bishops, Lasso de la Vega, Bishop of Mérida, and Salvador Jiménez, Bishop of Popayán, both of whom had been supporters of Spanish rule, but who were won over by Simon Bolívar, the liberator of much of Latin America. They were able to assure the Pope that the new governments were not hostile to religion. It was particularly important that the Pope should agree to the consecration of new bishops where these were needed. In Argentina, for instance, the Church was crippled by the lack of bishops. But it was not until 1827 that the Pope acted. Pope Leo XII then named the first six bishops for Colombia, much to the joy of Bolívar who exclaimed, 'We are today united in the greatest cause: the good of the Church and the good of Colombia.' In 1831 Pope Gregory XVI named six bishops for Mexico, and the reorganization of the hierarchy in other parts of Latin America soon followed. The bishops who were appointed were Latin Americans, not Spaniards, and they were appointed directly by Rome: the *patronato* had ceased to exist.

The political and economic situation was unstable, however, and the Church found it difficult to respond to rapid changes of government and policy. From 1841 to 1889 Brazil was a monarchy under King Pedro II; Mexico was ruled by conservative governments between 1824 and 1857; Bolívar's hopes for a confederacy of small states fell apart after he resigned in 1831; the leaders of Venezuela, Argentina, and Ecuador at first supported the privileges of the Church. After some initial chaos, Chile settled to a period of government during which the Church was protected by the state, but nevertheless some of its powers were slowly taken away. The uncertainties of the period, and the identification of the Church with the forces of conservatism, meant that the night was indeed dark for it during this period. Nor could Latin America expect help from Europe, where the Church was going through a missionary crisis of its own. In short, the circumstances were such that any hope for renewal seemed remote.

Meantime, during the first half of the nineteenth century, those areas of the North Amerian continent which had been colonized by Spain, but which are now part of the United States, were gradually passing out of Spanish hands. Louisiana was ceded to France and thence to the USA in 1803, and in 1848 Texas was the last area to be handed over. In this way there emerged a Latin American people within the USA who were Spanish speaking and Roman Catholic. They were left with almost no pastoral care, and became part of the mainstream Irish-dominated Catholicism that came into being, though with their own distinctive cultural identity.

We have already noticed that those Latin American countries which encouraged immigration from Europe soon found themselves admitting Protestants. Brazil was one of the first to do so, though there was opposition to the arrival of Protestants, and the Roman Catholic clergy were intolerant of their presence. In 1824 a treaty was signed between Brazil and Britain. In this there was a clause which gave Britons living in Brazil the right to build chapels for Anglican (Church of England) worship. The first chapel was built in 1826. Lutherans and Calvinists arrived in 1824, when German immigrants first settled in southern Brazil. Their numbers were considerable (there were some three quarters of a million Lutherans in Brazil by the 1970s), but they were not allowed to have any influence in the country. For a long time the German Churches considered them as traitors and fugitives, and the first German pastors did not arrive until 1886. They found the Lutherans organized into lay communities with unqualified preachers. The newly-arrived pastors despised these preachers, and much harm was caused to the Protestant Churches.

Argentina too encouraged Protestant immigration, and the first Argentinian Constitution of 1819 guaranteed freedom of thought. The first Protestant service was conducted in Buenos Aires in 1819. In 1825 a treaty was signed between Argentina and Britain, and British immigration was encouraged by this. The British government built several Anglican chapels in Buenos Aires for these immigrants. Scottish colonists also arrived in 1825 and built their first chapel in the capital. In 1836 Methodists from the USA introduced their own form of worship for some of the English-speaking immigrants in Argentina.

Shortly after Venezuela's independence in 1821 that country too welcomed the arrival of Protestant immigrants, and in 1834 the Congress proclaimed freedom of practice for all religious groups. In the same year an English-speaking congregation was formed in Caracas with the right to maintain its own cemetery.

In Uruguay and Costa Rica Protestants arrived rather later. Between 1850 and 1860 members of the Waldenses (a Calvinist group from northern Italy) began arriving in Uruguay. The government gave them arable land, and the Waldensian community began to grow. They did not content themselves with providing for their own religious needs, but sought to spread their religion. In time they became the largest Protestant community in Uruguay. In Costa Rica the first Protestant services took place around 1848, in private homes. The first Protestant chapel there was built in 1865. We can see that the gaining of independence in Latin America favoured the Protestant presence in the area. If the Protestant form of the Christian faith was to spread, it had to do so by converting people one by one, either through evangelism or friendship. The Protestants could not rely, as the Roman Catholics could, on a large proportion of the people being nominal adherents of their Church, to whom they had easy access.

Break with the Past 1850–1929

During this period it was not only Protestant religious influence that began to be felt by the Latin American nations, but also the technology, engineering and commerce of Northern Europe and North America. French influence was strong in the arts and in philosophy, and French attitudes against privileges for the clergy were spread. Worker groups inspired by European socialism were formed among the landless proletariat and urban immigrants, slowly at first, but more quickly towards the end of the century.

From the 1850s onwards the Church began to break away from its colonial past, in which it had been a privileged organ of the state and could count on the nominal adherence of most of the population. In Colombia a religious persecution began under the liberals who were in power from 1849 to 1886. In 1853 the Church there was separated from the state, and some years later the Church was deprived of the right to hold property, other than buildings used for worship, and the religious orders were suppressed. Naturally the bishops resisted, and Archbishop Antonio Herrán did so with such vigour that he was imprisoned for sedition. Other bishops were also imprisoned or exiled. The situation did not improve until after 1880, when the Church was granted a proper status in law, and was able to act freely and own property. The Church also found itself in difficulty in Chile, Uruguay, and Bolivia.

In Mexico there was intense friction between Church and state. The very conservative clergy there tried to retain all their former privileges, and the state passed legislation which deprived the Church of almost all its rights. If this legislation had been enforced, the Church would scarcely have existed. Each side in the dispute pushed the other to extremes. However, the laws against the Church were not strictly enforced, and the Church recovered much of its wealth and influence during the course of the century. But the laws remained on the statute books, and for a brief period in the 1920s, they were enforced, and even strengthened. Schools were closed, all foreign-born priests were expelled, and the number of priests allowed to function was drastically reduced. In protest against this, the bishops withdrew the clergy, and no religious services were held for three years. The situation did not improve until after a new President had taken office, and even then, the position of the Church remained unsatisfactory.

The old pastoral practices of the Latin American Church proved to be ineffective in dealing with the new developments in society. The Church could not meet the needs of people from the rural areas who crowded into the growing towns and cities, nor of the immigrants from Europe who came to settle in Latin America. Anti-religious feeling grew in the universities and in political parties. By the end of the nineteenth century, the future for the Church seemed very bleak.

However, there was one new development which gave hope for the future. Archbishop Mariano Casanova of Chile urged that all the bishops of Latin America needed to meet together to discuss the situation of the Church, and as a result, thirteen Archbishops and forty-one bishops met together in Rome in 1889. It was the first council of its kind for Latin America. The bishops discussed not only their pastoral concerns, but a wide range of topics such as the legal standing of the Church, its relations with the press, the continuation of pagan and superstitious practices among nominal Christians, and the Church's attitude to socialism. The most important result of this Council was that the bishops saw the need to meet and act together with a common mind.

We must note one other important development, the increasing activity of Protestant missions. From 1850 onwards, Protestant Churches in Europe and North America became interested in evangelizing Latin America. Presbyterians reached Brazil in 1860, Argentina in in 1866, Mexico in 1872, and Guatemala in 1882. Next on the scene were the Methodists, who reached Mexico in 1871, Brazil in 1876, the West Indies in 1890, and Costa Rica, Panama and Bolivia in 1895. Ten years after the arrival of the Methodists, the first Baptists arrived. They reached Brazil in 1881, Argentina in 1886, and Chile in 1888. The Anglican South American Missionary Society also started work. At first they had little success in making converts. On the eve of World War II in 1939 they still had only about 100,000 members. But their work was to grow, and they held a number of missionary congresses: in Panama in 1916, in Montevideo in 1925, and in Havana in 1929. These meetings were inspired by the World Missionary Conference held in Edinburgh in 1910. This conference had not discussed Latin America because its population was reckoned to be already Christian. But Robert E. Speer, a missionary leader in the USA, saw the need for Protestant missions working among the still unevangelized peoples of

Latin America to meet together, so the Committee on Co-operation in Latin America was formed, and this series of conferences was held under its auspices.

During this period, Protestant missions concentrated on education, especially secondary and university education. A number of outstanding American Colleges were founded, as well as Bible Colleges and institutions for theological training. By the end of the period, there were about 3,000 Protestant missionaries in Latin America, with some 10,000 Latin American co-workers.

Developments in the Church 1930–1962

The events which mark the beginning and end of this stage of Church development are the inception of Catholic Action in 1930, and the calling of the Second Vatican Council in 1962. In this period, the Roman Catholic Church recovered the unity it had possessed during the period of Spanish rule, but without the disadvantages it suffered during that era.

Catholic Action was a lay movement which sought to deepen faith and to encourage lay people to take a more active part in the life of the Church. The first Latin American country which it reached was Argentina. Catholic Action absorbed many smaller movements, and it attracted a large membership. In Chile the Young Catholic Students' movement was particularly strong.

At another level of the Church's life we find CELAM, the Conference of Bishops of the Roman Catholic Church in Latin America. Bishop Larraín of Chile was instrumental in founding this.

In the universities Christian thinkers were beginning to respond to the challenges of modern thought which sought to do without God and religion. New theological and philosophical journals were founded in which Christian scholars could put forward their views and share ideas.

The Church's social concern is expressed in the Latin American Confederation of Christian Trades Unions. These are directed by Christians who are concerned for justice and freedom in society. They are part of the Christian response to the challenge of Marxism. Roman Catholic Christians in Latin America have also learnt the importance of being involved in politics, and a number of Christian political groupings have been formed.

A whole book would be needed to describe all the ways in which the life of the Church in Latin America has been undergoing renewal. There has been a rebirth of religious communities devoted primarily to prayer and worship; there have been new developments in theology; liturgies have been renewed; there are new developments in pastoral work; and above all, there is a surge of new interest in biblical studies which is the most important source of new life in the Church. This has partly been due to the presence of Protestants in Latin America. The Second Vatican Council gave a further impetus to the study of the Bible by clergy and lay Catholics alike.

The number of Protestant missionaries grew very rapidly during these years, and so did the number of converts. Many Protestant missionaries who had to leave China found a new sphere of work in Latin America, and at a later date these were joined by other missionaries who were no longer able to work freely in the Arab world. By the 1960s there were some 7,000 Protestant missionaries, with 30,000 local pastors and lay-workers, 45,000 places of worship, and a total Church membership of twelve and a half million. They were most numerous in north-eastern Brazil and in Chile, and least numerous in the countries of north-western South America. The chief purpose of their work in this period was to build up and instruct Christian congregations.

A NEW AGE: LATIN AMERICA SINCE 1962

Since the early 1960s Latin America has been in revolution, a revolution whose roots go back to the beginning of the century. The small wealthy minority, who were once in total control, have been losing their power to the military or to the rising proletarian and peasant classes ever since the serious economic crisis which hit the world in the 1930s. The first 'people's revolution' was the 1910 uprising of Mexican peasants; the most successful was the 1959 Cuban revolution. The people of Latin America are waking up to the fact that many of their countries are 'dependent' and 'oppressed' colonies of the United States and other developed countries. They are therefore setting out on a course of political, economic, and cultural liberation. This has direct repercussions on the Church.

The Second General Conference of Latin American Bishops of the Roman Catholic Church, held in 1968 in Medellín in Colombia, was an important event, and was related to this 'revolution of the people'. The bishops disscussed the implications of the Second Vatican Council for the Church in Latin America. The conference documents state that all the signs 'indicate that we are on the threshold of a new historical age on our continent, and an age full of yearnings for complete emancipation, for liberation from all servitude'. The bishops realized that 'foreign neo-colonialism' was the worst enemy of this liberation. In these circumstances they found themselves forced to the conclusion 'that Latin America in many places is in a situation of injustice which can be called one of *institutionalized violence*'. That is, the law, the police, the security forces, the ways in which land is held and in which work and wages are organized, the tax system, and all the institutions of government *forcibly* prevent the mass of the people from expressing themselves freely and acting to better their condition. In many countries the mass of the people remain desperately poor, and unless the system can be changed, there can be no chance of any improvement.

The Roman Catholic Church is becoming more and more allied with the liberation movement in Latin America. Increasingly it denounces the neo-colonial pact between the rich and powerful Latin American élites and rich and developed areas such as the United States, Europe, and even the Soviet Union. Bishop Pironio, secretary general of CELAM, the Conference which brings together Latin American bishops in the Roman Catholic Church, states: 'We have become more painfully aware that we are living in a state of subordination and of internal and foreign oppression.' Co-operation between Latin American countries is increasing (this should not be confused with the Pan-Americanism which is fostered by the United States for its own ends). The existence of CELAM is one aspect of this co-operation.

At the same time, Latin American intellectuals are rediscovering indigenous Latin American culture. For too long Latin America has been culturally dependent on Europe and North America. Now there are the beginnings of cultural liberation. A. Salazar Bondy has said that 'in worldwide competition the differences between developed and underdeveloped countries are growing deeper. ... But there is still a possibility of liberation; hence we must act decisively to keep hope alive and bring it about.'

Only a decade after the calling of Vatican II it seemed clear to many Latin American Christians that a new stage had begun in the history of their Church. It was characterized by the abandonment of efforts to restore the older Christian patterns through movements such as Catholic Action or politically through Christian Democracy. A new kind of Christian action needed to be mapped out for the future.

Vatican II and the Medellín Conference of Roman Catholic Bishops

In 1966 the first attempt to apply the new spirit of Vatican II had been made at a conference in Mar del Plata, but it was unsuccessful. The conference held at Medellín two years later was more successful than anyone had dared to hope. The conference produced a document on 'the presence of the Church in the transformation of Latin America today' which contained findings that are increasingly being put into practice. The Conference dealt at length with the question of peace and justice, and a new language and a new spirit are apparent in what was said and written. Medellín was a watershed for the Roman Catholic Church in Latin America.

Between 1962 and 1975 there were a whole series of military coups in Latin America: in Brazil (1964), Argentina (1968), Peru (1968), Uruguay, Bolivia and Chile (1973). These increased the number of military

A statue of Simon Bolívar 'the liberator' in Venezuela recalls the enormous changes in Christian life in Latin America since the end of Spanish rule; while the beggar huddled on the steps of a splendid—but boarded up—church doorway in Colombia symbolizes the contrast between the Church as centre of wealth and power and as haven and help of the poor.

Poverty and under-development in the Caribbean area is much like that in South America, but local Christians have to find their own answers. Here a rural Church group discuss how to achieve better working conditions.

114

governments, which also existed in Paraguay, Haiti, and, in a different sense, Santo Domingo and Puerto Rico. The Roman Catholic Church has changed its position on politics. In the past it spoke out to defend its own rights and privileges. Now it speaks out in favour of justice for the poor, and freedom for Christians and non-Christians alike. It has left its old defensiveness behind, and has taken upon itself a prophetic role, denouncing evil and tyranny where necessary, with all the political consequences of doing so.

What happened in the Church in north-eastern Brazil is an example of this. This is an area where there is extreme poverty, and where wealthy plantation owners have practically enslaved sections of the population. Bishop Helder Camara was appointed Archbishop of Recife a few days after a right wing coup in 1964. He took advantage of the situation to speak out clearly, fearing that it he did not do so then, he would never dare to do so. Eventually, because of his outspokenness against torture, imprisonment, and the repressive policies of the Brazilian government, the press was forbidden even to mention his name, and in this way he was largely silenced. Yet he is an unwavering opponent of violence. During the 1960s and 1970s hundreds of Brazilian Catholics were tortured, imprisoned and killed. Among them was Fr Pereira Neto, a martyr of modern times. He was warned that his life was in danger, but he refused to flee and went on with his work as Chaplain to Roman Catholic students. On the night of 26 May 1969 an extremist group dragged him off, half-naked, tied him to a tree, and shot him three times. In spite of the terror, some valiant bishops continued to champion the oppressed. In Haiti and Paraguay the bishops have also challenged the government, but in Argentina the bishops have been more conciliatory towards the government, and have even been implicated in some of the severe oppression in that country. If there was a measure of improvement in one country, as there was in Brazil, then matters became worse elsewhere. Eventually in March 1980 the world was shocked by the murder of Archbishop Oscar Romero of Salvador, shot in front of the congregation as he was saying mass.

The Roman Catholic Church and Socialism

The attitude of the Roman Catholic Church towards events in Cuba also points to a new age. In the period just before the Communist revolution there the Church was weak, and most of the priests were foreign-born, and were expelled. In 1959 a national Roman Catholic Congress chanted 'Down with Communism!' But when the United States blockaded Cuba in 1969, the bishops declared, 'We denounce this unjust blockade which causes unnecessary suffering and places more difficulties in the way of development.' Later the same year they called on all men of good will, 'atheists or believers' to contribute to the cause of liberation.

Many Christians in Latin America, laymen, priests and bishops, are speaking of the possibility not only of dialogue with socialism, but also of a Christian socialism. Bishop Carlos González of Talca in Chile said in a pastoral letter, 'In today's circumstances we cannot fail to recognize the right of lay Christians to seek a revised kind of socialism.' In Mexico lay people have reassessed the earlier revolution of 1910. They saw that those Christians who died then were defending the Church's privileges rather than Christianity itself (though this was understandable at the time). In Chile a group of Christian political activists were among those who elected the Communist president, Allende, and they energetically supported his Popular Front Coalition. Elements in the Church openly supported radical reform under Allende. A movement called *Cristianos para el socialismo* (Christians for Socialism), which arose in Chile in 1973, spread throughout Latin America as well as to several European countries. Eventually United States intervention brought Allende's government to an end. Since then, Chile has suffered under one of the most repressive governments on the continent, that of General Pinochet. Thousands of Chileans have been imprisoned, tortured and murdered, or else have 'disappeared'.

The Roman Catholic Church and Violence

The Church is gradually forming new attitudes towards violence, attitudes which try to combine faithfulness to the gospel with commitment to liberation. Fr Camilo Torres, a Colombian sociologist and specialist in development, only turned to armed combat as a final resort when it seemed to offer the last remaining possibility for liberation. His death, on 15 February 1966, shows how bloodshed simply leads to more bloodshed, and holds no solution. Nevertheless, many other Christians have chosen the same option, in Colombia, Venezuela, Bolivia, Guatemala, and Argentina, including some other priests.

But there are many kinds of violence. There is the violence of oppression used by dominant social classes and countries; there is the violence of armed subversion used by guerrilla fighters; and there is the violence of coercion used by the army and police. The worst type of violence is the violence of oppression, institutional violence, for it is used against the poor who cannot defend themselves. Prophets rise up against this type of violence; they denounce it and teach people how to recognize it. But oppressive governments often respond to the voice of prophecy by using violence against it. Those who prophesy in Latin America are always prepared for police violence, and many have suffered from it. They consider their experience to be similar to that of Christians in the days of the Roman Empire.

Some of the Christians of Latin America ask whether Christians in Europe and North America realize that their fellow-Christians in the Third World are being persecuted for opposing a system of world trade which benefits the wealthy nations of the West, but exploits the people of the under-developed countries. Many Latin American Christians fear that only a few Christians in the West realize the extent to which their wealth depends on the prices of Third World products being kept low, whilst the manufactured goods which under-developed countries need to import are constantly rising in price. In Latin America, theology that does not come to grips with the question of poverty and inequality is not fully relevant to the situation.

Bishops and Clergy in the Roman Catholic Church

Latin American bishops today hold widely differing views. On the one hand there are bishops such as Bishop Sigaud of Diamantina, Brazil, who has written an 'anti-communist catechism' in which he defends every kind of private ownership. On the other hand there are men such as Bishop Fragoso of Cratéus and Bishop Candido Padim of Lorena, Brazil, who are politically progressive. Bishop Padim wrote a courageous book to show how the militarism of the Brazilian government confuses Christianity with Western culture, and how the Brazilian Armed Forces treat as subversives anyone, whether communist or Christian, who questions their policies. One could give a long list of distinguished bishops in Latin America who have tried to defend their people against oppression, and who have worked for justice and peace. We have already mentioned the two who have become best known outside their own countries: Archbishop Helder Camara and Archbishop Oscar Romero.

Priests in Latin America have sometimes found themselves in conflict with their bishops. They are closer to the people, and can sympathize with them in a way that bishops cannot always do. Many of them have been more anxious than the bishops to implement the new spirit of the Second Vatican Council. In most countries of Latin America priests have their own national conferences where they can decide on policies and action, and can discuss their problems. On the other hand foreign priests, Spaniards, Belgians, and Maryknoll Fathers from the United States, have been expelled from a number of countries. Such priests have become involved with development projects among the very poor in their parishes, and this has brought them into conflict with wealthy landowners who did not wish to see the peasants liberating themselves. Some foreign priests have been accused of being subversive or even communistic. Priests are playing an enormously important role in Latin America today.

Lay People

In Latin America, as elsewhere, lay people are only just beginning to play a significant role in the life of the Church. For many lay people the Church still seems to be too much in the hands of the clergy. However, lay people are beginning to make themselves heard, and even demonstrating to make their point, as happened in 1966 in Montevideo, Uruguay, when a group of Christians occupied the Church of Corpus Domini to protest when their parish priest was moved. The older lay movements such as Catholic Action are ceasing to attract people, and Christians prefer to join secular trades unions rather than Roman Catholic unions. Young people who formerly supported Christian Democrat parties are now joining the militant left. On the other hand, history is being made by the development of 'basic communities'. These are small groupings of Christians at parish level who combine to help and support each other in living out the faith. In a basic community each person is known and valued, not simply a passive member of a congregation. In north-eastern Brazil, where the movement started, there were some 1,500 basic communities by the mid-1970s, each consisting of about 150 Christians. The Medellín Conference called these basic communities 'the primary and fundamental core of the Church'.

At the same time, Christians in the universities are moving away from the old ways of thinking, and trying to relate their work more closely to the needs of society, and to the liberation of an oppressed and dependent people. They are searching for ways in which they can help to form a new society in which there will be neither slaves nor oppressors.

The major contribution of Latin American theologians to Christian thinking in the modern age is 'Liberation Theology'. In this, theologians have tried to apply the insights of Scripture to the problems facing them in Latin America, and particularly to the economic and political oppression from which large sections of the population suffer. One of the best known writers is Fr Gustavo Guttiérrez of Peru. Born in 1928, he studied medicine for five years, but then decided to become a priest. He studied theology and philosophy in Peru, Belgium, France, and in Rome. Increasingly he came to feel that the theology he had learnt in the West was inadequate to meet the problems of Latin America. Here is how he explains this:

A goodly part of contemporary theology seems to take its start from the challenge posed by the *nonbeliever*. The nonbeliever calls into question our *religious world*, demanding its thoroughgoing purification and revitalization. ... In a continent like Latin America, however, the main challenge does not come from the nonbeliever, but from the *nonhuman*—i.e., the human being who is not recognized as such by the prevailing social order. There are the poor and exploited people, the ones who are systematically and legally despoiled of their being human, those who scarcely know what a human being might be. These nonhumans do not call into question our religious world so much as our *economic, social, political and cultural world*. The question is . . . how to proclaim God as Father in a world that is not human, and what the implications might be of telling nonhumans that they are the children of God. (Quoted in R. Gibellini, *Frontiers of Theology in Latin America* (SCM 1980), p. x)

Gutiérrez has been developing his thought since 1964. His chief work, written in 1971, is *A Theology of Liberation* which has been translated into many languages. Gutiérrez is Professor of Theology in the Roman Catholic University in Lima, Peru, and a national adviser for the National Union of Catholic Students.

A number of liberation theologians are Roman Catholic priests, and several belong to the Jesuit Order. However, Enrique Dussel of Argentina, who now works in Mexico, is a Catholic layman, and Protestants are also represented. Rubem Alves, a Brazilian, was a Presbyterian who left his Church because of its refusal to become sufficiently involved in the acute economic and social problems of Latin America. The Rev. José Míguez Bonino is a Methodist. Born in 1924, he studied in his own country and in the United States. Since 1954 he has taught at the Evangelical Theological College in Buenos Aires, and has been deeply involved in the ecumenical movement. His most important book is *Doing Theology in a Revolutionary Situation*, published in 1975. He has been particularly concerned with the problems raised by the use of violence.

Although these theologians have dealt with problems which are specially urgent in Latin America, their thinking has been a challenge to theologians and Christians everywhere, in the advanced industrialized countries of Western Europe and North America as well as in the Third World.

The Protestant Churches

The Fourth Assembly of the World Council of Churches met in Uppsala, Sweden in July, 1968, and its agenda included many topics which were especially relevant to the Latin American scene, such as 'the revolutionary ferment of our time', 'the social and economic problems of the third world', 'war and peace', and 'race'. The Assembly recommended that the Churches should work towards a renewal of mission, programmes of social and economic development, and the fight against injustice and in favour of peace in international relations.

It appealed for faith in Christ as 'the Man for others', and for the Christian community to see itself as existing for the sake of others. But many of the Protestant Churches in Latin America are not affiliated to the World Council of Churches, and look upon the ecumenical movement as the enemy of true faith. They think it is Communist dominated, and that Communism is the greatest evil in the world today. Indeed the Protestant Churches as a whole in Latin America are theologically conservative, and have hesitated to be involved in the burning social, economic and political issues of that continent today, though some are rethinking their position. Others, however, are strong supporters of right-wing governments, no matter how repressive, since they fear that the only alternative is Communism, which they regard as even worse. The fastest growing Protestant group in Latin America this century has been the Pentecostals, who have avoided involvement in politics at national level, though they may be involved in local social issues.

An important development among the Protestant groups has been the growth of Theological Education by Extension (TEE). The Latin American Churches pioneered this, and it has now spread widely. TEE seeks to meet two needs: the need for clergy to be trained without taking them out of society for long periods into theological colleges, because these are expensive to run, and the Church cannot afford full-time clergy on the European model in anything like the numbers needed. TEE also seeks to meet the needs of lay people for theological training. TEE material is sent out to small groups who meet in their own locality and in their own time to work through the reading that is set, and to discuss together the questions raised. In particular they try to relate theology to their own lives and to the lives of the communities in which they live. In the 1960s and 1970s the World Council of Churches helped in this venture through its Theological Education Fund. We saw how Liberation Theology was developed to meet the needs of a particular situation, and then proved to have a much wider relevance. The same has been true of TEE. We can see that Latin American Christianity is growing in importance for the rest of the Christian world.

THE CARIBBEAN

We have already mentioned Haiti, Cuba and Puerto Rico which became Spanish possessions. The smaller Caribbean islands and a few areas on the mainland belonged to Britain, France and the Netherlands, and had a different history from the rest of Latin America. In particular they did not have the large Spanish (and therefore Roman Catholic) element in the population. The original Carib people were wiped out, and the majority of the Caribbean islanders are now the descendants of slaves imported from Africa. The exception is Trinidad, which was Spanish for 300 years, and therefore has a larger proportion of Roman Catholics than most other islands, as well as Muslims, Sikhs and Hindus who were recruited from India as labourers at the time when slavery was abolished. Something of the same mixture is found in Guyana.

The largest of the islands in the Caribbean which did not belong to Spain is Jamaica. This was a British colony, where the Church of England was the official Church until 1870. Before the nineteenth century not much was done to evangelize the black population: slave-owners even resisted attempts to convert their slaves, lest their status as Christians might mean that they could not so easily be exploited. As a result of the Evangelical Awakening, things improved during the nineteenth century. Anglican, Baptist, Methodist, Presbyterian and Moravian missionaries arrived from Europe and North America, and a large part of the population became Christian, at least in name. Roman Catholic missionaries, previously forbidden, were now allowed to come to Jamaica, and the Jesuits took responsibility for Roman Catholic work in 1837. The African Methodist Episcopal Church of the USA played a part in evangelism in the Caribbean, and Caribbean Christians in their turn have helped to evangelize Africa (see p. 132). Most practising Christians come from the rather better off groups; the very poor, especially those living in the deprived areas around Kingston, the capital of Jamaica, for example, do not feel at ease in the smartly-dressed Sunday morning congregations, and do not find answers to their problems in the Churches.

In Jamaica and elsewhere, independent Churches, and cults which combine elements of African traditional religions with elements from Christianity and Islam, flourish among the poor. The best known of these is perhaps the Ras Tafari movement which draws on the biblical images of exile and exodus on the one hand, and on Jewish and Muslim food-taboos on the other. The Rastafarians describe their present condition as being in exile in Babylon. Their true African homeland is symbolized for them by Ethiopia, and the former Emperor Haile Selassie (whose name before he was crowned was Ras Tafari) is looked upon as divine. His death has made no real difference to Rastafarian belief. They do not have much in the way of cult worship, but often smoke cannabis together, which they explain by reference to Rev. 22.2, which speaks of the tree in the New Jerusalem whose leaves were for the healing of the nations. The Rastafarians attracted many who were alienated from society, and they are looked down upon by the more 'respectable' citizens and churchgoers. Yet they speak eloquently of the need for the gospel to become good news for the poor.

Throughout the Caribbean, Christian teaching on Christian family life has had to face the results of slavery which uprooted people from their homelands and destroyed family life. A man could be sold away from his wife and children, and slave marriages had no legal standing. Patterns of family life have had to be recreated with the mother in the dominant role. In recent times family structures have been further distorted by emigration away from the West Indies to the USA and Britain. Often the breadwinner emigrates to find work, and may only much later be able to bring his wife and children and older dependent relatives to join him. Emigration to Britain has been a particularly bitter experience for Caribbean Christians, who found themselves unwelcome, even in many of the Churches, because of continuing British racial prejudice. Many of the people from the Caribbean now living in Britain who have remained Christian have joined together as Black Churches, many of them Pentecostal in type, where worship is vigorous and lively, and where black Christians may feel more at home than in the rather staid traditional British pattern of services. These black Christians have much to give to Christianity in Britain, as white Christians are just beginning to recognize. To some extent the same sort of prejudice has been faced by Puerto Ricans and others from the Caribbean who have gone to find work in the USA, though it must be said that their expectations of opportunities to better themselves have probably been lower.

The poverty and underdevelopment of the Caribbean area, and the way in which its people continue to be exploited by the great powers, has much in common with the situation in Latin America. Both Liberation Theology and Black Theology are beginning to be heard in the Caribbean, but the different history and cultural heritage of the people means that answers from Latin America cannot be taken over easily. Caribbean Christians have to make their own application of the Christian gospel.

Some encouraging signs that problems of diversity and distance may eventually be reduced, even if not overcome, have appeared in the present century. Most of the mainstream Churches at least attempt to co-ordinate their work for the Caribbean area as a whole, and initial steps towards united action on a wider scale were taken with the formation in 1962 of an ecumenical committee 'to plan missionary strategy on a regional basis'. Three years later ten denominations joined together in setting up a United Theological College at Kingston, Jamaica. There are still many impediments to progress, however, chief among them perhaps being the problem of poverty and consequent lack of adequate education, and in some island groups the advent of Independence has not been an unmixed blessing.

STUDY SUGGESTIONS

WORDS AND MEANINGS

1. Explain briefly what is meant by the following terms as used in this chapter:
   (a) *Patronato real* (or *padroado*) (b) Amerindians (c) Mestizos (d) Waldenses (e) Rastafarians

REVIEW OF CONTENT

Latin America

2. (a) To which Church did the Spanish and Portuguese conquerors of Latin America belong?
   (b) What was the relationship between the colonial governments and that Church in the three centuries before 1800?
   (c) What advantages did the Church enjoy as a result of this relationship, and what were its disadvantages?
   (d) What was the relationship of the colonial governments to the Amerindian peoples of Latin America?

3. (a) To which religious order did many of the Spanish clergy in Latin America belong in the seventeenth and eighteenth centuries?
   (b) What was the effect of their expulsion from Latin America when the order was suppressed in Portugal and Spain in the 1760s?

4. Explain what is meant by the 'Golden Legend' and the 'Black Legend' regarding Spanish and Portuguese domination in America.

5. What important change took place in the political situation of many Latin American countries during the nineteenth century? How did this affect the relationship between the Church and society, and what was the attitude of the Churches to the new situation?

6. (a) In what chief ways was the life and organization of the Church disrupted as a result of the Wars of Independence in the early nineteenth century?
   (b) In what chief ways did the influence of social, political, economic and technological development in Europe and North America affect the lives of ordinary people in Latin America in the late nineteenth and early twentieth centuries?

7. Give a brief account, with dates and details of the denominations involved, of the Protestant missionary work in:
   (a) Brazil (b) Argentina (c) Mexico (d) Venezuela (e) Uruguay (f) Costa Rica (g) Bolivia
   In what field of activity did Protestant Missions chiefly concentrate their activity?

8. Give a brief account of the restrictions and/or persecution experienced by the Church in:
   (a) Mexico, in the mid-nineteenth and early twentieth centuries
   (b) Colombia between 1850 and 1881

9. What were or are the chief concerns or aims of the following, and who were the participants in each case?
   (a) the Committee on Co-operation in Latin America,
   (b) Catholic Action,
   (c) CELAM,
   (d) the Confederation of Christian Trades Unions.

10. In what chief ways did the attitudes and ideas of the Churches in Latin America change and develop in the period 1930 to 1962?

11. (a) In what chief way was the form of government in all the major Latin American countries (Brazil, Argentina, Peru, Uruguay, Bolivia and Chile) changed between 1962 and 1965?
    (b) What were the results of this change which gave rise to the statement of the second General Conference of Roman Catholic Bishops at Medellín in 1968, that the situation in Latin America in many places 'can be called one of institutionalized violence'?
    (c) In what way has the Roman Catholic Church changed its position with regard to politics as a result of those events?

12. What is the importance of each of the following in the Church's stand against oppression in Latin America?
    (a) Bishop Helder Camara (b) Fr Pereiro Neto (c) Archbishop Oscar Romero.

13. Describe some of the ways in which lay people are beginning to play a significant role in the life of the Church in Latin America.

14. What are the chief concerns and insights of 'Liberation Theology', and who are some of the Latin American theologians currently involved?

15. In what chief ways have the Protestant Churches in Latin America responded to the changing political situation, and to what extent has their response differed from that of the Roman Catholic Church?

The Caribbean

16. Which denominations have chiefly been involved in missionary work in the Caribbean?

17. What are some of the social and economic problems faced by the Churches in the Caribbean?

18. (a) In what chief ways do political conditions in the Caribbean today resemble those in Latin America, and in what chief ways do they differ?
    (b) What differences make it unlikely that either Liberation Theo-

logy—or Black Theology as understood elsewhere—can be applied directly to the Caribbean situation?

DISCUSSION

19. The problems in Latin America under Spanish domination 'were not the result of mixing Christianity with Amerindian culture, but of trying to combine Christianity and *Spanish* culture' (p. 105). How far do you think this is true? How far could the same be said of the relationships in your country between Christianity, indigenous culture(s), and the culture of any colonizing power, and what have been any resultant problems?

20. 'Many "superstitions" are not pagan survivals, but grew up in the nineteenth century when the Inquisition no longer kept an eye on lay catechists and missionaries' (p. 105). What superstitious ideas or practices do you notice among Christians in your own country? Find out all you can about the origins of such superstititions. How far do you think that better training of clergy and lay leaders might help Christians to abandon such superstitions?

21. A century of renewal began in 1869. Since then 'Protestants have concentrated on education, ... Roman Catholics learnt the importance of involvement in politics.' Read again the paragraph describing the many examples of renewal in Latin America (p. 111). In which of these ways, if any, has your own Church experienced renewal? In which, if any, do you think it needs to? What sort of events in the life of a Church are likely to lead to a period of renewal?

22. 'Lay people are beginning to play a significant role ... history is being made by the development of "basic Christian communities"' (p. 118). How far do you think it is a good thing for such communities to develop, alongside the normal Church structures but with their own lay leadership? In what ways can it strengthen the Church—and what are any possible difficulties?

23. 'The major contribution of Latin American theology to Christian thinking in the modern age is "Liberation Theology"' (p. 118). Find out all you can about Liberation Theology, and about the parallel Black Theology (in Africa and North America). What are the chief differences between them? In what ways, if any, is either Liberation Theology or Black Theology relevant to the situation in your own country? How far is either likely to be applied to that situation?

24. Not all clergy in Latin America have accepted Liberation Theology. Some priests have found themselves in conflict with their bishops. To what authority do you think a priest should turn in such circumstances?

6
Africa: The Nineteenth Century
by Louise Pirouet

In this chapter we study Christianity in nineteenth-century Africa in four parts of the continent. First we look at Ethiopia, the one place in black Africa where Christianity has had a continuous history since the early centuries of the Church. Then we look at three main areas of nineteenth-century missionary advance: northward from the Cape of Good Hope; along the West African coast from Freetown in Sierra Leone; and inland from Zanzibar in the east. By the end of the century there were the beginnings of Christian witness in almost every country of Africa.

ETHIOPIA

The conversion of Ethiopia in the fourth century was described in Vol. 1 of this TEF Church History Guide (Ch. 8). Then in the seventh century the rise of Islam meant that Ethiopia became cut off from most of the Christian world. In the centuries that followed, however, the Ethiopian kings gradually extended their rule southwards, and the peoples whom they conquered became Christians. The churches carved out of rock, which are among Ethiopia's greatest cultural treasures, are thought to date from the twelfth century onwards, and are associated with King Lalibela, who is honoured as a saint. There was a revival of literature and monastic life in the thirteenth and fourteenth centuries, and by the beginning of the sixteenth century Ethiopia was at the height of her power.

At about this time Portuguese travellers first reached Ethiopia, and were greatly impressed by the wealth and the Christian devotion of the people. At first relations were good, but later there was disagreement, when the Portuguese tried to bring the Ethiopians into obedience to Rome. They wanted the Ethiopians to make sweeping changes in the liturgy, and said that the people should be rebaptized and the priests re-ordained. The Ethiopians were deeply insulted at this refusal to recognize them as true Christians.

They rose in rebellion against the king who had agreed to enter into negotiations with Rome, and he was forced to abdicate his throne. He then told his people that he had misled them, and urged them to return to the Christianity of their ancestors. The Roman Catholics were expelled from the country, and it was a long time before Ethiopians overcame their distrust of foreigners.

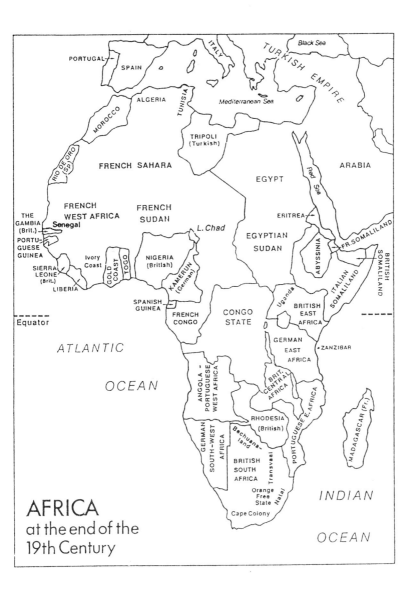

PORTUGAL
SPAIN
ITALY
Black Sea
TURKISH EMPIRE
ALGERIA
TUNISIA
Mediterranean Sea
MOROCCO
RIO DE ORO (Sp.)
TRIPOLI
(Turkish)
FRENCH SAHARA
EGYPT
ARABIA
Red Sea
FRENCH
WEST AFRICA
FRENCH
SUDAN
L. Chad
ERITREA
FR. SOMALILAND
THE
GAMBIA
(Brit.)
Senegal
PORTU-
GUESE
GUINEA
Ivory
Coast
GOLD COAST
TOGO
NIGERIA
(British)
KAMERUN
(German)
EGYPTIAN
SUDAN
ABYSSINIA
ITALIAN SOMALILAND
BRITISH SOMALILAND
SIERRA
LEONE
(Brit.)
LIBERIA
SPANISH
GUINEA
FRENCH
CONGO
CONGO
STATE
Uganda
BRITISH
EAST
AFRICA
Equator
ATLANTIC
OCEAN
GERMAN
EAST
AFRICA
ZANZIBAR
ANGOLA -
PORTUGUESE
WEST AFRICA
BRIT.
CENTRAL
AFRICA
RHODESIA
(British)
PORTUGUESE E. AFRICA
MADAGASCAR (Fr.)
GERMAN
SOUTH-WEST
AFRICA
Bechuana-
land
Transvaal
BRITISH
SOUTH
AFRICA
Natal
INDIAN
AFRICA
at the end of the
19th Century
Orange
Free
State
Cape Colony
OCEAN

AFRICA
at the end of the
19th Century

By the nineteenth century the Ethiopian kings had lost their power, and there was chaos in the country. The *abuna* (bishop), who by ancient custom came from Egypt, was unable to exercise any authority, and the monasteries, which were the only places of education, were torn by theological controversy. However, the real strength of Christianity lay in the parishes. The people expressed their devotion by fasting, observing Church festivals, and obeying dietary rules like those in the Old Testament. Few of the clergy had much education, but the Church was at the centre of life, and the people were deeply loyal to what they knew of their faith.

When missions revived in the nineteenth century, they looked for ways in which to help the Ethiopian Church, and a Roman Catholic mission had some success in the north of the country. A number of Ethiopian Orthodox priests and their congregations were brought into communion with Rome, but were allowed to keep their liturgy and customs almost unchanged. Bishop Justin de Jabobis, a French missionary, is still remembered for his saintliness by people in the area around Adwa and Adigrat where he worked.

By the end of the nineteenth century Ethiopia had been reunited by forceful rulers who conquered large areas in the south, and efforts were made to evangelize the newly-conquered peoples. Unlike the rest of Africa, Ethiopia was not brought under colonial rule. The Red Sea Coast was annexed by Italy, but the Ethiopians resoundingly defeated the Italians when they tried to advance further. Africans elsewhere began to hear of this independent African country whose rulers and core culture were Christian, and Ethiopia became an inspiration to many, both because of her freedom from colonial rule, and because of her ancient Christian culture.

WEST AFRICA

New Beginnings

There had been some Christians on the west coast of Africa since the late fourteenth century. Roman Catholic priests and Protestant clergy had been attached to trading posts, and had converted some Africans as well as serving their own people. The Reverend Philip Quaque (1745–1816), one of these converts, was one of the first Africans to study in Europe. After ordination as an Anglican he returned to the Gold Coast (now Ghana) where he worked as a chaplain-schoolmaster until his death. His work was continued by a group of Africans trained in Britain who started a Bible Band, and asked the Methodist Missionary Society for help. The Methodist Church in Ghana is thus the end result of Quaque's work. But for the most part Christianity in West

Africa had disappeared by the nineteenth century. There had never been anything that could properly be called a Church there, and a new beginning was needed.

The story of how this came about begins in America. During the American War of Independence some slaves fought for Britain. In return, the British promised them their liberty and land to settle on, but the British lost the war, and the freed slaves waited in vain for their land. Eventually they agreed to be resettled in Africa, so early in 1792 several shiploads of freed slaves reached Sierra Leone. They were already Christians, and there were teachers and preachers among them. Christopher Fyfe, a leading historian of Sierra Leone, has described their arrival thus:

> When the people first landed, their pastors led them ashore, singing a hymn of praise, to a cotton-tree standing, tradition says, near where St George's Cathedral later stood. There like the Children of Israel which were come again out of captivity they rejoiced before the Lord who had brought them from bondage to the land of their forefathers. (*A History of Sierra Leone*, 1962, p. 37)

The town which they founded was named Freetown. The settlers experienced many difficulties, and they appealed for help to the Church Missionary Society in Britain. The CMS missionaries who arrived in 1804 did not come to evangelize, but to provide pastoral care and education for the Christian community. They soon had plenty to occupy them, for the population was swollen both by new arrivals from America, and also by people from further along the west coast. We must see how this came about.

In 1807 Britain made it illegal for her citizens to engage in slave trading, but for years afterwards the trade continued illegally, so a squadron of warships was sent to stop it. When a slave-ship was caught, the slaves were set free in Sierra Leone. Many were young men and boys, and they were educated and cared for by the missions and by the Christians of Freetown. They saw the hand of God in their release, and many became Christians. The mission established primary schools in Freetown and the surrounding villages, and from these the more able pupils went on to Freetown Grammar School. A few then progressed to Fourah Bay Institute to train as teachers or clergy, and others trained as artisans. The standard of education was high, and the students were trained for leadership. By the middle of the century many held posts of responsibility in the Church, in education, and in the civil service.

Henry Venn's Missionary Policies

The Reverend Henry Venn (1796–1872) was responsible for CMS

policy during this period, and was immensely influential in missionary circles. He believed that the task of missions was to establish as quickly as possible Churches that were self-supporting, self-governing, and self-propagating. Once this was done, he said, the missionaries should move on to evangelize new areas. He realized that indigenous priests and leaders must be trained. He knew many Africans personally, and had great faith in the possibilities of a local Church. In 1860 Venn persuaded the CMS to go part of the way towards realizing this policy in Sierra Leone. A 'Native Pastorate' was established, and nine congregations in and around Freetown were put wholly under the care of African clergy, and a constitution was drawn up for their administration. By 1872 there were 14,000 Church members, nineteen African clergy, nearly sixty catechists, and over a hundred Sunday School teachers. But some missionaries began to be concerned about what they called a 'spirit of rather petulant independence'. A new generation of missionaries had less trust in Africans than had Henry Venn.

The Move Eastward: Nigeria and the Gold Coast (Ghana)

By the 1840s the Africans who had been released from slave-ships and converted in Sierra Leone began to make their way back to their original homelands. Soon they were asking for teachers and pastors for themselves and their children, and both black and white missionaries were sent from Freetown in response to these requests. At the beginning of the century missionaries had hoped that the Church in Sierra Leone would be the means of bringing the gospel to the whole of West Africa: now this hope began to be fulfilled.

Bishop Samuel Adjai Crowther (1806–1891) was one of the first to go from Sierra Leone to Nigeria. He had been seized as a slave in boyhood, rescued from a slave-ship, and brought to Freetown. In 1843 he was ordained, and he went to Nigeria three years later. In 1864 he was made Anglican Bishop on the Niger Delta. He evangelized his enormous diocese with the help of a team of clergy and catechists trained in Sierra Leone. He tried to make each mission house and school the centre of a new way of life based on Christian values, but at the same time he increasingly appreciated African values and culture. He travelled extensively, supervising the diocese and encouraging African enterprise.

The Reverend Thomas Birch Freeman (1806–1890), of part-African parentage, was a pioneer missionary in the Gold Coast. From 1838 to 1890 he led the Methodist Church whose seeds had been sown by Philip Quaque. Freeman selected and trained African pastors, and arranged with African chiefs for these pastors to work in their territories. In 1849 he sent teachers to help Methodist Christians in Nigeria. On the Gold Coast, Methodists went inland to Kumasi, capital of the powerful

Left Samuel Adjai Crowther, first African to be made an Anglican bishop, 'a gracious and heroic man who became a legend in his own lifetime'.

Right Henry Venn, CMS Chief Secretary and outstanding missionary leader and thinker, whose vision of a self-supporting, self-governing and self-extending indigenous Church has inspired many Christians since his day.

Left Robert Moffat, pioneer LMS missionary in Southern Africa, famous for his friendship with Matabele and Botswana chiefs.

Right Apolo Kivebulaya, a shining representative of the many devoted evangelists who spread the gospel in East Africa, often under persecution.

Asante kingdom. When the Gold Coast Methodist Church celebrated its jubilee in 1885, Freeman played a leading role.

In 1828 the Swiss Basel Mission began work in the Gold Coast, and in 1843 a group of freed slaves from Jamaica arrived to help. They formed the nucleus of the Church at Akropong, and gave long service, which the Swiss missionaries were seldom able to do because of sickness and death. The Basel missionaries concentrated on education, and encouraged the converts to live together around the church building: they feared that they would be drawn back into the old religion otherwise. This separation of Christians from the rest of society may have delayed the spread of Christian values. The dilemma of how to be 'in the world, but not of the world' was often acute.

New Developments

1. THE REVIVAL OF ROMAN CATHOLIC MISSIONS

By the mid-nineteenth century changes had begun to occur. First, new life in the Roman Catholic Church in France led to a revival of Catholic missionary work. In 1861 the newly-founded Society of African Missions arrived to start work in Dahomey (Benin). They were helped by Bishop Kobès, of the Holy Ghost Fathers, who were already training African priests and sisters in Senegambia. The new missionaries settled at Ouidah on the coast where there was a mixed population of Dahomeans, the descendants of Dahomeans who had married Portuguese traders, and ex-slaves from Brazil. Some people in the last two groups knew a little about Christianity. The missionaries began to teach, but it was a long time before the King of Dahomey allowed them to make converts among his subjects.

Nigeria became another centre of Roman Catholic missionary work. In Lagos, as in Dahomey, the missionaries found a group of ex-slaves from Brazil. They continued to practise their faith under the leadership of a man called Pa Antonio who had spent some time in a seminary. Pa Antonio gathered them together every Sunday and said the prayers of the Mass with them. He baptized dying children, blessed marriages, and prayed with those who were dying. In 1878 the missionaries began to build a cathedral in Lagos to seat 2,000 worshippers, but it was soon too small. It was in Nigeria that Catholics first felt that they were securely on the way to planting the Church in West Africa. In the mean time the Holy Ghost Fathers established missions in Guinea, Sierra Leone and Liberia, and to the east of Nigeria in Cameroun, Gabon and Congo.

2. CONTACT WITH ISLAM

A second development was that missions in West Africa came increasingly into contact with Islam. For instance, in the 1880s Roman Catholic missions reached those parts of French West Africa known today as Niger, Chad and the Central African Republic. All these countries were sparsely inhabited, mostly by Muslims. By the middle of the century Islam had spread southward and westward from the semi-desert interior, and had already reached the coast in some places at about the same time as Christian missionaries. One such area was Senegambia, where Christian missions were only successful on the coast. In Ghana and Eastern Nigeria the missions had much greater success because the advance of Islam had been slowed up by strong tribes living to the north. The missions had very little success in converting Muslims, and it became part of their policy to try and prevent the further spread of Islam.

3. THE SCRAMBLE FOR AFRICA

The third and most far-reaching change was the so-called 'Scramble for Africa' when the European powers seized large areas of the interior of Africa in order to protect their trading interests on the coast. Missionaries were able to enter these areas freely after annexation, and they came to feel that they needed the protection of a colonial government if the Church was to spread, though, as we have seen, Christianity had already begun to spread widely before colonialism, largely because so many of the missionaries were Africans.

The colonial powers justified their empire-building by a doctrine of racial superiority. White people began to think of themselves as having a natural ability to rule people of other races, and when missionaries became infected with such thinking, they refused to work under African Church leaders. Such attitudes led to the formation of the first independent African-led Churches in West Africa in the 1890s.

4. REVIVALISM

Fourthly there was a change in missionary personnel. The Protestant missions began to recruit people who had been influenced by Evangelical revivals, and by the Keswick Movement in Britain which grew out of these. The revivals laid great stress on the need for holiness of life and for evangelism. People were encouraged to give up drinking alcohol, smoking, dancing, and other 'worldly pleasures', and great importance was attached to personal prayer and Bible-reading. The revivals produced many very dedicated missionaries, who set high moral standards both for themselves and for others. But zeal and charity do not always combine easily together, and some of the new generation of missionaries were harsh and unforgiving of what they took to be sin in African Christians. It was a group of such missionaries who brought about the resignation of Bishop Crowther in Nigeria.

After Venn's death in 1872, a new generation of CMS leaders continued to agree in principle with his ideas, but felt it was far too soon to put them into practice. Roman Catholic missions were equally dedicated to planting an indigenous church, but they too drew back. The Holy Ghost Fathers gave up the attempt to train African sisters and priests, and decided, like the Protestants, that the time was not yet ripe.

SOUTHERN AFRICA

Setting the Scene

The Cape of Good Hope was the base from which missions extended their work throughout Southern Africa in the nineteenth century. Dutch settlers had been at the Cape since 1652. They acquired slaves, and found another source of cheap labour in the remnants of the indigenous peoples whom they called Hottentots and Bushmen. The 'coloured' community of South Africa is largely descended from slaves, Hottentots and Bushmen, and people of mixed descent. There is also an Indian community in South Africa.

The beginning of the nineteenth century was a turning-point in the history of Southern Africa. First, in 1806 the British succeeded the Dutch as rulers of the Cape (which led to the abolition of slavery as such in 1834). Secondly, missionaries of many nationalities came to South Africa as the modern missionary movement got under way. Thirdly, the colonists began to come into conflict with the Nguni, black, Bantu-speaking peoples to the east, whom they saw as another source of cheap labour. There was a series of wars in which the Nguni were gradually dispossessed and driven into small enclaves, or forced to seek work on white farms.

The Dutch colonists, who called themselves Afrikaners, were members of the Dutch Reformed Church who had fled from the Netherlands to avoid persecution under Spanish rule. They saw themselves as representatives of white Christian civilization in a land of heathen darkness, but they did not feel the need to evangelize. They were determined to defend their way of life, and lived in constant fear of being overwhelmed by the blacks. By the 1830s some of them found British rule so irksome that they travelled further into the interior to find new lands. They began to think of themselves as God's chosen people being led, like the Israelites of old, into a new land which God had given them. They believed that, like the Israelites, they must separate themselves from the heathen who already lived in the land. In this Afrikaner folk-religion the black and coloured peoples were equated with the 'hewers of wood and drawers of water' of Joshua 9.21. The Afrikaners needed cheap labour for economic reasons, and they justified their exploitation of blacks and coloureds by reference to this religious myth. The initiatives for evangelizing the indigenous peoples of Southern Africa therefore had to come from overseas.

Missionary Beginnings

The earliest systematic missionary work was done among the coloured people of the Cape. Moravians and missionaries of the London Missionary Society established settlements where people could support themselves by agriculture or trade. Within a few years the LMS settlement at Bethelsdorp had several hundred settlers, and a Christian community of 100 Church members with their own deacons and deaconesses. There was daily as well as Sunday worship, and on moonlit nights and at sunrise people would sometimes slip out into the bush and kneel to pray. There seems to have been a similar practice in pre-Christian times, which the converts adapted.

In 1815 James Read, an LMS missionary at Bethelsdorp, enraged the Afrikaners by bringing thirty-six charges against them of murdering or using violence against coloured people. Twelve of the charges were proved, and the guilty sentenced. The Afrikaners were furious, and never forgave the LMS for 'blackening their name' as they put it, and British missionaries were not welcome in Afrikaner areas. During the next twenty years, Dr John Philip of the LMS led the missions' campaign on behalf of non-whites. The missions played a creditable part in trying to secure justice, but they lost the overall war in spite of some minor successes. No-one seriously questioned the justice of colonialism itself, or the existence of an economic system which could only function if a large part of the population was reduced to semi-slavery. By 1850 most of the coloured people living within the Colony had accepted the ideals of white society as their own. Their tragedy was that white society refused them any place within it.

Christianity in the Eastern Cape and Natal

Just when the colonists came into conflict with the Nguni, the Nguni themselves were in a state of upheaval because one section of them, the Zulu, had embarked on wars of expansion. As the missions moved into the area, they made their first converts among the Mfengu, refugees who had fled from the Zulu armies and had regrouped into new social units. The converts were

> the poor in spirit, kingdomless men who were glad enough to find a place in the kingdom of heaven. They were the meek, landless men who longed to inherit the earth. . . . They must have been heartened by the thought that an act of belief would transmute them into the salt of the earth and the light of the world. (Norman Etherington,

Preachers, Peasants and Politics in South-East Africa, 1835–1880, p. 115.)

As has happened in some other parts of the world, the first converts came from among the misfits and the social outcasts.

The most southerly of the Nguni were the Xhosa. They had allowed many Mfengu to settle among them. They too were threatened by the advance of the colonists, and Chief Ngqika was in the front line. Some of his councillors advised armed resistance, but among those who advised caution was Ntsikana (c.1760–1820), who saw Christianity not as something totally new and alien, but as something which fulfilled what he already knew. The Xhosa explain that he was converted before he ever met a missionary. He is remembered as a prophet who made many correct predictions, and also as a poet. In his *Great Hymn* Ntsikana sometimes speaks to God, and sometimes speaks about him. Here is a paraphrase of part of it:

> It is he, the great God, who is in heaven!
>> It is you indeed, our true shield;
>> It is you indeed, our true fortress;
>> It is you indeed, the true forest where we can take refuge.
> He who created life below also created life above.
> It is that same creator who made the heavens and the stars.
>> A star flashed forth—it was telling us;
>> The hunting-horn sounded—it was calling us;
>> In his hunting he hunts for souls.
>> It is he who reconciles enemies;
>> He, the leader who has led us,
>> He, the garment we put on.
> Those hands of yours, they are wounded;
> Those feet of yours, they too are wounded;
> Your blood, why is it flowing?
>> Your blood was shed for us.
>> You paid the great price; and we didn't even ask you.
>> You made a home for us, before we even knew we wanted it.

This hymn is in the form of a Xhosa praise poem, and the imagery is African even where it is also biblical. Ntsikana made a path along which a section of the Xhosa was eventually able to follow him into Christianity, and he is remembered annually on 10 April as a saint, and as a forerunner of African nationalism.

The Reverend Tiyo Soga (1829–1871) was of a later generation of Xhosa Christians. He was educated by the LMS, and when war disrupted the area, he was taken to Scotland to finish his education, where he was ordained and married a Scottish girl before returning to

Africa. He spent much of his life at Mgwali, where he built a large church which still stands, and trained catechists to help him evangelize the area. Like the white missionaries, he found the Mfengu more receptive to the gospel than anyone else. Within ten years there was a congregation of 350, and his wife's sister had joined him and was teaching nearby. The best-known of Soga's writings are his translation of *Pilgrim's Progress* and his many hymns, some of which are still sung. Soga suffered from living in two worlds: he and his Scottish wife were never fully accepted by either whites or blacks. But his pioneer achievements in education, literature and the Church blazed a trail for others to follow.

The school where Soga started his education was Lovedale, begun in 1841 by Scottish missionaries. In 1855 industrial training was added, and girls' education a little later. Under the Reverend Dr James Stewart (Principal from 1870 to 1905) there was great expansion. In 1872 there were 300 students; by the time of the school's golden jubilee in 1891 there were 650, and numbers continued to rise. Many eminent South Africans of all races were educated at Lovedale.

In 1857 the main body of the Xhosa were persuaded that if they destroyed their crops and sacrificed their cattle, the ancestors would rise from the dead, and help them drive the whites out of the land. Starvation and terrible suffering followed the cattle-killing. The Churches were massively involved in relief work, and they reported that after this tragedy people were more willing to listen to their teaching.

Ten years later diamonds were discovered, and then gold. This transformed the economy of South Africa, and more and more blacks left home to become migrant workers. Schools began to be seen as a way into the new society that was developing, but just when blacks were beginning to demand education, ideas about the kind of education suitable for them began to change. African education was redirected so as to enable them to serve their own people and the needs of white-dominated society, rather than as a means of bringing about greater equality.

From the 1840s the American Board Missions started work among the Zulu, but there was little response. In 1879 the Zulu were finally defeated, and it was at this critical point in their history that the Roman Catholic Mariannhill Mission was founded to work among them. It was started by Trappist monks, who serve God primarily through prayer and silent adoration, and support themselves by farming. It was hoped that their example of work and prayer would be a Christian witness in Africa as it had been in Europe. The Trappists became excellent missionaries, but they were unable to live the silent life to which they are called. In 1909, therefore, the Mariannhill missionaries, who by then had some twenty stations, became independent. School work dates from 1884, and the Mariannhill schools offered a high standard of education, both academic and practical.

The Tswana and Sotho

The pioneer missionary to the Tswana was Robert Moffat of the LMS (1795–1883) who worked in South Africa for fifty years at Kuruman. He reduced the Tswana language to writing and translated the whole Bible, printing it on the Kuruman Press. Moffat helped to establish missions to the north, partly through his good relations with chiefs. His daughter married the great missionary traveller, Dr David Livingstone (1813–1873), and Moffat helped him on his journeys. Livingstone's books were immensely important in publicizing the needs of missions in Africa.

In 1833 Chief Moshweshwe (c.1798–1870) of Lesotho invited the Paris Evangelical Mission to his country. He had just become chief, and faced a difficult task because the Sotho had suffered greatly as a result of the Zulu wars. Moshweshwe encouraged his people to attend the mission, and by 1848 there were 2,000 baptized Christians, 1,000 catechumens, 600 pupils in school, and six mission stations. The missionary Eugene Casalis acted as his advisor and gave wise counsel to Moshweshwe in his dealings with the whites. However, the missionaries had taught that accepting Christianity brought peace and prosperity, and when peace was disturbed and prosperity threatened by white people who also claimed to be Christians, many Sotho were angry. They said the mission had cheated them, and for a time Christianity suffered a setback. In 1862 Roman Catholic missionaries reached Lesotho, and towards the end of Moshweshwe's life both Catholics and Protestants battled for his soul, but he died before he could be baptized. Catholics called their mission *Motsi va Ma-Jesus* (village of the mother of Jesus), but Protestants nicknamed it Roma, and the nickname stuck. Roma is today the site of Lesotho's university, and Catholic Christians are in a majority in the country.

The Ngwato are a northern branch of the Tswana. In 1860 a chief's son called Khama (1837–1922) was converted. In 1875 he succeeded to the chiefdom, and in the interests of unity among his subjects he allowed no mission other than the LMS in his country. He was greatly respected by both blacks and whites. 'Khama was a gift of God to the people', said Tsogang Sebina, a retired teacher who remembered his reign. 'He was not educated. . . . He had only a Tswana education, but he was, in religion and rule, what they call a sage' (quoted in Bessie Head, *Serowe, Village of the Rain Wind*, 1981, p. 23). Both Khama and Moshweshwe succeeded in preventing the whole of their countries being annexed by South Africa, and Botswana and Lesotho became independent nations in the 1960s, with largely Christian populations.

Independent Churches

The missions in South Africa were particularly slow to give black and coloured people responsibility in the Churches. In the 1880s the Methodists ordained some pastors, but the move came too late to prevent impatience from spilling over. In 1884 the Reverend Nehemiah Tilé left the Methodists to found the Church of the Tembu people, with the chief as its head. A little later the Ethiopian Church was founded in the gold-mining area, and it brought together people from many tribes. It claimed a biblical foundation in such verses as Ps. 68.31 and Acts 8.27. In neither case was there any quarrel over doctrine or Church order. Those who founded these Churches simply wanted to be free of white missionary control. Since then an enormous number of Independent Churches have appeared throughout Africa, and many have included the word 'Ethiopian' in their titles. They have in mind, not only biblical references to Ethiopia, but also the model provided by the existence of an ancient Church free from Western domination. Independent Churches which have grown simply out of a desire to be free from white rule are often called 'Ethiopian' Churches. In the twentieth century, as we shall see, more radical Churches, often referred to as 'Zionist', have been founded, which reflect a more deeply-rooted dissatisfaction with the sort of Christianity in the mission-founded Churches.

By the end of the nineteenth century the thrust of the missions based in the Cape had taken them as far north as the present countries of Zambia and Zimbabwe, in both of which areas work had just begun. In the east and west, Roman Catholic missions had come to life again in the Portuguese territories of Mozambique and Angola, and Protestant work had just begun in these countries. German Lutherans were at work in what is now Namibia, and Scottish missions in Malawi. In central Africa too, missions had started work, and the spaces on the map were being filled in.

EAST AFRICA

Freed Slaves on the East Coast

By the middle of the nineteenth century the East Coast slave-trade had reached huge proportions. Slave-traders coming down the Nile from Egypt and those working their way inland from Zanzibar had almost linked up. A little further south, Arab traders had made their way as far inland as Lake Tanganyika. They made alliances with stronger peoples such as the Ngoni and Nyamwezi of Tanzania, and encouraged them to raid their neighbours and organized slave caravans to the coast.

Dr David Livingstone, who travelled widely in south and central Africa, drew the attention of Europe to the extent of the slave-trade, and to its cruelties. He said it could only be stopped if other sorts of trade were introduced as an alternative. His writings caught the attention of missions and attracted them to the area, and the British tried to make the Sultan of Zanzibar declare the trade illegal. The Sultan was unwilling to do so because the economy of Zanzibar depended on slave labour. However, by 1874 he was forced to outlaw the trade, though, as in West Africa, it continued illegally for some time.

Before 1874 freed slaves had been cared for by missions in India because of the risk that they would be recaptured if returned to Africa. They lived in settlements similar to those in Sierra Leone, and were educated in the hope that one day they would return to Africa as evangelists. After 1874 some of them returned to work for other freed slaves near Mombasa where the CMS had opened a settlement. William Jones and Ishmael Semler, who had been brought up in India, and David George, a local catechist, became the leading African Christians on the Kenya coast, and worked as evangelists and teachers. Within a few years a mature Church developed near Mombasa, and its leaders persuaded the people of the Taita Hills to accept evangelists: the missions had been unable to win their confidence. It seemed as though an independent pastorate might come into being on the lines of the one in Freetown.

But in the 1880s new missionaries attacked the work of the African Christians in much the same way that Bishop Crowther's work had been attacked. There was such bitterness that an experienced missionary was sent to find out what had gone wrong. He wrote praising the work of the African leaders, and advising that several of them should be ordained: 'They are spiritually-minded, possess many gifts and qualifications, speak English and Swahili, and for more than fifteen years have worked faithfully.' When James Hannington arrived in 1885 as the first bishop, he ordained William Jones and Ishmael Semler, but David George had died the previous year.

Roman Catholic missions were also at work in East Africa. The Holy Ghost Fathers started in Zanzibar and moved to the mainland in 1868, and founded Christian villages where freed slaves were trained as artisans and catechists. An attempt to train priests and sisters in the 1870s was not successful. The mission hoped that the orderly and prosperous life of the villages would attract others and make converts. By 1886 six settlements had been founded, but they did not attract the surrounding villagers, except in times of danger or hunger, when people turned to them for help. Perhaps they were run too much like monasteries to be suitable for lay people. The greatest success of the Holy Ghost Fathers in the nineteenth century was to train catechists, who went and established schools in the interior among non-Muslims who were more open to the gospel.

Anglican missionaries of the Universities' Mission to Central Africa (UMCA) also helped freed slaves, and hoped they would evangelize the interior. They, too, began work in Zanzibar, but in 1875 and 1876 they moved to the mainland and set up missions at Masasi and Mbweni. A few years later, in 1882, Masasi was attacked by the Ngoni in a raid for slaves, and many people were carried off. Charles Suleiman, a freed-slave catechist, helped to get some released, but others were never seen again. The mission withdrew for safety, but Suleiman stayed on working as a catechist. He was still at work when the mission returned in 1893, and soon there was a good sized group of Christians as a result of his work.

In spite of some success, freed slaves in East Africa did not take Christianity as far or as widely as freed slaves had done in West Africa. The coastal people of East Africa were mainly Muslims, and so were hostile to Christianity. The economy depended on slaves, and the missions' campaign for their emancipation only increased Muslim hostility to Christianity. Work was therefore very slow. The freed slaves did not make their way back to their original homes as they had done in the west, probably because there was no comparable pattern of trade to attract them. So the plans made by the missions did not fully work out. But many freed slaves did become Christians and worked as catechists, and when work began further inland, they began to meet with more success.

The Move Inland to Uganda

It was in Uganda, however, that the East African missions met with their most spectacular success in the east. In the mid-1870s travellers reported that Mutesa, the king of Buganda, wanted Christian missionaries in his country. This was true, though not primarily because he was interested in their religion. His country was threatened by Egypt, whose traders were advancing down the Nile in search of ivory and slaves, and were approaching his northern borders. Anglican missionaries of the CMS arrived in 1877 in response to his appeals, and Roman Catholic White Fathers two years later. Mutesa was disappointed when he found that the missions were not willing to supply him with firearms, and the missions were equally disappointed to find that he was more interested in guns than in the gospel.

At Mutesa's court there were many young men in training for future positions of leadership. Some had already been converted to Islam by

Left Memorial to Bernard Mizeki, martyr, painted by African artists at Cyrene School, Zimbabwe. Anglican and Roman Catholic shrines at Namugongo honour Uganda's many martyrs, both early and more recent. *Right* is the Roman Catholic memorial.

Today the Ethiopian Church consecrates its own bishops, and uses Amharic in worship (pp. 128 and 151), but it still retains much of its ancient liturgy and ritual.

142

Muslim traders from the coast, and had begun to learn to read the Qur'an. The Christian missionaries also taught literacy, and soon a number of the most intelligent young men from the court had attached themselves to the missions. Mutesa and his chiefs were drawn into intense debates on religion.

Mutesa's successor was a young man called Mwanga, who came to the throne in 1884. He was a less able statesman than his father, and he made enemies. Like all new rulers of Buganda, he found at his court young men who wanted a share of power, and older men who did not want to share the power they already had. The older men included priests and office-holders of the traditional religion. They and the Muslims joined together and took every opportunity to suggest to Mwanga that the Christians were a political danger. During 1885 and 1886 a series of misfortunes was blamed on the Christians, and many died for their faith. The greatest slaughter took place on 3 June 1886, when thirty-one young men and boys were burnt alive at Namugongo. The names of another twenty martyrs are known, and as many as 200 may have died altogether.

The leader of those who died at Namugongo was Charles Lwanga (c.1860–1886), a palace official who had become a Roman Catholic and who baptized several of the martyrs the night before they were led away to execution. He died alone before the others. One of the leading Protestants was Robert Munyagabyanjo (?1836–1886). He encouraged the others in words which a Ugandan writer has recorded thus:

> I appeal to all of you gathered here to have firm minds. Never fear those who kill the body but cannot kill the spirit. We sympathize with those of you who are going to remain in this world of extreme hazards. We are happy because in a short time we shall be in this place which Jesus Christ has prepared for us, not by ourselves, but with all those who love him and happily await his coming. You who have seen us, go and tell our brothers that we have broken Satan's chains, and that we shall soon be with our Saviour. (Translated by Dr J. A. Rowe from the writings of James Miti.)

The youngest martyr was Kizito (c.1872–1886), only fourteen or fifteen years old, whom the missionaries thought too young for baptism in such dangerous times. He was baptized by Charles Lwanga. In 1964 the Roman Catholic martyrs were recognized as saints by their Church, and the first visit ever made by a Pope to Africa was made by Pope Paul VI in 1969 to do honour to the Uganda Martyrs. Protestants and Roman Catholics joined together for part of these celebrations as the martyrs had done eighty years before in suffering and martyrdrom. St Charles Lwanga and his companions are commemorated on 3 June each year.

Only four years after these martyrdoms a revolution took place in Uganda. Christian leaders seized power after both they and the Muslims had been further threatened by Mwanga. After that, anyone who wanted to be successful in Buganda had to be literate, and that meant being a Christian. It is sad that in the political strife of the 1890s bitter rivalry grew up between Catholics and Protestants, and Muslims were pushed into third place and acquired genuine grievances which were to have serious results later.

The new Christian leaders in Buganda encouraged evangelism and made themselves responsible for building churches and providing land for catechists. Political and religious motives were often mixed in their passion for evangelism. They used the Churches to strengthen their own positions, and even to spread the influence of Buganda into other areas of Uganda, but many also had a deep personal commitment to Christianity. They set the pace in the evangelism of Uganda, and the white missionaries found it difficult to keep up with all the demands made on them.

One of the best-known Ugandan Anglican missionaries was the Reverend Apolo Kivebulaya (1864–1933). Baptized in 1894, he went as an evangelist to western Uganda the following year, and then on to the Congo (Zaire). Here he worked among the pygmies of the Ituri Forest, and translated part of St Mark's Gospel into their language. He was loved by all who knew him, and radiated happiness. He received only a tiny salary, and gave away most of what he possessed. He died in 1933, and his saintly life has been an inspiration to many. Yohana Kitagana (1858–1938) was a Roman Catholic missionary catechist who was contemporary with Kivebulaya. He too worked in western Uganda, and then went south to the border with Rwanda. Like Kivebulaya he pioneered in places where no white missionary had been. Kitagana is remembered for his zeal and devotion, and for caring for widows and orphans. He was decorated by the British for his services to the people of Uganda.

Stanislaus Mugwanya (1849–1938) was one of the greatest of the Christian chiefs, and he represents another aspect of the Christian impact on Uganda. He was baptized as a Roman Catholic in the year of the martyrdoms, and became one of the most powerful men in Uganda. He was a leading supporter of Catholic schools, and he paid the fees of many poor pupils. He also pioneered the growing of cotton and coffee. In 1914 he travelled extensively in Europe, as well as visiting the Holy Land and the headquarters of the White Fathers Mission, which was then in Algiers. Like many Ugandans he was a writer, and published a book describing his travels. He was honoured by both the British Government and the Roman Catholic Church.

Already by 1900, then, there was a sense in which Christianity 'belonged' in Uganda. In spite of setbacks, this sense that the Church belongs still exists.

Conclusions

In this chapter we have studied the three main lines of Christian advance in Africa in the nineteenth century: from Sierra Leone in the West; from the Cape in Southern Africa; and from the East African coast. In the final quarter of the century the map began to fill up, and in most of the countries of modern Africa the Church had been founded by the end of the century, though in several only a very small beginning had been made, and many of the peoples of Africa had not been reached at all. Only a tiny part of the population was Christian, even where Christianity had been present longest. No one could possibly have guessed at the transformation which was to take place in the next century. But already, by the end of the nineteenth century, hundreds of Africans were dedicated to spreading their new faith. We have met the Sierra Leonians who evangelized the Niger Delta under the leadership of Bishop Crowther, and the chiefs and catechists of Uganda who ventured far afield, so that when white missionaries arrived, they found an embryo Church already in existence. Some people have suggested that Christianity was more or less forced on Africans by the colonial powers: the dedication of thousands of evangelists shows that the truth is something quite different.

We conclude this chapter by mentioning Bernard Mizeki (c.1861–1896), a founder-saint of the Anglican Church in Zimbabwe, who sums up this spirit of evangelism. Born in Mozambique, he was converted to Christianity in Capetown where he had gone to work, and in 1891 he volunteered to help establish the Diocese of Mashonaland. He died in the Mashonaland Rising of 1896, having refused to save his life by fleeing from danger because he felt he must stay and try to protect a disabled man whom he was caring for. The place where he lived is today a centre of pilgrimage for Christians in Zimbabwe.

STUDY SUGGESTIONS

WORDS AND MEANINGS

1. What do you understand by the following terms used in this chapter?
   (a) Abuna (b) Gold Coast (c) The 'scramble for Africa'
   (d) 'Coloured' people in South Africa (e) Afrikaners (f) Nguni

REVIEW OF CONTENT

2. (a) In what way has the history of the Church in Ethiopia been different from its history in all other countries of Africa?
(b) What was the political situation in Ethiopia during the nineteenth and early twentieth centuries?
(c) What was the state of the Ethiopian Church at that time, and the attitude of Ethiopian Christians to the Church elsewhere?

3. (a) Give a brief description of the events which explain why Freetown in Sierra Leone came to be founded and why it was given that name.
(b) For what special purpose were CMS missionaries sent to Sierra Leone in 1804?

4. Who were the following and where did they work? Describe briefly, with dates, the aims and achievements of each.
(a) Philip Quaque (b) Henry Venn (c) Samuel Adjai Crowther
(d) Pa Antonio

5. At what dates did the following societies start work in West Africa, and in which countries?
(a) The Basel Mission (b) The Society of African Missions

6. What was the effect on Christian missionary work, and on the specific aims and attitudes of missionaries themselves, of:
(a) the spread of Islam south and west from the Sahara?
(b) the establishment by European powers of colonial governors to protect their trading interests in Africa?
(c) the recruitment by Protestant missions in Britain and Europe of people influenced by Evangelical revival and the Keswick movement?

7. (a) Approximately when, and why, did Dutch colonists (Afrikaners) first come to settle in South Africa?
(b) For what three chief reasons can the beginning of the nineteenth century be regarded as 'a turning point in the history of southern Africa'?

8. (a) Which were the first missionary societies to work systematically in the Cape, and what form did their work take?
(b) What was the relationship between these missions and the Afrikaners?

9. Who were the following? Describe briefly the aims and achievements of each.
(a) Ntsikana (b) Tiyo Soga (c) Robert Moffat (d) Moshweshwe
(e) Khama

10. What was the effect on people's lives, and on the work of missions, of each of the following events in South Africa during the nineteenth century?

(a) The Zulu wars of expansion (b) The Xhosa cattle-killing (c) The discovery of diamonds and gold.

11. Give a brief account, with dates, of the founding and work of the Mariannhill Mission to the Zulu people.

12. What were the chief reasons for the founding of independent Churches in South Africa? Why did some of them include the word 'Ethiopian' in their titles?

13. Slavery as such ended in South Africa in 1834. Why was it not outlawed in East Africa until forty years later?

14. Give a brief account, with dates, denomination and sending countries, of the early work in East Africa of each of the following: (a) The Holy Ghost Fathers (b) The Universities' Mission to Central Africa
For what chief reason was their work on the east coast of Africa less successful at first than it was later on?

15. (a) In what ways did the early development of the Church in East Africa in the second half of the nineteenth century resemble that of the Church in Sierra Leone and neighbouring West African countries in the first half of the century?
(b) Who were the leading African Christians on the Kenya coast at that time?

16. (a) For what chief reason did King Mutesa of Buganda invite Christian missions to work in his country, and which missions responded?
(b) Which groups of people in Uganda were first among those who became Christians?

17. (a) What were the events which led up to the persecution and martyrdom of many Ugandan Christians in 1885 and 1886, and in what ways have the martyrs since been commemorated?
(b) What subsequent political events in Uganda encouraged evangelism and Church growth?

18. Give a brief account, with dates, of the lives and achievements of the following:
(a) Apolo Kivebulaya (b) Yohana Kitagana (c) Stanislaus Mugwanya (d) Bernard Mizeki

DISCUSSION

19. Henry Venn believed the task of missions was to establish local Churches which could run and support themselves, and then to move on quickly to evangelize new areas. Others believed that new Churches needed continuing missionary control, coupled with the training of indigenous catechists and teachers to carry on the evangelizing. What is your opinion? How far do you think the choice of such policies should depend on local circumstances?

20. In some areas missions have encouraged new converts to live in close-knit communities, to avoid reverting to pre-Christian practices. What are any other advantages of such an arrangement, and what are any possible disadvantages?

21. Some worship practices in Christian settlements established by the LMS and Moravians among coloured people in South Africa, seem to be adapted from those of pre-Christian times. What do you see as the benefits of adapting traditional practices, or the possible dangers?

22. 'Ntsikana saw Christianity, not as something new and alien, but as fulfilling what he already knew' (p. 136). Do you think many people see Christianity in this way? How far, if at all, does it reflect your own experience?

23. 'Christian leaders in Buganda built churches and provided land for catechists. Political and religious motives were often mixed in their passion for evangelism' (p. 144). 'Some people have suggested that Christianity was forced on Africans by the colonial powers: the dedication of thousands of evangelists shows that the truth is quite different' (p. 145). What connections, if any, do you see between these two statements?

7
Africa: 1900–1950
by Louise Pirouet

This history of Christianity in Africa in the nineteenth century was a story of heroism and adventure, a modern 'Acts of the Apostles', in which individual missionaries and African Christians stand out for their heroic witness. The story of the first half of the twentieth century is rather different. From one point of view the period from 1900 to 1950 was a success story. There was a steady growth in the number of missions and missionaries, in the number of converts, in the number of Christian schools and hospitals, and in the number of languages into which the Bible was translated. But for African Christians there was often a keen sense of disappointment, even frustration, because missionary control increased, and there seemed less and less hope of achieving an autonomous Church in the foreseeable future. Yet if we look more closely we shall find that the missions were less in control than sometimes appears. Much of what they did was in response to African demand, and it was not always the mission who generated that demand. The wind of the Spirit was blowing, though it was not always recognized.

ETHIOPIA

The Emperor Menelik who had defeated the Italians died in 1913. His successor, Lij Iyasu, was rejected because of his leanings towards Islam. From 1916 to 1974 the effective ruler of the country was Ras Tafari, who took the throne name of Haile Selassie when he became Emperor in 1930. Haile Selassie recognized his country's need for modernization, but he believed that change must come slowly if it was not to be disruptive. The revolution which began in 1974 has shown that his reforms were too slow and too paternalistic. He was faced with three sets of problems. First, there were the feudalistic powers of the royal family and nobility (which, of course, he shared). He did not realize that these were incompatible with modernization and democracy. Secondly, there was the difficulty of forging national unity among recently conquered peoples who were both ethnically and religiously different from the people of the Christian heartland of Ethiopia. Thirdly, there was the extreme backwardness of the country and of the Church, even the priests being largely illiterate.

The first moves towards Church reform had in fact been made in the nineteenth century, when Menelik's predecessor had persuaded the

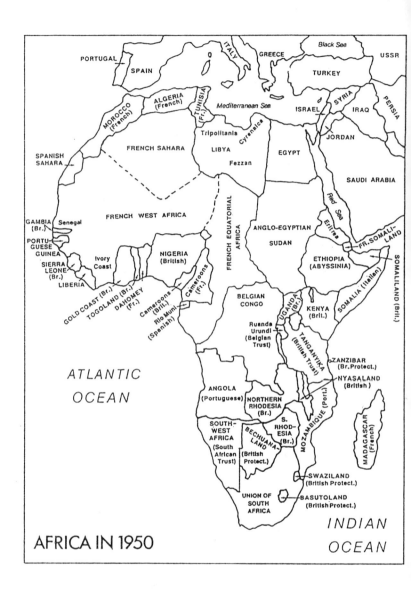

AFRICA IN 1950

Patriarch of Alexandria to consecrate four bishops, rather than just one; but these were all Egyptians, and they were not replaced when they died. In 1929 a new *abuna* (bishop) was consecrated, and the Patriarch agreed to consecrate five Ethiopians to serve under him. For the first time dioceses were demarcated, and a bishop placed in charge of each. This was a first step towards better Church administration.

Further reforms in Church and state were disrupted in 1935, when the Italians invaded the country and annexed it as a colony. There was strong resistance, and the Italians had great difficulty in imposing their rule on the Church. Bishops Mikael and Petros were executed for their opposition, and many monks and clergy were massacred on the suspicion of resistance. The *abuna* Qerillos refused to co-operate with the Italians, and returned to Egypt. Bishop Abraham was made *abuna* in his place, and was forced to declare the Ethiopian Church independent of Egypt. He and those who co-operated with him were excommunicated by the Patriarch of Alexandria because of this. The Italians also tried to use the Church to make their rule more acceptable to the people, and they had some success, for although many people rejected the new *abuna*, many others did not. They welcomed greater independence from Egypt. *Abuna* Abraham and his successor were able to consecrate several bishops, and about 2,000 priests were ordained. The Italians also tried to win the support of the Muslims—who were almost as numerous as the Christians, but had little power or influence—by granting them favours and opportunities which they had not possessed before.

Ethiopia was liberated in 1941 with British help, and the following year *Abuna* Qerillos returned and was reinstated, and all Ethiopian Christians were restored to the fellowship of the Church. But the clock could not be put back, and the Ethiopian Church leaders insisted that greater independence from Egypt was needed. After years of debate an agreement was reached in 1948. Five Ethiopian monks were consecrated as bishops in Egypt, and it was agreed that the next *abuna* would be an Ethiopian, and would be empowered to consecrate bishops himself instead of depending on the Patriarch of Alexandria. This was effected in 1959, when an Ethiopian monk was consecrated as *Abuna* Basileos.

Better education for the clergy was also introduced, with help from trained Egyptians. A theological college was started in Addis Ababa which later became the theological faculty of the university. Priests now received a general as well as a theological education. The Church's finances were put on a better footing, and Amharic (the language of the dominant Christian ethnic group) began to be used in worship as well as the ancient liturgical language, Ge'ez, which not many people understood. The Bible was translated into Amharic and other vernaculars, which helped to increase people's understanding of the Scriptures.

Missionary societies were permitted to work in Ethiopia, but only under strict controls. In the Christian areas of the country they were allowed to do medical and educational work, but they were not supposed to convert people away from the national Church. Elsewhere in the country they were encouraged to evangelize. The Emperor sincerely wished to encourage evangelism, and the national Church as well as the missions worked among non-Christian peoples. But the authorities also hoped that if people were converted to Christianity they would be more loyal to the Christian state. The missions had considerable success among the followers of African traditional religions, such as the Oromo people of the south-west where Lutherans were at work. The Mekane Yesus Church which they founded there has about half a million members.

NEW MISSIONS AND MORE MISSIONARIES

The revival of Roman Catholic missions in Africa had already begun in the last part of the nineteenth century. Roman Catholic missionaries soon began to equal Protestants in number, and then to overtake them. Many new missions were set up specifically to work in Africa, such as the Society of African Missions, begun in 1856 to work in West Africa. Ten years later Italian missionaries, who had tried for years to establish missions along the Nile Valley, were reorganized as the Verona Fathers, and worked in Sudan and Uganda. The first White Fathers had arrived in Africa in 1869, working in North, East and Central Africa. The Italian Consolata Mission arrived in Kenya in 1900. Each of these societies had a related congregation of missionary sisters. *Propaganda Fide*, the Department of the Vatican responsible for missions, directed the societies to different areas so that there should be no overlapping.

New Protestant missions dated from a little later, and recruited as missionaries people who had been influenced by the Evangelical revivals of the late nineteenth century in England and America. These missions too were specially founded to work in Africa. They were interdenominational, and their purpose was to evangelize individuals rather than to plant denominational Churches or become involved in 'secular activities' such as schools or hospitals. They were often deeply suspicious of the older denominational missions, suspecting that their missionaries were not properly converted. Before long, however, the newer missions realized that they could not avoid establishing Churches, and that if they did not provide schools and hospitals, their converts would go off to other missions which did. Among the new Protestant missions were the South Africa General Mission (1889), the

Africa Inland Mission (1895), and the Sudan United Mission (1902) which worked throughout the Sahel, the region just south of the Sahara Desert. Protestant Church development was less orderly than that of the Roman Catholic Church, because there was no overall authority to direct the Protestant missions. They often competed with one another, though in some places they entered into what were known as 'comity' agreements among themselves, and in others governments forced such agreements upon them. Roman Catholics rarely entered voluntarily into such agreements with Protestants, but occasionally they were imposed, as in the Sudan. Since there were never enough missions and missionaries to work everywhere on the continent, it was often a matter of geographical accident rather than choice that determined which Church African Christians belonged to.

The Roman Catholic missions usually included lay-brothers who were skilled builders, and many of the churches and mission houses which they built are landmarks for miles around. On a typical Catholic mission, an imposing church stands on the highest ground, with a house for the priests, a convent for the sisters, schools for boys and girls, and a hospital or dispensary, all clustered around it, and gardens and farmland to help feed the community. There may also be a training college for teachers, a seminary, a printing press, a bookstore, and so on. On Protestant missions the church itself is often less imposing and built with local labour, and a row of bungalows for married couples and single missionaries replaces the priests' house and the convent. In other ways the missions were similar, since all aimed to provide the same range of institutions to serve the Christian communities. The missions called people to leave their old ways and customs, so they needed to provide all that was required for their new life as Christians. A network of out-stations surrounded the central mission, each with a church or chapel in charge of a catechist. Missionaries visited these out-stations from time to time.

Schools and Hospitals

The educational and medical work of the Churches in Africa has been so important in promoting their growth that we must look at it in more detail.

In Freetown, Sierra Leone, and elsewhere on the West African coast where people had been in contact with European traders for a long time, education was in demand from the time that missions first arrived. Nearly everywhere else people resisted education at first because they could see no point in it, and because they thought (quite correctly) that it would disrupt their society. However, when they saw that change could not be resisted, then they demanded education because they saw that schools offered a way into the new society that was emerging. Many Africans clamoured for education because it offered a way of escape from the constrictions of subsistence agriculture. With a little education a person might become a clerk in government service, or find his way into paid employment, or become a teacher or nurse. The missionaries looked at education from a different point of view. For Protestants, the basic reason for providing schools was so that people could learn to read the Bible. But education could not stop there. Through the schools they also hoped to train Christians who would become the leaders of their society as well as pastors and teachers. Roman Catholics, like Protestants, wanted to train Christian leaders, but they also needed to train indigenous priests. Since all Catholic priests whether African or European had to have the same level and kind of training, this meant establishing seminaries, and a network of schools which would provide candidates for them. The seminaries in fact fulfilled a dual role. Some students who entered them were eventually ordained, but the majority were not. Their education was not wasted, since it enabled them to take their place among the lay Christian leaders of their communities.

The missions found it difficult to meet all the requests they received for teachers and schools. Sometimes Africans benefited from the rivalry between missions, and played off one against another in order to get the education they wanted. A striking example of this was in Eastern Nigeria, where the Igbo were willing to convert to whichever branch of Christianity would provide them with schools. Most Igbo became Roman Catholics because Fr (later Bishop) Joseph Shanahan and the Holy Ghost Fathers succeeded best.

Most of the schools which the missions managed were small village primary schools, teaching reading, religion, and perhaps writing and a little arithmetic. In the early years the teacher was usually a catechist; and when in the 1920s the roles of catechists and teachers were separated, the catechists continued to teach reading and writing to those who wished to be baptized. The primary school buildings were usually of mud and wattle with a thatched roof, and were put up by the local people. Equipment and furniture were almost non-existent, and children and adults sometimes learnt together. Central schools at mission stations offered a more extensive education for the ablest pupils from the village schools, and taught geography and history (of Europe, not Africa!), a European language, arithmetic, and perhaps woodwork and some agriculture. Religion was at the centre of the syllabus.

There was much discussion about the sort of education that should be given, in particular whether education should be mainly literary or mainly practical. For a time some students at Livingstonia in Nyasaland (now Malawi) took an advanced Arts course which included philosophy, and ancient and modern European languages and literature. The teacher was a gifted enthusiast, and some of the students found the course greatly stimulating. But for the most part Livingstonia concentrated on training people in practical trades, which enabled them to find work with European employers, mostly in South Africa. It is not clear that this sort of practical training contributed anything to the development of Nyasaland as it was intended to do. In the 1920s surveys were made of both Protestant and Roman Catholic schools. The Phelps–Stokes Commission reported on Protestant schools and praised them for their work. It called on governments to give more assistance to education so that better standards could be reached, particularly in the village primary schools, which were often sub-standard. The Commission recommended that much more attention should be paid to training in agriculture, and thought that the schools were too 'bookish'. The missions welcomed the report, the governments increased their grants, but the schools were not successful in promoting agriculture. People came to school to escape from agriculture, not to return to it. Msgr Arthur Hinsley was sent from Rome to tour the Roman Catholic mission schools. He too urged co-operation with government, and told the missions to accept all the government help they could get. The missions were gaining most of their converts from among those being educated in their schools, so Hinsley's advice to the missions was, 'Where it is impossible for you to carry on both the immediate task of evangelization and your educational work, neglect your Churches in order to perfect your schools.' The schools were proving to be the main evangelistic agencies. All the missions agreed that teachers needed to be better trained, and training colleges were opened.

Girls' education generally lagged far behind that of boys, though the Annie Walsh Memorial School in Sierra Leone, started by the CMS in 1849, was an exception. It provided secondary education for girls almost a century before any other school in Africa. St Monica's Girls' School at Onitsha in Eastern Nigeria had its roots in a school started in 1895 by Edith Warner of CMS. Like most girls' schools before the 1940s, it concentrated on homecraft and babycare. At Mbereshi in Northern Rhodesia (Zambia) a remarkable LMS missionary, Mabel Shaw, ran a girls' school and worked to help Lunda women and girls in the 1920s and 1930s. She had a most unusual appreciation of African cultural values, which she deeply respected. In a book called *God's Candlelights* she gives a sympathetic account of aspects of Lunda culture, and tells of her efforts to express Christianity in Lunda terms in school. The 1940s saw the beginnings of secondary education for girls in most parts of Africa. Mother Kevin of the Franciscan Missionary Sisters founded Mount St Mary's School in Uganda in 1940 as a full secondary school. Among its former pupils was the first African

Left The Lutheran church in Dar es Salaam, Tanzania, where Lutherans remain the largest Protestant group 60 years after German rule ended.

Right William Wade Harris, prophet and preacher in Sierra Leone, Ghana, and the Ivory Coast where the independent Harrist Church still flourishes.

Below Africans have welcomed Western medicine often without forsaking traditional methods. A mother in Burkina Faso looks on as Fr Claude Blanc of the White Fathers examines her child.

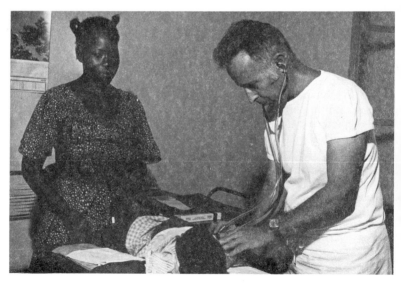

woman in East Africa to gain a science degree, and the first woman doctor in East Africa, Dr Josephine Namboze.

The missions pioneered medicine throughout Africa. Most missionaries thought of hospitals as opportunities for evangelism, but a few people realized that if Africans were told to give up traditional medicine because it involved religious rituals, some replacement must be provided. The positive aspects of traditional medicine were not understood. Africans were quick to take advantage of Western medicine, but they seldom gave up traditional medicine entirely. African attitudes to sickness and health were part of their whole philosophy of life, and people cannot change their whole way of perception even if they want to. Africans appreciated both the effective medical treatment and the good nursing care available in mission hospitals, however, and many patients were converted.

The best-known mission hospital in Africa was probably Lambaréné in Gabon, run by the German theologian, musician and doctor, Albert Schweitzer. He gave up a brilliant career to work in Africa. The hospitals which made the greatest contribution to African development were those that pioneered the training of nurses and medical orderlies. Kikuyu Hospital in Kenya started training Africans in 1911, and when World War I broke out in 1914 it was the one hospital in East Africa able to provide trained African medical personnel for the forces. Roman Catholic training of nurses was somewhat hampered until 1936 by a rule which prohibited nuns from practising midwifery. One of the first Roman Catholic lay missionaries was Dr Evelyn Connolly, who started training nurses in Uganda in 1921 because the nuns were not able to do so. When the ban was lifted in 1936 a new era began for Roman Catholic hospitals. With the help of specialist societies such as the Medical Missionaries of Mary, founded in 1937, they soon caught up with the Protestants. In medicine, as in education, the missions were able to meet a felt need, and hence were successful.

Training Church Leaders

Some missions began to train African clergy very early. We have already seen examples of this at Fourah Bay in Sierra Leone and Lovedale in South Africa. For the most part, however, Protestant missions were slow to train African clergy, and did not attempt to provide the same sort of training that they themselves had received. The missionaries argued that it was sufficient for men to be filled with the Spirit. But it was difficult to hand over administration to under-educated men, so missionaries held all the key posts, and this led to great frustration. Roman Catholic policy, on the other hand, was to give African priests just the same kind of training that priests anywhere in the world were given, even though this meant learning Latin and spending twenty years in the seminary. The Protestants were able to ordain far more Africans than the Roman Catholics, but African Catholic priests were the intellectual equals of missionary priests in a way that African Protestant clergy were not.

The first African Roman Catholics were ordained in Uganda in 1913. Frs Brazilio Lumu and Victoro Mukasa had entered the seminary in 1893, the year of its foundation by Bishop Streicher, who had gone ahead with plans for an indigenous clergy in spite of the doubts of some of the other White Father missionaries. In 1939 the Masaka District of Uganda was placed under an African bishop, the first Roman Catholic to be consecrated, Msgr Joseph Kiwanuka. He had a staff of 33 priests, 43 brothers and 262 sisters, all of whom were Africans. But it was a long time before any other area was treated in the same way. By 1950 some long-established African dioceses still remained without any indigenous priests at all, and for a long time Msgr Kiwanuka remained the only African Catholic bishop.

The Roman Catholic Church has far more African sisters than priests, and again Uganda was in the lead, having the oldest congregation of African sisters, the Bannabikira, or Daughters of the Virgin. This sisterhood was founded in response to repeated requests from African women and girls. The first Bannabikira made their preliminary vows in 1910, and in 1924 Mother Cecilia Nalube became the first African Superior General of her congregation. The blue-clad sisters soon became a familiar sight in Masaka District, and the success of this congregation led to the foundation of others. In West Africa, for instance, the Little Sisters of the Poor were founded in Eastern Nigeria in 1913, and the 1920s and 1930s saw the founding of many other congregations, often at the request of a bishop who realized how much African sisters could offer to the life of the Church.

One group of Church leaders, the catechists, received less and less training during the period from 1900 to 1950, yet it was they who kept the Church in existence in the villages of a continent that was still very largely rural. Catechists taught the rudiments of literacy and religion, they visited the sick, they led daily prayers in the village churches, and on Sundays they either led worship themselves or escorted their congregations to worship at the central mission church. They made no conscious attempt to indigenize, but the whole atmosphere of the prayers and worship which they led was unmistakably African, even where they used a set liturgy, and an unnoticed process of adaptation went on in their preaching and teaching. Village congregations were lucky to receive one visit a year from an ordained clergyman; some were never visited by a white missionary at all. To missionary eyes village Christianity seemed uninspiring, and there were large areas of African life and thought which remained untouched by Christianity, but often the catechist and his Church blended into the rural background and had long ceased to appear alien. Some catechists were more aggressive. They had themselves made a clean break with much of the traditional way of life, and they demanded that their congregations should do the same. Ngugi wa Thiong'o, the Kenyan novelist, has described such a catechist in the person of Joshua in *The River Between*, whose uncompromising attitudes did more harm than good. Catechists and Protestant pastors who had little education themselves often went to great lengths to secure a good education for their children, and many leading Africans of the next generation are the children of such men. President Kenneth Kaunda of Zambia, son of a Presbyterian minister, comes immediately to mind.

AFRICAN INITIATIVES

Perhaps it is misleading to call this section 'African Initiatives', since we have seen already that from the beginning Africans did not just passively receive what missions came to give. The developments in education and medicine, and the beginnings of African sisterhoods, were responses by missions to African demands. But the pattern and framework of all these activities was provided by the missions, and had been developed in a different cultural context. Catechists who unconsciously indigenized were adapting something that already existed rather than creating something new. But as time went on innovation rather than adaptation took place both within the Churches founded by the missions and outside them, and arose in response to people's felt needs.

Traditional African life revolves around the extended family; difficulties are shared, and decisions are taken by the community. If Africans were to feel at home in the Church, they needed to experience something of the closeness of the extended family within the Christian family, and too often this did not happen. Just after World War I, during a severe flu epidemic, Nigerian Christians felt keenly the need for prayer and fellowship to see them through this time of trouble, and the people who felt the need most were the poor and illiterate who did not count for much in the mission-founded Churches. They began to pray in small groups, meeting together out of doors near their own homes. In these groups everyone felt free to take part, and they shared the burdens of life. At first the prayer groups were additional to Church worship, but as more and more people joined them who had no previous connexion with the Churches, the groups tended to *become* Churches. These independent 'Aladura' (praying) Churches have spread throughout West Africa.

A similar need for fellowship arose in South Africa. There it became the custom for the Churches to hold women's fellowship meetings on Thursday afternoons, and these *manyanos*, as they were called, met the same needs for South African women as the Aladura Churches for people in West Africa, through the same means of praying and sharing each others' burdens. And for women in South Africa the problems were particularly acute, since racial discrimination and economic repression were destroying family life. In East Africa the Revival, which started in the Anglican Church in Rwanda in the 1930s and spread to other Churches throughout the region, shared many of the same characteristics. Revival was a close-knit fellowship of those who confessed their sins and could testify to being 'born again', and it reached across tribal and natural boundaries, as did the Aladura Churches. Most of the members remained in their Churches, sometimes forming a self-righteous élite of those who were 'saved'. The Revival demanded high ethical standards, encouraged evangelism, and brought new life to congregations which had lost their first zeal. In its close fellowship, people who felt adrift in a rapidly changing world could find reassurance, and a strong community spirit such as had characterized the extended family.

Some of the most remarkable innovators have been African prophets: Ntsikana, the Xhosa prophet (see p. 136), was only one of many. Some of them have been John the Baptist-like figures, forerunners, who have called on people to repent, turn to God for help and protection, and join the Churches. William Wade (or Waddy) Harris (1865–1929), a Liberian, preached for two years (1913–1915), mainly in the Ivory Coast, and baptized some 120,000 people, before being arrested by the French authorities, who were afraid of him because of his immense influence. The Methodist Church was unable to cope with all his converts, so those who could not be absorbed into the Methodist Church formed the independent Harrist Church which is still strong in the Ivory Coast. In 1921 the prophet Simon Kimbangu (1889–1951) started out on an equally short preaching career in the Congo (Zaire), and his message met with the same sort of response. The mission Churches were flooded with those he had converted, but the missionaries and the Belgian authorities became alarmed at the extent of his influence. He was arrested and condemned to death lest he might lead an uprising. However, the missionaries joined in the outcry against the sentence, and it was commuted to life imprisonment. In the mean time the mission churches had emptied when the missionaries turned against Kimbangu. His followers were exiled to different parts of the country, where they spread his message far and wide. After Independence the ban on the Kimbanguists was lifted, and the 'Church of Jesus Christ on Earth through the Prophet Simon Kimbangu' now flourishes throughout Zaire and beyond. It is a member Church of the World

Council of Churches, and may have as many as 5,000,000 members.

Other prophets broke more decisively with orthodox Christianity. Johane Maranke (1912–1963) began to preach in Southern Rhodesia (now Zimbabwe) in the early 1930s, at a time of great social and economic deprivation. He consciously likened himself to John the Baptist. He called on people to give up the protective charms used in traditional religion; he cast out evil spirits; he called people to obey an elaborate set of rules by which they could avoid sinful uncleanness. His followers feel that life in their community is life in Zion, an anticipation of life in heaven. The leadership of this movement is quite differently organized from anything found in the mission Churches, and the Apostles of Johane Maranke are not fully orthodox in their beliefs. They teach the need to avoid uncleanness by obeying rules rather than finding salvation in Jesus Christ, for instance. But they are deeply influenced by Christianity, they read the Bible extensively, and it may be that as they do so they will become more orthodox, as has happened with other movements.

The most controversial African prophet was the Zulu, Isaiah Shembe (1870–1935). His followers saw him as the Messiah for black people, but since his death his successors have insisted that he never made such a claim for himself. Shembe's followers are called the Amanazaretha, the people of Nazareth, and their chief place of worship is Ekuphaka-meni, the place of exaltation. Amanazaretha worship, with beautiful hymns set to Zulu tunes, recaptures for the worshippers some of the past glories of the Zulu kingdom. Unlike the other movements we have mentioned, this one is confined to a particular ethnic group, and it is difficult to see how anyone other than a Zulu could belong to it, for it is so closely linked with Zulu culture.

These are just a few examples of new religious movements and Independent Churches which are found in Africa. Not all Independent Churches show innovation. Some arose because Africans were frustrated by the way in which missionaries clung to power. The Independent Churches they founded differed little from the mission Church from which they had sprung. Others, like Isaiah Shembe's Amanazaretha or Johanne Maranke's Apostles show much innovation. In some, internal differences of opinion have led to further secessions. Many Independent Churches permit African customs such as polygamy, but others are even more outspoken in denouncing African traditions than the missions have dared to be. The more innovative Churches have colourful rituals, vestments and uniforms, bands and newly-composed hymns; and women may play a major role as leaders. The Maria Legio Church of Kenya which broke from the Roman Catholic Church is one of several whose founder and leader is a woman. We have already noted that the Ethiopian Orthodox Church has been an inspiration to

African Christians, and that 'Ethiopian' forms part of the title of a number of Independent Churches.

In the years 1900 to 1950, the missions of the mainline denominations regarded the Independent Churches with disfavour and their members as heretics, much as Roman Catholics have traditionally regarded Protestants. Towards the end of the period we are considering, however, missionary attitudes began to change. In 1946 a Lutheran missionary, Bengt Sundkler, who later became a bishop, published his *Bantu Prophets in South Africa*, which showed clearly that racial discrimination within the Churches in South Africa was a major cause of secession from the mission Churches. Missions began to re-examine their attitudes to the Independent Churches, and relations between them and most of the Mission Churches have improved. By this time it was also clear that Independent Churches were far too numerous to be ignored.

CHURCH AND STATE

Between 1900 and 1950 most of the missions accepted the fact of colonial domination without question. Some went so far as to see it as part of God's plan for the evangelization of the world. This did not mean that they approved of everything that the colonial governments did. At times they acted to try and protect African rights, and a few individual missionaries were a constant embarrassment, both to the governments and to their missions, because of the strong stand they took.

By 1900 Africa had been divided between the European powers. Britain had the largest share, then France, Portugal, Belgium, Germany and Spain. Germany lost her colonies after World War I. Many of the colonial governments preferred to have their own nationals as missionaries, but only the Portuguese came anywhere near to achieving this, and their monopoly was broken because Portugal could not supply enough missionaries from her small population. Some colonial authorities had a clear religious bias. In the Belgian Congo (Zaire) Roman Catholic mission schools received large subsidies, whilst Protestant schools received none. The largest degree of co-operation between governments and missions was in the sphere of education. Only after the Phelps–Stokes Commission did British colonial authorities give realistic grants-in-aid, but from 1920 onwards co-operation grew increasingly close. The French government took a more active role in providing schools, and by the time of Independence about half the schools in French territories were in government hands. The Germans also planned and provided education, and subsidized mission schools to teach the German language.

Between 1876 and 1908 the Congo was virtually the private property of King Leopold of the Belgians, who exploited it ruthlessly. The building of the railway to Leopoldville (now Kinshasa) cost thousands of lives. British and French missionaries were prominent among those who exposed the scandals. As a result the Congo's status was changed. Another occasion when missions intervened was in 1919, when missionaries in Kenya, with the assistance of Dr J. H. Oldham of the International Missionary Council, succeeded in stopping plans which would have introduced forced labour under another name. This was not the only occasion when Dr Oldham and the International Missionary Council took effective action on behalf of African interests in situations where Africans had, as yet, no effective voice of their own. On the whole, missions preferred to act behind the scenes, by getting their leaders to lobby in London or Paris, rather than risk a public row which might endanger government support for, or toleration of, their work.

A few missionaries, however, were prepared to be far more outspoken and controversial. The Reverend Arthur Shearly Cripps (1869–1952), an Anglican missionary in Southern Rhodesia (now Zimbabwe) from 1901 until his death, worked to protect African interests. He would walk miles to defend in court an African who, he felt, was being unjustly accused, and he worked through the press and through influential friends in London in defence of African land rights. He won the affection of Africans and the respect of government, but he embarrassed many of his missionary colleagues by his uncompromising stand, and by the Franciscan simplicity of his manner of living. During the 1920s and 1930s Archdeacon W. E. Owen (1878–1945) became detested by white settlers and feared by the colonial administration in Kenya for his defence of African rights. It was well known that when he went to court over injustice to Africans, he won his case. Although the actions of such men reduced the harsh effects of colonialism for some of those whom they championed, they did not attack the system itself.

It was in South Africa that the rights of the non-white population were most seriously at risk, and where the Churches were least effective. The Act of Union of 1910 brought the Boer Republics of the Transvaal and the Orange Free State into the Union of South Africa, but that union was achieved at the expense of the rights of non-white peoples. The limited rights which blacks, coloureds and Asians had in the Cape Province were not extended to other parts of the Union, and were gradually lost in the Cape. The Churches made occasional statements, but these were ineffectual because the Dutch Reformed Church stood aloof, and the rank and file of Church members connived at the system because of what they gained from it.

Conclusion

By 1950 Christians were still in a minority in almost every country in Africa, and in some a very tiny minority. But because of the extent to which education was in mission hands, almost all the emerging élite in Africa south of the Sahara had been through mission schools, and identified themselves as Christians. The Churches were heavily mission-dominated, and there was little sense of urgency over training indigenous clergy.

Yet under an apparently calm surface a ferment was at work, and the whole continent was about to enter a period of vastly accelerated change. World War II (1939–1945) profoundly affected the European colonial powers, as well as the thinking and expectations of African peoples. The use of radios was encouraged during the war for propaganda purposes, and it continued to grow afterwards. This alone ensured that Africans were increasingly drawn into world thinking. Many served overseas, made new contacts, and learnt from Indians and black Americans and others of a world-wide struggle of oppressed peoples to win their freedom.

Besides the cataclysm of World War II, three other events in the 1940s were of worldwide importance and influence, and pointed the way to what lay ahead. The first of these occurred in 1947, when India and Pakistan became independent. This ensured that the rest of the colonial empires would eventually follow along the same road, though at the time not many people realized that this was inevitable, or that it would happen so swiftly. But there were small signs of forward thinking. In British Africa university colleges were founded in Ibadan (Nigeria), Legon (Ghana), Khartoum (Sudan) and Makerere (Uganda). These would help to provide the trained manpower for the future transfer of power. Except in Khartoum, where the students were Muslims, chapels and chaplaincies were part of the university establishments from the start. This was to be important for the Churches.

The second event, which happened just a year after Indian independence was the inauguration of the World Council of Churches (WCC) in 1948. The new spirit of co-operation among Protestant Churches was largely the result of working together in mission. The WCC, in turn, intensified the desire for co-operation and unity among the mainline Protestant Churches, though a number of fundamentalist groups refused to have anything to do with the WCC. A few years later the International Missionary Council was merged into the WCC, and the 'younger churches' of Africa and Asia began to be seen as partners rather than as mere recipients.

The third event also took place in 1948, when the first Nationalist government came to power in South Africa and began to implement the twin policies of *apartheid* (racial segregation) and white supremacy.

The Dutch Reformed Church (DRC) in South Africa supported this programme, and said it was theologically and morally acceptable provided that it was administered with justice. Only a tiny handful of DRC theologians had misgivings. The Nationalists claimed that apartheid was essential in order to preserve white, Christian civilization. The synods of the other Churches regularly passed resolutions objecting to apartheid, but most white Christians were apathetic: they benefited from the system and had no wish to see black Africans on an equal footing with whites. The most effective protest against apartheid in the 1940s came from the Reverend Michael Scott (1907–1983), an Anglican priest who was twice imprisoned for his protests. He suddenly became a world figure when Chief Hosea of the Herero of South West Africa (Namibia) sent him to the United Nations as his representative, to give evidence on the repression of his people by South Africa. Michael Scott had little support from the bishops of his own Church, who were embarrassed by his outspokenness. In 1950 he was prohibited from re-entering South Africa, and became one of a long line of Christians who have been deported, refused re-entry, or detained and imprisoned because they have taken action against apartheid. The coming to power of the Nationalists in 1948 was an ominous portent for the future of South Africa.

STUDY SUGGESTIONS

REVIEW OF CONTENT

1. (a) What three sets of problems faced the Emperor Haile Selassie of Ethiopia in his efforts to reform and modernize his country?
   (b) What further difficulties occurred in the period of Italian occupation?
2. (a) What were some of the changes and reforms in Church organization and practice effected in Ethiopia, between liberation from Italian occupation in 1941 and the appointment of an Ethiopian as *Abuna* in 1959?
   (b) What sorts of work were undertaken by the missionary societies permitted to enter Ethiopia during that period?
3. List some of the new missions founded specially for work in Africa which began to operate in the latter part of the nineteenth and early twentieth centuries. In what important ways did Roman Catholic missions differ from the Protestant ones?
4. (a) Why did Africans in many areas at first resist the development of educational institutions?
   (b) What were some of the many different reasons why Protestant and Roman Catholic missions were anxious to provide education, and Africans eventually came to demand it?

5. (a) Describe briefly the scope of the education offered by mission schools in most African countries.

(b) What recommendations for the work of Protestant schools were made by the Phelps–Stokes Commission in the 1920s, and for Roman Catholic schools by Monsignor Arthur Hinsley?

(c) What were some of the more important centres of girls' education at that time and later?

6. (a) What was the general attitude of Africans in the early twentieth century towards the treatment offered by mission hospitals?

(b) What was the chief contribution such hospitals made to African development at that time?

7. (a) What was the chief difference between the aims and methods of Protestant missions in training African clergy and Church leaders, and those of the Roman Catholics, especially in the training of women?

(b) What was the range of work generally undertaken by Catechists at this period, and how much education and training for their task did they receive?

8. 'As time went on innovation took place in response to people's felt needs ... prayer groups tended to become Churches, and these independent Churches spread' (p. 159). What sort of need was it that gave rise to the spread of 'independent' Churches in many parts of Africa?

9. Describe briefly the particular characteristics which distinguish the Independent Churches as they developed:

(a) in West Africa,

(b) in Southern Africa,

(c) in the form of 'Revival' in East Africa.

10. Describe briefly, with dates, the aims and achievements of each of the following, and the particular practices of their followers and the Churches they founded.

(a) William Wade Harris (b) Simon Kimbangu

(c) Johane Maranke (d) Isaiah Shembe

11. Give some examples of the sort of relationships that existed from 1900 to 1950 between Churches and colonial governments in different parts of Africa, with regard to:

(a) education (b) exploitation of African labour (c) political structure and moves towards independence (d) racism and human rights

12. What did the following people have in common? J. H. Oldham, Arthur Shearly Cripps, W. E. Owen, Michael Scott.

DISCUSSION

13. The Emperor Haile Selassie 'believed that change must come

slowly if it was not to be disruptive'. What sort of disruption do you think he feared? Some Churches, on the other hand, experienced disruption because they failed to change quickly enough. What has been the experience of your own country in this respect?—of your own Church?

14. 'For Protestants the main reason for running schools was so that people could learn to read the Bible' (p. 154), and Monsignor Hinsley advised that 'schools were proving to be the main evangelistic agencies'. But the Phelps–Stokes report on Protestant schools recommended that much more attention be paid to agriculture. What do Church-run schools in your country regard as their primary purpose? Some Christians believe the Church should run schools *only* to win converts. What is your opinion?

15. 'Innovation took place in response to people's felt needs' (p. 159). The Church has always tried to model its teaching and worship practices as closely as possible on those of the apostles and their followers. In what circumstances do you think Churches are right to innovate, and to what authority should they look for guidance about the sort of changes that are justified?

16. 'Besides World War II, three events in the 1940s pointed the way to what lay ahead' (p. 164). What were those events, and how far can we say that the developments they seemed to point to have actually come about? Give examples.

8

Africa Since 1950

by Louise Pirouet

A PERIOD OF CHANGE

Since 1950 there have been immense changes in Africa. The most obvious are the political changes. In 1950 there were only four independent nations in the whole continent, Egypt, Ethiopia, Liberia, and South Africa. In 1975 there were only four states which were *not* independent, Spanish Sahara, Namibia, Afars and Issas (Djibuti), and Rhodesia (Zimbabwe), and the last two of these became independent a few years later. Many of the newly-independent states experienced far-reaching political upheavals, and a number were involved in war either before or after Independence. As we shall see in this chapter, the super-powers made sure that it was almost impossible for African countries to remain non-aligned, as most of them wanted to do, and against their will they were sucked into the world capitalist or socialist systems. Social and economic changes were equally far-reaching. There was a rapid growth of social, educational, and medical services; industry grew; towns and cities grew faster than people could find jobs or housing; people developed new expectations of life; and economic growth could not keep pace with population growth.

These years also saw a renaissance of African culture. In 1950 African students were still being taught about French, Portuguese or British history, geography, and literature, and were trained in the cultural values of the European colonists. By 1975 a whole new literature had developed, and writers such as Chinua Achebe, Léopold Sédar Senghor, Wole Soyinka, and Ngugi wa Thiong'o had achieved international reputations. African history was being rediscovered, and the universities were working to provide the materials for Africanizing every aspect of the syllabus. Much African literature discusses the effects of change, and one of the best ways to begin to understand modern Africa is to read the novels and poetry and plays which are being written. The study of African traditional religion has played an important part in the cultural renaissance.

During these years, the population of Africa has doubled and the number of Christians much more than doubled. By the mid-1970s the vast majority of Africans south of the Sahara identified themselves as either Muslims or Christians. In West Africa there were more Muslims than Christians, but in Zaire, Uganda, and Rwanda, for instance, over seventy per cent of the people claimed to be Christian by 1975. This

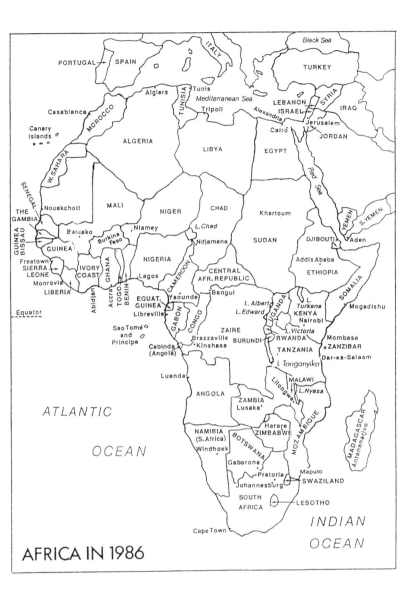

PORTUGAL SPAIN

ITALY

Black Sea

TURKEY

Casablanca

Algiers Tunis
TUNISIA
Mediterranean Sea

Tripoli

LEBANON SYRIA
ISRAEL IRAQ

Alexandria
Jerusalem

Cairo JORDAN

Canary
Islands

MOROCCO

ALGERIA

LIBYA

EGYPT

W. SAHARA

Red Sea

SENEGAL

THE
GAMBIA

Nouakchott

MALI

NIGER

CHAD

Khartoum

YEMEN S. YEMEN

GUINEA
BISSAU

Bamako

GUINEA

Niamey

Burkina
Faso

L. Chad

Ndjamena

DJIBOUTI Aden

Freetown
SIERRA
LEONE

Monrovia

LIBERIA

IVORY
COAST

GHANA

Lagos

NIGERIA

SUDAN

CENTRAL
AFR. REPUBLIC

Addis Ababa

ETHIOPIA

Equator

Abidjan

Accra

TOGO
BENIN

EQUAT.
GUINEA

CAMEROON

Yaounde

Bangui

SOMALIA

Mogadishu

Libreville

GABON

CONGO

ZAIRE

L. Albert
L. Edward

UGANDA

L.
Turkana

KENYA

Nairobi

Sao Tomé
and
Principe

Brazzaville
Kinshasa

BURUNDI

RWANDA

L. Victoria

Mombasa
ZANZIBAR
Dar-es-Salaam

Cabinda
(Angola)

TANZANIA

L. Tanganyika

Luanda

ANGOLA

ZAMBIA
Lusaka

MALAWI

Lilongwe

L. Nyasa

ATLANTIC

OCEAN

NAMIBIA
(S. Africa)

Windhoek

BOTSWANA

Harare
ZIMBABWE

MOZAMBIQUE

MADAGASCAR

Antananarivo

Gaborone

Pretoria
Johannesburg

Maputo
SWAZILAND

SOUTH
AFRICA

LESOTHO

Cape Town

INDIAN

OCEAN

AFRICA IN 1986

massive Christian présence ensured that the Churches were involved at every level in the changes that were sweeping through the continent.

THE 1950s: TOWARDS INDEPENDENCE

In 1950 few people would have believed that in only ten years half of Africa would be independent. Even the more far-sighted were over-taken by the speed of events. In 1951 the first clear sign of what was to happen came when Kwame Nkrumah of Ghana won an overwhelming electoral victory, although still in prison at the time. The following year the pent-up anger of the Kikuyu of Kenya, who were hemmed in by white settler farms, exploded into the violent 'Mau Mau' rebellion. In 1954 something of a new era dawned when Nasser came to power in Egypt to lead his country on a revolutionary course, and to encourage African nationalism. Sudan gained independence in 1956, Morocco and Tunisia the following year, but the breakthrough for black Africa came in 1957 when Ghana became independent under Nkrumah. French Africa followed in 1960, and so did the Belgian Congo. The Belgians had done nothing to prepare for Independence, and the country broke apart in violence which resulted in lasting instability in the area.

Further south there was regress, not progress. In 1953 a Central African Federation was formed of Northern and Southern Rhodesia and Nyasaland (Zambia, Zimbabwe, and Malawi), pushed through by a Conservative Government in Britain against the wishes of Africans who feared increased association with white settlers in Rhodesia. The Portuguese did not envisage eventual independence for their colonies, but intended them to become parts of 'Portugal Overseas', and Africans, who were sufficiently assimilated to Portuguese culture, to become Portuguese citizens. In South Africa laws were brought in to implement the policies of apartheid and white supremacy, which deprived blacks of most of their rights.

The Churches and Independence

Church and mission attitudes to Independence varied considerably. In the Congo (Zaire) and the Portuguese territories of Guinea-Bissau, Angola, and Mozambique, relations between the Roman Catholic Church and the state were governed by a Concordat (agreement) between the Vatican and the colonial power. This gave the Church a privileged position within the state in return for a measure of state control over the Church. The Church benefited so greatly from this relationship that its leaders feared change of any kind. In Zaire the Church was very strong, with three and a half million members in 1950. In Mozambique it was very weak in spite of Portugal's long period of rule. When the Concordat was signed with Portugal in 1940, non-Portuguese Catholic missions were allowed to work in the country for the first time. There were individual missionaries elsewhere who feared change as much as those in Congo and the Portuguese territories, but there was nowhere else in Africa where a particular Church was so closely identified with a reactionary regime, except for South Africa, where the Dutch Reformed Church occupied a privileged position.

The changing attitudes of Protestant Churches and missions to independence can be traced over the years in the Anglican Church Missionary Society's *Newsletter*, written by Canon Max Warren. He was a leading missionary thinker, and his regular *Newsletter* was widely read in missionary circles. He tried to help missionaries and their supporters to understand the growing demand for independence, and to play a part in equipping the so-called 'younger Churches' for their new role. African leaders recognized that he understood some of their problems and aspirations, though the missionaries on the spot sometimes lacked his degree of understanding. Some of the *Newsletters* dealt with the other world religions, and introduced missionaries to new and more positive attitudes towards them instead of the old outright condemnation.

Some of the Churches feared not just a loss of influence in newly-independent states, but also a resurgence of 'heathenism'. The Mau Mau rising in Kenya appeared to give some ground for such fears. The Kikuyu of Kenya, who were restricted to living in overcrowded reserves in the so-called 'white highlands', bound themselves, by an oath incorporating traditional religious rituals, to overthrow the Europeans by violent means. This provided an excuse for those who wished to see Mau Mau as a return to heathen savagery. At about the same time traditional religion was given a new lease of life in one area of Uganda during a political crisis.

However, when independence came, most missionaries were able to welcome it, and many of the independent governments paid handsome tributes to the missions and Churches for the part they had played in preparing people for Independence through their contribution to education. The majority of the leaders who came to power at Independence had been educated in mission schools, and they were at least sympathetic towards the Churches, even if they were suspicious of continuing missionary control.

An Indigenous Ministry

During the 1950s the Churches became increasingly involved in education. Networks of primary schools were expanded, and more secondary schools were developed, with increasing numbers of missionary teaching staff. Soon the missions found they could not supply enough qualified staff, and schemes were begun for Christian teachers to work in Church schools for limited periods, and without committing themselves to a mission.

There was also a massive increase in theological education. The Protestant Churches were concerned that few of their ordained clergy had an adequate standard of education, and it was difficult to find men to fill posts of responsibility. The Roman Catholic Church had ordained far fewer Africans, but those they had ordained were much better educated than all but a few of the Protestants. It has been noticed that the Protestant missionaries retreated upwards, keeping key senior positions in their own hands, while the Roman Catholics retreated sideways, opening some positions to Africans at all levels in the Church hierarchy. But in spite of these developments, all the Churches remained over-dependent on the missions.

Yet theoretically most of the Churches were autonomous by the end of the 1950s. The Roman Catholic Church led the way. The hierarchy was established in British West Africa in 1950, and in British East Africa and South Africa the following year. The Anglican Province of West Africa was inaugurated in 1951, and of East Africa in 1961. In Cameroun the Presbyterian Church became autonomous in 1957, three years before the country became independent. But as long as much of the leadership remained in missionary hands, this autonomy was more apparent than real. The 1950s saw the beginning of an enormous effort to improve and expand the education of African clergy.

An important step forward was taken in 1957 with the establishment of the Theological Education Fund. It was started by the International Missionary Council (later absorbed in the World Council of Churches) with a mandate to strengthen theological education in the 'younger Churches' of the Third World. It assisted theological colleges and university departments of Religious Studies when these came into being, helped to build up theological libraries, and helped to fund advanced theological education for those who would become tutors in theological colleges, where it gave the impetus for rethinking the syllabus. The Fund also helped in the setting up of Departments of Religious Studies in several African universities, and supported local programmes of theological textbook publishing in twenty-five or so different language areas (as well as initiating this continuing Study Guide series).

In spite of the increase in theological education which began in the 1950s, the supply of African clergy still did not begin to meet the increase in the number of Christians to whom they had to minister. The number of people claiming to be Christians seems likely to have doubled during this decade alone. In 1950 the estimated number of Christians in Africa was twenty-three million. By the mid-1960s a fairly conservative estimate put the number at sixty million. The Churches themselves did not claim so many, but when people were asked, for example when a census was taken, far more people said they were Christians than the Churches included in their returns. Because of the shortage of clergy, the Churches depended more and more on catechists to look after the growing congregations. For various reasons many of these new Christians were not communicants. Perhaps there were marital irregularities; perhaps they had simply been married by local custom because they could not afford a Church wedding. The lack of the Eucharist did not seem to such people to be very important, because they could not take part in it. Dr Adrian Hastings has pointed out that what was emerging in Africa was a largely lay Christianity, even, for example, in Roman Catholic and Anglican Churches which set great store by the sacraments.

Independent Churches

In one group of Churches things were different. These were the Churches which, as we have seen, did not need to *become* independent because they had never been anything else, and where there was no shortage of clergy because they had not tried to copy the European model. In 1950 there were about three million members of Independent Churches, and these Churches continued to multiply. Some of the newer ones were very small, and quickly disappeared, but others were large and became important. Among these was the Church of Christ in Africa which broke away from the Anglican Church in Kenya, and had 16,000 members. This was a schism which should never have happened, and was largely the result of missionary tactlessness. In 1954 the Lumpa Church in Zambia appeared in response to the message preached by a prophetess, Alice Lenshina. It spread to Tanzania and Malawi, and its membership rose to over 100,000, but it was forcibly suppressed by the Zambian authorities in 1964 when its members refused to pay taxes. By contrast the Church of Christ in Africa, whose membership continued to grow, became a member of the National Christian Council of Kenya, and of the World Council of Churches.

FROM MISSION TO CHURCH 1960–75

Aid and Development

During the 1960s, most of Africa north of the Zambezi River became independent, sixteen countries becoming free of colonial rule in 1960 alone, and most of the rest by 1965. Hope and confidence were in the air, and all the talk was of development. Missions found themselves increasingly involved in development projects, and National Christian

Councils became involved in co-ordinating development and channelling funds. More and more posts of responsibility in the Churches and on the Christian Councils were filled by Africans rather than by missionaries, and soliciting development funds from Europe and America became a major preoccupation of both governments and Churches.

Yet this overseas aid created a new form of dependence, and in two different ways the Churches found themselves in a new kind of bondage because of it. On the one hand, more and more of their senior personnel were African nationals; on the other hand, the administrative structures of the Churches and of Church institutions (like those of the governments) were based on European models, and many needed continued funding from overseas just to keep going. Bishops, for example, were expected to administer large areas, and each required a secretariat in order to do so. This ate up funds and trained personnel. The Roman Catholic Bishop Kalilombwe of Lilongwe Diocese in Malawi has described his horror when he realized the extent to which his diocese was dependent on funds from abroad. He found himself asking the question, 'What is a really local Church?' The Catholic Bishops' Conference of Eastern Africa decided that a local Church must be 'self-ministering, self-supporting, and self-propagating', and went on to spell out what this meant:

> We believe that in order to achieve this we have to insist on building Church life and work on basic Christian communities in both rural and urban areas. Church life must be based on the communities in which everyday life and work takes place: those basic and manageable social groupings whose members can experience real interpersonal relationships and feel a sense of communal belonging, both in living and working. We believe that Christian communities at this level will be best suited to develop real intense vitality and to become effective witnesses in their natural environment. (Quoted in E. Fasholé-Luke and others. *Christianity in Independent Africa* (Rex Collings 1978), p. 93.)

In other words, neither passive Church attendance nor reliance on the clergy would produce a truly local Church: small, close-knit groups of Christians in which each shouldered a share of responsibility were needed if the Church was to become truly local. And only a truly local Church would be able to find the will to be self-supporting.

Dependence on overseas development aid created another kind of bondage as well. Aid agencies would support those projects which appealed to them, not necessarily those which were most important or which matched local felt needs. Most aid agencies found ways of consulting with local Churches and working in a proper partnership,

In the 1950s secondary and university education developed rapidly in Africa, and many independent governments later paid tribute to the contribution of missions and Churches. But in some countries economic problems are now making it hard for Church and State alike to provide more than primary teaching, in small schools like this one in Zaire, for the great majority of their populations.

Two outstanding theologians of the Dutch Reformed Church who have courageously demonstrated their unshakeable opposition to apartheid:
Left Dr Beyers Naudé, Director of the Christian Institute in Johannesburg, and
Right Dr Allan Boesak, President of the World Alliance of Reformed Churches in South Africa.

175

but this did not always happen, especially at first. African Christians also had to learn which projects would simply become a drain on future resources, and which ones would help people to become more independent. Ox-ploughs, for instance, were less prestigious than tractors, but were more dependable in many rural areas where it was difficult to get spare parts and find mechanics to fit them. By the mid-1970s there seemed to be a danger in some countries that the Churches would become so busy with development that they might neglect their primary tasks of evangelism and building people up in the faith.

Africanization

The take-over by nationals of decision-making in the Churches was one aspect of making Christianity at home in African culture, but there were others of equal importance. Departments of Religious Studies had been started at Legon University (Ghana) and Ibadan University (Nigeria) in the 1950s, and at Makerere University (Uganda) in the early 1960s. These soon began to make a significant contribution to the education of clergy, though the majority of those who studied in them became teachers. It soon became clear that the new generation of African Christian scholars was interested in two subjects in particular: the relationship between African traditional religion and Christianity, and the history of the African response to the preaching of the gospel. Students in university Departments of Religious Studies and in theological colleges and seminaries took part in research in both these fields, and study of these topics was a part of the new syllabuses introduced in this period. The Second Vatican Council of the Roman Catholic Church which was opened in 1962 encouraged this development. Two important books were published that year. From Ghana came Professor Christian Baëta's *Prophetism in Ghana*, and from Nigeria Professor Bolaji Idowu's *Olodomare: God in Yoruba Belief*. In 1969 the Kenyan Professor John Mbiti published *African Religions and Philosophy*, and also from Kenya came Ernest Wanyoike's biography of his grandfather, *African Pastor*. These are just a few of the early studies issued, forerunners in the richly diverse and growing stream of theological writing by African scholars.

Another new development was the use of African art-forms and music. The Roman Catholic Church led the way here. The doors of the Catholic Chapel at Ibadan University in Nigeria are a superb example of Christian art in an African idiom. In Zaire the beautiful *Missa Luba* was regularly sung in Luba-speaking churches, and in Tanzania Fr Stephen Mbunga composed the *Missa Baba Yetu* (Mass of Our Father). In Uganda an oratorio on the Uganda Martyrs was composed in 1964, the year in which they were canonized. In 1965 the Xhosa-speaking dioceses in South Africa held a conference on African liturgical music. The Protestants were rather slower, perhaps because for them there was nothing comparable to Vatican II to set the seal of approval on African music. But when the Assembly of the World Council of Churches was held in Nairobi in 1975, the new WCC hymn-book, *Cantate Domino* (Let us sing to the Lord), contained African hymns from the Swahili collection made at Makumira Lutheran Theological College in Tanzania, and in Yoruba, a Nigerian language. In many parts of Africa Protestants as well as Catholics are using African music and writing original words with increasing confidence. Some Churches have also produced successful recordings of these, both LPs and singles, to raise funds for local development projects.

INDEPENDENCE AND CONFLICT

A more sombre task for the Church in Africa was to formulate a response to the violence which afflicted the continent. In the Mau Mau conflict of the 1950s, Christians had faced an acute dilemma. Kikuyu Christians shared their people's grievances, but some among them were deeply troubled by the indiscriminate use of violence, and by the manner of the Mau Mau oath, which involved blood sacrifice. 'We have drunk the blood of Jesus in Holy Communion; how can we drink any other?' they asked, and this refusal cost some of them their lives. Murang'a Anglican Cathedral with its commemorative paintings by Elimo Njau is a memorial to the Kikuyu martyrs. Among the Christians who resisted but survived was the Presbyterian pastor, the Reverend Wanyoike Kamawe (1888–1970) whose life story by his grandson we have already mentioned. When there was renewed oathing during a period of political stress in 1969, it was again the Churches who led successful protests to get it stopped, but not before a Presbyterian elder, Samuel Githingi, had paid with his life for refusing to take the oath. Most white Christians, including missionaries, failed to understand Kikuyu grievances, and saw Mau Mau simply as a return to savagery, but there were a few who understood the situation better, and who saw that the security forces too were guilty of brutality, and spoke out against it. One such was Canon Bewes, Africa Secretary of the CMS. In 1952 he reported on this, and described one particular incident: 'I saw a hospital ward of inoffensive, yet badly injured men; had they been beaten up by Mau Mau? No, they had been "questioned" by the police' (T. F. C. Bewes, *Kikuyu Conflict*, p. 56).

In the violence which followed independence in the Congo (Zaire) and in Rwanda, churches and missions were often attacked, and both missionaries and African Christians killed, often because of their efforts to curb violence. In the Congo a rebel military court asked a Congolese pastor why he had sheltered a white woman missionary.

'Because she is my sister in Christ, the child of my own Heavenly Father,' he replied. The court condemned him to death, but an officer was so impressed that he set him free (quoted in T. A. Beetham, *Christianity and the New Africa*, p. 142). There are many such tales of courage from both countries.

Independence in the Sudan led to more prolonged violence. The South had been developed far less than the Muslim North, and although there was a change of policy in 1946, this came far too late for Southerners to be able to play a proper role in the new state. In 1960 the government attempted to force Islam on the South in an effort to unite the country. This met with massive resistance from the Southerners whose tiny élite were all Christians. All missionaries were expelled in 1964, and terrible repression and massacres followed. Some 300,000 Southerners became refugees in the surrounding countries, including almost all the clergy of all Churches, who were prime targets, and other Southerners took to the bush to fight a guerrilla war which did not end until 1972. Christianity became something of a rallying point for the South, and the Churches increased as never before. The Churches and aid agencies were willing enough to help the refugees, but Christians who had remained in Sudan felt abandoned by the rest of the Christian world, as indeed they very largely were. The reluctance of the outside world, and especially Christians, to recognize what was happening in Sudan is still unexplained. In 1972 an agreement was reached which ended the war. Both sides were ready for mediation, and when the first attempt failed, the WCC and the All Africa Conference of Churches were able to step in, and their mediation succeeded largely because of the patience and tact of Mr Kodwo Ankrah, a Ghanaian, who had been a Refugee Officer with the WCC for some years.

In 1966 civil war broke out in Nigeria when 'Biafra', as the Eastern Region named itself, tried to secede. Far from standing aside, as had been the case in Sudan, the Christian world became massively involved on one side or another in this conflict. The largest ethnic group in Biafra were the Igbo, the majority of whom were Catholics. Caritas International and other international aid agencies flew thousands of tons of food and other supplies into the shrinking Biafran enclave to help its beleaguered peoples. The Federal Government accused them of prolonging the war, and there may have been some justice in the accusation. On the other hand, the people of the Eastern Region could not accuse the rest of the Christian world of ignoring their plight as the Southern Sudanese did. There has been an immense amount of heart-searching by Nigerian Christians about the moral issues raised by this war. Among the many books which have appeared is *Christian Concern in the Nigerian Civil War*, a collection of extremely thoughtful articles which appeared in the periodical *Nigerian Christian*. In this war, both sides claimed with equal forcefulness that God must be on their side, and much newspaper writing described the war in biblical terms. Yet in this book we find Provost F. O. Segun writing thus:

> War has come upon us as members of a nation which has chosen selfish and godless ways of life. We in this nation have been, and still are, guilty of shameful social evils. There have been horrible things done in the conduct of the present hostilities. Our immediate duty is not so much to protest that we are right and that surely God must be on our side, as to learn humility and repentance. We have to find out what kind of personal and national behaviour will bring us to the side of God, and make us true soldiers of Christ, the Captain of the host of the Lord. Are *we* on *God's* side? (*Christian Concern in the Nigerian Civil War*, p. 94.)

In the same publication, Dr Obaro Ikime of Ibadan University argued that the right to conscientious objection should be acknowledged, a brave stand to take in time of war. The writer Wole Soyinka was detained by the government for appealing to governments throughout the world to refuse to supply arms to *either* side. Some of Soyinka's best writing has come out of his experiences during the war: *A Man Died*, *Season of Anomy*, and *A Shuttle in the Crypt*.

Ethiopia's apparently peaceful progress was marred by an abortive coup in 1960. In 1962 the federal status of Eritrea (the area by the Red Sea) was dissolved, and the region made part of Ethiopia. The government at first underestimated the determination of Eritreans to resist being incorporated into Ethiopia. Christians and Muslims joined the movements fighting for secession, and the government was unable to crush these. This long-running war was one of the reasons for the revolution of 1974. The Marxist revolution achieved important and necessary land reforms, and has run successful literacy campaigns. But it has also attacked intellectuals (including university students), people connected with the old regime, and both Christians and Muslims. The leaders of the revolution have used detention, imprisonment without trial, torture, and unlawful killing against those whom they suspect of opposition. In spite of much suffering, Church attendance increased, and many Christians have been sustained by their faith during this period.

Relations Between Church and State

During the colonial period in Africa, the missions usually enjoyed good relations with governments, particularly in the field of education. We have seen that some missionaries spoke up against injustice, but those who did were often something of an embarrassment to others. When Independence came, the Churches had little experience of being in a position where they needed to question the actions of government on moral or religious grounds, and in the following years they were often severely tested in this regard. Missionaries could do little to help, and some did less than they should, fearing to jeopardize the work of their missions if they criticized what the authorities were doing.

In many countries relations between Church and state remained unchanged for a time after Independence, and in some the good relations have continued. In Tanzania, for instance, there was open and frank discussion on a number of issues, and most difficulties have been worked through satisfactorily. But in Zaire, President Mobutu began to demand something that looked to the Churches dangerously like worship; in Burundi, Equatorial Guinea, the Central African Republic and Uganda there has been fierce oppression and massacre; in Ethiopia the socialist revolution was followed by the 'Red Terror' directed against Muslims and Christians alike. In that part of Africa which lies just south of the Sahara there has been conflict between Muslims and Christians, though politics and culture have usually been a more important cause of it than religion, and Christians have not always known how to act. We cannot here look at every country in detail, but the following are two examples of countries where Christians found themselves in a dilemma.

1. GHANA

One of the first tests for the Churches came in President Nkrumah's Ghana. The people did not experience extreme oppression, but there were aspects of Nkrumah's rule which Christians found worrying, like the inscription on Nkrumah's statue in the capital, Accra: 'Seek ye first the political kingdom, and all other things will be added unto it.' This seemed to be a deliberate mocking challenge to the gospel. They were unhappy about Nkrumah's use of the title 'Saviour' for himself. And they were much more disturbed by the far-reaching type of loyalty which Nkrumah's Convention People's Party demanded of Ghanaians, and particularly of its junior branch, the 'Young Pioneers'. The heads of several Churches spoke out on what was due to Caesar and what was due to God, and for a while the Anglican Archbishop, who was then still an expatriate, was deported. Ordinary Church members also acted. When a Catholic priest was detained without trial, massed choirs sang outside the prison for two full days. Ghanaian Christians felt relieved when Nkrumah fell from power.

2. UGANDA

Uganda under the dictator Idi Amin was a more extreme situation. The last year of President Obote's first period of office had seen increasing repression and lawlessness, and people hoped for an improvement. It was some time before the Churches recognized the nature of Amin's rule. His expulsion of the Asian population was popular with most Ugandans, and though individual Christians tried to help the Asians, the Churches as institutions did not act. In 1972 the Roman Catholic Church was appalled by the murder of a leading Catholic layman, Benedicto Kiwanuka, who was the country's Chief Justice. On several occasions he had tried to use the law to curb the army. On 21 September 1972 soliders dragged him from his office in the Law Courts, and murdered him. Christians suffered greatly in the years that followed, and not even the Muslim community escaped Amin's terror. The Churches rose magnificently to the task of caring for the widows and orphans of those who were killed, but Amin's erratic and vindictive rule made it difficult for them to do much to prevent violence, though on several occasions Church leaders pleaded with him. In 1977 more outspoken protests resulted in the murder of the Anglican Archbishop Janani Luwum. The ending of Amin's rule has, sadly, not brought peace or security to Uganda, and the Churches have suffered further.

SOUTHERN AFRICA

Zimbabwe (Rhodesia), Angola, Guinea-Bissau, and Mozambique

In these four countries independence was won by armed struggle against exceptionally repressive white rule. The three Portuguese territories were colonies proper; in Rhodesia (now Zimbabwe) a white settler, Ian Smith, declared Unilateral Independence in 1965, and his illegal government was given a good deal of undeclared support by the West. Smith maintained that he was defending 'white, Christian civilization' against communism and godlessness, a claim the other white regimes in Southern Africa also made. The majority of white Christians in these countries, and some missionaries, accepted govern-ment propaganda, condemned the 'terrorism' used by the nationalist guerrillas, and fiercely defended their own living standards. A minority of white Christians, though, including some missionaries, recognized the injustices under which Africans suffered, and the institutional violence practised against them by the state. In Mozambique the Roman Catholic Bishop of Beira was prepared to question the regime, and he invited the White Fathers Mission to work in his diocese. This mission had taken a lead in training African priests and working towards an indigenous Church. He died in 1967 and was succeeded by an exceptionally reactionary bishop. By 1971 the White Fathers reached a point where they decided they must leave Mozambique. They had waited for the bishops to act 'in face of injustice and brutality', but they had not done so. The White Fathers themselves were not free to speak out, and feared that if they stayed, their presence might lend support to the regime. Their departure drew international attention to the worsening repression in Mozambique, and seems to have given other missionaries the courage to speak out more boldly: there was a series of deportations of priests and nuns in the following years. The massacre of 180 people at Wiriyamu in December 1972 was reported on in detail by Catholic missionaries, and exposed in *The Times*, a leading London newspaper, a day or two before the Portuguese Prime Minister visited Britain. The horror this incident aroused drove yet one more nail into the coffin of the Portuguese government, which was already seriously weakened by the long-running African colonial wars. The government fell in 1974, and Angola, Mozambique and Guinea-Bissau became independent in 1975.

Zimbabwean independence still lay five years in the future. Among the most effective Christian critics of the regime were Guy and Molly Clutton-Brock, Anglican lay-people, who had great success in working with Africans on an equal footing at St Faith's Farm. This was broken up in 1970, and the Clutton-Brocks were deported. In 1971 opposition to proposals for very limited progress towards possible independence in the far distant future was led by the Methodist Bishop Abel Muzorewa, almost the only African leader of standing who was not either in prison or in exile. African opposition to these proposals was so overwhelming that the British government would not permit the plan to go ahead. Armed opposition to the Smith regime grew, and Mozambican independence greatly assisted the Zimbabwean nationalist guerrillas. At that stage Roman Catholic missionaries, led by Bishop Daniel Lamont, found it rather easier than did Protestant missionaries to sympathize with African aspirations, though most ordinary white Roman Catholics shared the views of other white settlers. The Roman Catholic Justice and Peace Commission played an important role in exposing torture and injustices practised by the Smith regime.

The Marxist governments which came to power in all these countries were the direct result of Western assistance to white domination in Southern Africa. They are not, however, opposed to Christianity.

Namibia and the Republic of South Africa: Under the Shadow of Apartheid

We now turn to two countries where freedom still seems far away. The 1960s began with the Sharpeville Massacre in South Africa in which sixty-nine Africans were shot in the back by police who broke up a peaceful demonstration against the extension of the pass laws to women. Under these laws all blacks had to carry passes at all times, and anyone who failed to produce a pass on demand would be arrested, and might be removed out of the area. The pass laws were a cornerstone of apartheid. The Sharpeville Massacre caused a tremendous outcry, but nothing changed in South Africa. In this brief survey we cannot trace all the complicated history of the Churches and apartheid in South Africa. We can only look at some important characteristics of Church involvement, and try to understand why it is that the Churches have been unable to achieve any modification of apartheid, in spite of making numerous statements against it, and in spite of the courageous stand taken by a series of outstanding individuals.

First, however, we must understand that apartheid is not only about racial differences and prejudice. As far as whites are concerned, it is also, perhaps mainly, about preserving their own standard of living, which they have achieved at the expense of blacks. Apartheid is not primarily about racial prejudice as far as blacks are concerned either, nor even about economics. It is primarily about enfranchisement, that is, the right to vote, and therefore, to share political power. If blacks shared political power in South Africa, the sharing of wealth would follow automatically, as blacks are four times as numerous as whites, and would dominate in any democratically elected government.

Secondly, the Churches are not able to act together to resist apartheid because the Dutch Reformed Church has officially supported it. Some theologians of that Church have questioned apartheid, the most important being Dr Beyers Naudé, whose statements caused the government so much embarrassment that he was 'banned', that is, nothing he said might be published or quoted, and he was virtually a prisoner at his own expense. Eventually, too, the World Alliance of Reformed Churches declared apartheid a heresy because it is contrary to the Bible, and the Reformed Churches in South Africa split on the issue, but that did not happen until 1982. By then a number of other theologians had followed Dr Beyers Naudé's lead, and had recognized apartheid as unscriptural. But the Dutch Reformed Church is the largest Church amongst whites in South Africa, and so long as it continues to support the government, the Christian voice is seriously weakened.

Nor are the other Churches able to speak fully effectively. Their synods make pronouncements, some individuals run costly risks in defence of justice (and if they are bold enough to be effective, run the risk of being banned or detained or deported), but rank-and-file members are apathetic because they benefit from the system. The government knows this full well, and can therefore safely ignore the pronouncements of the bishops and synods.

In one respect, however, some of the Churches have been successful. The English-speaking Protestant Churches and the Roman Catholic Church have resisted attempts to forbid multi-racial worship, and in some churches such worship takes place regularly. For many black

Christians this is a symbol of the unity which exists in Christ Jesus in spite of all attempts to break or deny it. There are others, however, who feel it is a sham for people to eat Christ's body together and drink his blood in the Eucharist when they cannot share any other form of social intercourse.

Although the Churches have failed to prevent the implementation of the apartheid legislation, the witness of such men and women as Archbishop Denis Hurley of Durban, Fr Cosmas Desmond, Bishop Ambrose Reeves, Hannah Stanton, Fr (later Archbishop) Trevor Huddleston, Dean Gonville ffrench-Beytagh, Bishop Colin Winter of Namibia, and many others who have been imprisoned and deported, has been a demonstration of the love of God which has saved many people from despairing about Christianity. How many more of the younger generation of blacks would have abandoned Christianity altogether had it not been for some white Christians such as these? Then, too, there has been a succession of black leaders who, at great cost to themselves, have refused to give in to despair and have kept hope and dignity alive and been the leaders of their people. Among these are two winners of the Nobel Peace Prize, Chief Albert Luthuli and Archbishop Desmond Tutu; the poet Dennis Brutus; Steve Biko, the murdered Black Consciousness leader; and the Reverend Dr Allan Boesak, President of the World Alliance of Reformed Churches. Such people have been able to understand the suffering in the light of the cross. Here is a poem about Christmas by Dennis Brutus, written out of his experience of political imprisonment.

For the children
for whom the flesh is not yet a burden
this is not an occasion for celebration
in quite this way at all:

but for us who know
just how massive was the cost
of adopting the garb of flesh
and the travail it entails

and who have plummeted
through the range of bestiality
that man is capable of
this transcendent act
of God assuming man's pathetic flesh
is something to be thankful for.
(From *Stubborn Hope*. Heinemann 1978)

We must remember, too, that Christians are not alone in resisting apartheid. People of many faiths and of no faith at all have been among those who have resisted it—to give just one example, the women's Black Sash movement, whose members work together to monitor human rights abuses, and to assist people who are unjustly arrested and detained, and their families.

Conclusion

The advent of independence did not slow down conversion to Christianity in Africa as some missionaries feared it might do. In some areas of the continent people seemed free for the first time to accept the gospel. In Central Kenya, for instance, old people who had shunned the missions all their lives were baptized by the thousand in the late 1960s. Because of the shortage of clergy, a form of lay Christianity has emerged all over Africa. The Independent Churches have continued to flourish in the post-independence period, but it has been suggested that they reached their peak in the 1960s, and that their importance may have declined somewhat as the mission-founded Churches lose their mission-dominated image. They have evolved patterns of leadership which do not depend on funds from overseas, but it is not yet clear whether these can be a pattern for other Churches. Some of the Independent Churches are aware that their leaders lack training, so they are sending people to the interdenominational Protestant colleges for theological education, and overseas aid has been given to several such Churches and associations of Churches for this purpose. Over much of the continent a lay Christianity has emerged which many people are not very happy about, but to which there seems to be no alternative at present.

In 1975 the World Council of Churches for the first time held its General Assembly in an African country, Kenya. This was the first time some Western Churchmen had gained any insight into the liveliness of Third World Christianity. It was also a sign that African Christianity had come of age.

STUDY SUGGESTIONS

REVIEW OF CONTENT

1. (a) Which four African nations were already independent in 1950?
   (b) Which African nations, if any, are still under colonial domination as you read this volume?
   (c) In what ways have many African countries, willingly or unwillingly, remained politically dependent on major powers?
   (d) In what ways have many African countries—and Churches—remained economically dependent?
2. In what important way did the future development envisaged for

their colonies by the Portuguese differ from the ideas of most other colonial powers for theirs, and what has been the result?

3. (a) What was the attitude towards independence of most Churches and missions in the 1950s?

(b) What were some of the steps taken by Churches and missions to prepare for independence?

(c) Give some examples of ways in which relationships between Church and state have changed in African countries since their Independence.

4. In the 1960s it was pointed out that 'what was emerging in Africa was a largely lay Christianity'. What were the reasons for this? What effect has it had on the relationship of the Churches to society as a whole?

5. When the Catholic Bishops' Conference of Eastern Africa decided that a 'Three-Self' policy (see p. 174) was called for, what changes did they say must be made in order to achieve this?

6. (a) What particular contribution to Church development have the African universities made?

(b) What two subjects have been of special interest to African theologians?

7. (a) Give some examples of Christians' response to increasing violence in many African countries before and since their Independence—e.g. in Kenya, Sudan, Nigeria.

(b) What particular dilemmas have the Churches had to contend with in situations of violence, e.g. in Ghana, Uganda, Zimbabwe.

8. (a) For what 'historical' reasons, and on what 'biblical' grounds, has the Dutch Reformed Church differed from the other Churches in its attitude to apartheid in South Africa?

(b) In what particular respect have the Churches in South Africa been successful in resisting legislation on racial segregation?

DISCUSSION

9. Under colonial rule in Congo and the Portuguese colonies a 'concordat' gave the Roman Catholic Church a privileged position in return for a measure of state control, so its leaders feared change. In what sort of situation do you think such a concordat can benefit the Church? In what circumstances might it harm the Church? Do you think it is right for government to control people's religion? Do you think it is possible? Give reasons and examples.

10. 'For various reasons many of these new Christians were not communicants ... the lack of the Eucharist did not seem very important' (p. 173). What were some of the reasons for this? Find out what rules are set by different denominations for admission to the Eucharist. How important do you feel the sacraments to be, for

the health and strength of a Church? How important are they to you yourself in your life as a Christian, and why?

11. 'Roman Catholic bishops decided that a local Church must be self-ministering, self-supporting, and self-propagating' (p. 174). On a self-support basis Christian communities have become active as a result. What are the chief advantages of the 'Three-Self' policy? What can be some of the dangers? In what circumstances, if any, is it *good* for a Church to depend on outside help? What light, if any, does 1 Corinthians 16.1–4 (or 2 Corinthians 8 and 9) shed on this subject?

12. 'Another new development was the use of African art-forms and music' (p. 176). In many other parts of the world as well, Churches are consciously introducing indigenous music, and also dance, into their worship. In the West too, new hymns and forms of music are being added to those that have been used for centuries. But some Christians find this disturbing rather than helpful. How far is your own Church indigenizing and up-dating its worship in this way, and what are your own feelings in the matter?

13. 'Apartheid is not only about racial prejudice. For whites it is also about preserving their standard of living achieved at the expense of blacks. For blacks it is primarily about the right to share political power' (p. 183). Even where all races are politically equal before the law, economic and social differences and prejudice remain. What is the situation in your own country? What can Churches as such do to overcome racial prejudice and mistrust? What can individual Christians do?

9
The South Pacific, Australia and New Zealand
from material contributed by Ian Breward

The Pacific Ocean covers a hundred million square miles, and is the largest expanse of open ocean on the globe. There are hundreds of islands and island chains in the Pacific area, yet only some twenty million people live in all the lands of the region we are to study. Some islands are tiny, like Niue with its population of 3,000; others, like Papua New Guinea, are huge; while Australia is of course a continent, though thinly populated. In this area there are four major ethnic and cultural groups. These are (1) Polynesians, living mainly in the central and south-eastern Pacific, (2) Micronesians, north of the equator, and (3) Melanesians to the west (the names mean, respectively, from regions of many islands, of tiny islands, and of islanders with dark skins). (4) This last group, of more recent newcomers to the area, including Europeans and people from various parts of Asia, are mainly in Australia and New Zealand.

POLYNESIA

Beginnings

The first missionaries to Polynesia were Spanish Franciscans from Peru, who landed in the Society Islands in 1772. They were unsuccessful, and left two years later. Next came the London Missionary Society (LMS) from Britain, who reached Tahiti in 1797 and the Marquesan and Tongan groups a little later. The British missionaries were mostly skilled craftsmen with little education, but with great zeal for preaching the gospel, and they had no idea of the difficulties they would face in translating Christian teaching into terms which the Polynesians could understand.

Problems of Mission

In Tahiti the missionaries had great difficulties in learning the language, and were shocked at many aspects of Tahitian life, which they did not understand. The people's sexual customs, and their attitudes to family life and property, filled the missionaries with fear and disgust—not the best foundation from which to proclaim the gospel. Many of them left for the safety of Australia.

However, one missionary, Henry Nott, remained in Tahiti and

persisted in learning the language and forming a relationship with the people. They began to see that although he could not provide them with the sort of European trade goods which were brought by visiting ships—as they at first expected—he could offer them two things: the secret of literacy, and a way of living together peacefully. Their religion was bound up with the achievement of success in house-building, war, and fishing. The superior wealth and technology of the Europeans led many of them to believe that the Europeans must have a more powerful god than they had.

In 1812 Pomare, one of the most important chiefs, asked for baptism. Within a few months other people began to follow his lead and enquire about Christianity. In 1815 Pomare defeated some of his rivals, and demonstrated the change that had taken place in his life. He did not kill or enslave those he had defeated as they expected him to, and as a result of his mercy to his enemies, interest in Christianity grew. But the missionaries hesitated to baptize him because of marital irregularities in his life, and he was not baptized until 1819. Throughout the 1820s and 1830s there were many baptisms and the beginnings of a Church in the Society Islands. By this time increased contact with Europeans had led to great changes. Old laws were no longer kept, and people began to attend schools run by the missions, and to acquire new skills. Traditional places of worship were destroyed and churches were built. Social and religious change inevitably went hand in hand, since religion was a part of the basic fabric of Polynesian society.

In some parts of the Pacific region radical changes had been made before the arrival of missionaries and traders. At the beginning of the nineteenth century some chiefs in Hawaii deliberately broke the most sacred customs concerning the boundaries between what was holy and what was profane. They seem to have believed that these no longer served any useful purpose. In 1820, after the traditional religion had been overthrown, and after consultation with the people of Tahiti, the Hawaiian leaders cautiously admitted American missionaries 'on trial'. By 1825 a number of important Hawaiians had become Christians, and a large number of the common people followed their example. The Hawaiians believed that they must modernize their community in order to retain their political and cultural independence, and the American missionaries helped the Hawaiian leaders to develop a new kind of society based on Christian principles. This Polynesian skill in using European religion and technology on their own terms, to meet the challenges which resulted from their contact with the West, is a striking feature of the history of the Pacific in the nineteenth century.

Polynesians saw Christianity as a vital part of their search for equality with Europeans. Word of the new religion was often spread ahead of the missionaries' arrival, by people who carried the news back

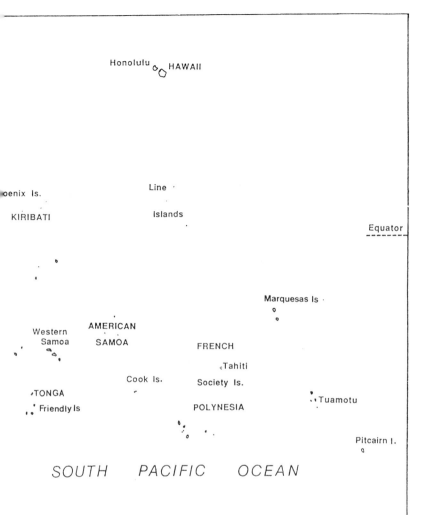

Honolulu HAWAII

oenix Is.

KIRIBATI

Line

Islands

Equator

Marquesas Is

Western
Samoa

AMERICAN
SAMOA

FRENCH

Tahiti

Cook Is.

Society Is.

TONGA

POLYNESIA

Friendly Is

Tuamotu

Pitcairn I.

SOUTH   PACIFIC   OCEAN

SOUTH PACIFIC, AUSTRALIA
AND NEW ZEALAND

to their villages, and great prestige came from adopting it and learning to read and write. By the 1830s Christianity had spread widely in Polynesia.

Polynesian Leaders

Missionaries of the London Missionary Society dominated the first stage of the expansion of Christianity in the Society Islands and in Samoa, and the Wesleyan Missionary Society pioneered in Tonga (1822) and Fiji (1835). But at village level much of the work was done by Polynesian missionaries.

Joel Bulu was a Tongan missionary who went to Fiji. He is remembered for his huge size, and for his strength and courage, as well as for the missionary work he did. He fought with sharks, settled inter-tribal disputes, and was frequently threatened with death. His courage was so impressive that sometimes his attackers could not strike him: he overpowered them with the force of his personality.

Another great Polynesian missionary was Papeiha, who was responsible for the conversion of Aitutaki (1821) and Raratonga (1823). He came from the island of Ra'iatea. He made a deep impression by his accounts of what the Christian faith had done for his own island, his ability to mediate in tribal disputes, his physical bravery, his patience when abused, his success in healing, and his possession of a Bible which told of the wonderful doings of Jesus Christ. To begin with his life was in danger, but gradually he won over important leaders, and soon the whole community had decided to forsake their old gods, keep Sunday and build churches for Christian worship.

By the end of the nineteenth century, the Bible had been translated into the major Polynesian languages, hymn books had been written, and quite a variety of books published in Polynesian languages. The Churches which had emerged by the end of the century were self-supporting financially. The Christians were ministered to by their own people, and, though there were many adaptations of European Christian patterns, a truly Polynesian Christianity had begun to emerge. This was especially clear in Tonga.

In Tonga these changes were largely due to King George Tupou (Taufaahau) (1798–1893), one of the most remarkable Polynesian rulers of the nineteenth century. He was a skilful soldier, a shrewd politician, and a great leader, and he was responsible for a series of reforms which changed the whole basis of Tongan society. He reformed land ownership, strengthened his own power, and brought the nobility under control. He produced a number of codes of law which show clearly how Tongan aspirations and Christian insights had come together. In addition to these internal changes, he was able to keep Tonga politically independent, and in 1885 he founded the Free

Left The Rev. Peter Vi, the first Tongan preacher and missionary, 'in the front rank among Polynesian ministers'.
Right Henry Nott, LMS missionary in Tahiti.
Below Wesleyan mission settlement at Viwa, Fiji, and interior of chapel at Lifuka, Friendly Islands, in 1839.

Methodist Church to end unacceptable missionary interference with Tongan custom. This was the first constitutionally independent Church in the Pacific. It was financially self-supporting, ran its own schools, and sent its missionaries abroad.

The results of Tongan missionary work can be seen most clearly in Samoa, where the LMS and the Wesleyan Missionary Society both worked. Although the Methodists had come to Samoa first, they agreed to withdraw and work in Tonga and Fiji, leaving Samoa to the LMS. However, the Tongans were not prepared to accept a decision that they had not been consulted about. Tongan missionaries therefore continued to work in Samoa and a strong Methodist Church was the result. The LMS missionaries deeply regretted this, but there was nothing they could do about it. The presence of another Christian group in Samoa made it possible for Samoans to accept or reject one Church rather than another, and so adopt Christianity more on their own terms.

Roman Catholic Missions in Polynesia

This choice was further extended with the arrival of Roman Catholic missions from 1834 onwards. The Catholics had a number of advantages. Their missionaries were unmarried, so they did not have to worry about supporting wives and children. They lived very simply, and they did not make their converts reject so much of their Polynesian heritage as many of the Protestant missionaries did. They were financially supported by the religious orders which they belonged to, and therefore did not have to make the same demands as Protestant missionaries who were concerned to establish an indigenous and self-supporting Church. The Roman Catholics were also willing to make gifts to people and to the chiefs, which accorded well with Polynesian custom, and enabled them to have a good relationship with the people among whom they worked.

One of the most important Roman Catholic missionary orders to work in the Pacific were the Marists from France. In 1836 Bishop Jean-Baptiste-François Pompallier (1801–1871) led a group of them to the South Pacific. He established missions in New Zealand, in Tonga, and on the Islands of Wallis and Futuna. The instructions he gave to missionaries in New Zealand show that he had a deep understanding of Maori culture, and also great pastoral and missionary insight. He and his missionaries were prepared to work very patiently, and they did not expect their converts to become brown Europeans. When the Diocese of Auckland was founded in New Zealand in 1848, he was appointed its Apostolic Administrator. His work among the Maoris was seriously disrupted in the 1840s and 1860s by wars in which the Maoris were eventually defeated by the whites.

By the end of the nineteenth century there were Roman Catholics in New Zealand, Samoa, Tonga, and the Society Islands, as well as in New Caledonia and the Loyalty Islands. In some islands, like Wallis, they were in a majority. There a Roman Catholic missionary had persuaded the whole population to be baptized within four months of his arrival in 1837. Many Polynesian villages adopted one of the varieties of Christianity available, and then forbade other Christian groups to come to their village. They believed that religious and social unity must not be separated.

Because of the importance of family life to Polynesian society, few men were willing to become priests, though a number became teachers or catechists. These were allowed to marry, but they could play no real part in the development of an indigenous Roman Catholic Church, and the leadership remained in the hands of priests and bishops from Europe.

Christianity and Polynesian Culture

Both Protestant and Roman Catholic missionaries played an important part in producing scientific works about the people among whom they were working. They also published dictionaries and grammars, and wrote books in the vernacular languages giving advice on political, social, and economic affairs. The result was that in both Protestant and Catholic areas the relationship between Christianity and Polynesian culture was close. Some missionaries felt that Polynesian culture was the dominant partner, a sure sign that the Polynesians had in fact made Christianity their own, and were no longer dominated by foreign patterns.

In Polynesia there are two interesting Independent Churches which bring aspects of traditional culture into Christianity. The Mamaia movement in the Society Islands and the Sivoli movement in Samoa accepted religious phenomena such as dreams and visions, and speaking when in a state of trance. These had occurred in traditional religion, but were discouraged by the missionaries of the time, although there are, of course, references to such phenomena in both the Old and New Testaments. The members of these movements also reverted to traditional patterns of marriage and family life, and in some villages most people left the mission-founded Church to join the new movements.

The best way of showing what the Christian faith could mean is described in this speech by an old Cook Islander who had spent his youth outside the Christian faith:

Friends, this is a new era to us—an era of love—which our fathers and forefathers never knew. God has loved us—even us—and therefore we love one another. During the domination of Satan over our land we had gatherings, but not like this. Of our food at our ancient feasts, we used to take a large portion to the gods, our false gods—but today we look to Jehovah. *He* is our God. He gives us all things. Formerly our wives were not allowed to eat with us, but today they are here, and our children are here, and we are not afraid to leave our homes—all is love, all is peace—this is surely in part fulfilment of what Jesus has said, 'My peace I leave with you.' And look at this new building, built by ourselves, and for what purpose? To teach our children the word of God. O how strange! How glorious! These are new things. And now let us give good heed to our children and put no hindrance in the way of their learning.

The Modern Period

The role of the Christian Churches in Polynesia has gradually changed during the twentieth century, and missionary control has been replaced by local control. The earliest example of this independence occurred when Samoan missionaries in Micronesia were withdrawn by the Samoan Church in 1900 because a newly arrived English missionary had insulted them. They did not return until the missionary had apologized. In the 1920s the Congregational Church of Samoa agreed to provide financial help for the LMS missionaries and institutions. The desire of Samoans to share control of Church finance was wrongly linked by some missionaries with a movement for political independence which was currently causing the authorities a great deal of concern. Eventually a solution was found when missionaries and Samoans agreed to meet jointly instead of on separate committees, and this system has since been adopted by Churches throughout the Pacific region.

The coming of political independence to many Pacific Island countries during the 1960s and 1970s speeded the process even further. Air transport has reduced the travel time between islands, and the Polynesian Churches have been growing steadily in Christian unity and identity. They have begun to understand anew the important cultural and religious links between them. The Pacific Conference of Churches met in 1966 and set up a series of seminars and consultations on Christian communication, marriage, and family life, as well as providing a forum in which the sort of theological education given at Pacific Theological College in Suva could be discussed. This college was opened in 1966.

Life in the village Churches, however, has not changed greatly for a century. Although the discipline of the past has been relaxed, the links between the rules of the Church and the rules of the village remain close. More significant changes can be seen in towns like Apia in West Samoa, or in cities like Auckland in New Zealand, where tens of thousands of Pacific Islanders have migrated since the 1950s. Migration, political independence, and the changes that have come through education and the beginnings of small-scale industry in some islands have posed sharp challenges for the traditional ways of Christian discipleship. Many village pastors and catechists do not have the education to preach the gospel effectively to the younger generation.

The whole issue of the relation of the gospel to the distinctive island cultures is being raised afresh. Younger ministers, as well as Church members, are now sufficiently distant from traditional religion to ask again whether customs and attitudes which were at first rejected by the Church for very sound pastoral reasons, need to be treated in the same way in the closing years of the twentieth century. In Samoa, people are beginning to use traditional Samoan music for hymns, something which was rejected in the last century. Re-examination of Christian attitudes to marriage, sexuality, and family life is also taking place. Such discussions can cause deep tensions between older leaders and younger members of the Church, tensions which are inseparable from the proclamation of the gospel, as the New Testament makes plain.

MELANESIA

The expansion of the Church into Melanesia is not yet complete. There are still parts of Papua New Guinea and the Solomon Islands which are hardly touched by the Christian faith. The task of preaching the gospel to Melanesians has been made more difficult by the huge number of languages they speak, and in Papua New Guinea, until the coming of air travel, by the sheer inaccessibility of most of the country. A missionary may have to spend a lifetime learning the languages of only a few hundred people.

Beginnings

The work of missions began in islands where whalers and traders had already made the people suspicious and hostile towards Europeans. The great pioneer missionary John Williams, who served in Tahiti and Ra'iatea and led voyages to the Cook Islands, Samoa and Tonga, was killed on attempting to land in the New Hebrides, and the Catholic Bishop Épalle suffered a similar fate in the Solomon Islands. It was not until John Geddie of Nova Scotia (1815–1872) came to Aneityum in 1848 that the situation changed. Geddie was a man of many gifts and great perseverance. He had trained as a printer, boat-builder, and carpenter, as well as learning medicine, before he came to the New Hebrides. After opposition and disappointments which would have broken the spirit of a lesser person, he gradually won the confidence of the people. By 1852 a small Church was in existence. Geddie was followed by other missionaries from the Presbyterian Church in Canada and the Reformed Church of Scotland.

Another important missionary movement into Melanesia came from the work of the Anglican Bishop of New Zealand, George Selwyn. His method was different. He believed that the Church could best be established by taking young men from the islands, training them in New Zealand, and sending them back, and he trained a number of men in this way. His policy was continued with great success on Mota and Banks Islands by John Coleridge Patteson, founder of the Melanesian Mission, who in 1861 became the first Bishop of Melanesia. In 1871 Patteson was murdered on Nukapu, in revenge for the recent kidnapping of some of the islanders by white traders for forced labour. Reaction in Britain to his death led to a great upsurge of interest in missionary work, and in labour conditions in the Pacific region generally. The training of Melanesian teachers and missionaries was continued throughout the nineteenth century, but their work was hampered by the vast distances between the islands, and the infrequency of the visits that the Bishop and other leaders could make to help and encourage them. Some of the teachers went back to traditional ways, but the majority were courageous pioneers of the gospel.

Ta'unga and other Polynesian Missionaries

An interesting example of the work of an indigenous missionary is described in the diary of the Cook Islander Ta'unga (1814–1898), who went as a missionary to the Loyalty Islands near New Caledonia. He gives a vivid account of the people's hostility to the new religion, which they associated with the new diseases brought into the islands by foreigners. There were frequent attempts to kill him, but Ta'unga refused to flee. The hostile chief went to confront him and called out, 'Who are you to create all this trouble? Where did you find these things that have caused all our customs and gods to disappear? Are you a chief that you should start all these new sayings? And when you are speared later on, who is going to save you then?' Ta'unga walked out of the house and went up to the chief, who was holding an axe and a spear, and greeted him in God's name. The chief was so taken aback by this boldness that he took an article of clothing and placed it on Ta'unga, which was a sign that he was accepted by the chief, and was safe. Ta'unga immediately explained why he had come to tell the people about Jesus. It was witness such as this that gradually won the hearts of the islanders to the gospel. Ta'unga was quite insistent that the people must forsake their old gods before they could pray to Jehovah.

Ta'unga was able to explain the Christian faith in ways which were easily understood by his Melanesian hearers, and his deep love for the people to whom he preached shines through his diary. After working in the Loyalty Islands for a number of years, Ta'unga served as a pastor in the Samoan island of Manua, before returning to his home in the Cook Islands, where he died full of honour among his own people.

It was difficult for Melanesians to understand some of the teachings of the missionaries. They asked searching questions on matters like creation. A most serious problem was the Christian teaching about God. As one Melanesian said, 'What! A god without a body! Who will believe that?' One village thought that the Bible the missionary carried round with him was his god. They said, 'See how he talks to it, and what his god says to him, he tells us. Wherever he goes, he carries it, and when he sleeps he has it near him. That is his god.' Melanesians also found it difficult to understand some aspects of the Christian teaching about sin as a personal responsibility. It was easy for them to understand that if they changed their religion, they must also change their behaviour, but it was much more difficult to understand the transformation of heart and mind which the missionaries believed was inseparable from accepting Jesus Christ as Saviour and Lord.

By the end of the nineteenth century the Christian Church had been established by Protestants and Roman Catholics on many Melanesian islands. The Congregation of the Sacred Heart of Issoudun (Roman Catholic) began work in New Britain in 1882. During the 1890s there were mass conversions, and by 1914 this mission had over 20,000 converts. Methodists began work in the Solomon Islands in 1875, and after a very difficult period of pioneering, they succeeded in establishing strong Churches in New Britain and New Georgia. By the 1970s there were 420 congregations and 13,000 confirmed members. Presbyterian and Anglican Churches in the New Hebrides had also grown steadily.

Social Change

The introduction of Christianity into the Melanesian islands led to important social changes. The missionaries brought the beginnings of Western education and medicine, and the conquest of some tropical diseases, but the most important change was the establishment of peace between previously hostile villages, and the growth of Christian villages whose whole way of life was influenced by the Christian faith.

The desire of plantation owners in the Pacific and in Australia for cheap labour from the islands created some problems until labour recruitment was abolished in 1901. Many young men went to work in Australia. Often they went willingly, but sometimes they were taken by force, with the result that the missionaries' work was severely hampered, because the people thought that they were connected with these unscrupulous labour merchants. Although such labour had its bad effects, it also meant that some islanders began to acquire new skills and gain a greater measure of wealth. Some of those who worked in

Australia became Christians while they were there. At the start of the twentieth century the South Seas Evangelical Mission extended its work so as to help the Churches founded by these converts when they returned home to the islands. This was the first of the interdenominational 'faith' missions to work in Melanesia. It has also been an important influence in the Solomon Islands.

PAPUA NEW GUINEA

Beginnings

The island of New Guinea remained closed to the gospel until 1872, when the London Missionary Society brought Polynesian teachers to Port Moresby. The first Papuan converts were baptized in 1881. Christian work in Papua New Guinea was made very difficult by the geography of the country, and travel was both slow and dangerous. The work of the missions was further hampered by the huge variety of languages, and by the lack of any overall political authority. One event which caused a great deal of discussion will serve as an example of the problems that missionaries faced. Several Fijian missionaries were massacred in New Britain in 1878. George Brown, the Methodist missionary in charge of the Church in the area, was placed in a difficult situation. The Fijian teachers said that if he did not punish the murderers and recover the bones of their countrymen, they would do so themselves. Brown organized a group which burned down houses in the village which had done the murders, and killed ten people. The bones of the Fijians were recovered, and the leaders of the people came and offered compensation for the murdered men in accordance with their custom, and Brown in turn gave them gifts to show that the matter was now settled. The result was that Brown and the leader of those who had attacked the murdered Fijians became firm friends, and this made it possible for the Church to be established in an area which had previously been hostile. The general feeling was that Brown had taken the only possible course of action in the circumstances, but nevertheless some people in Britain were bitterly critical of what he had done.

In 1884 the British and German governments annexed parts of the island. The British part was called Papua and the German part New Guinea. The remainder of the island was taken by the Dutch and now forms a part of Indonesia, called West Irian. Even after the British and Germans had established the beginnings of colonial rule, missionaries were often in danger.

The first Roman Catholic missionaries arrived in 1885, and the leading Catholic mission was the Society of the Divine Word which arrived in 1896. They used plantations to support their work, and spread rapidly. In 1922 a Vicariate-Apostolic (the first step towards a bishopric) was established, and by 1930 there were 19,000 Catholics ministered to by twenty-nine priests, and twenty-nine brothers and fifty-three sisters in religious orders. The Anglicans also developed a strong Church in the Solomon Islands, where Ini Kopuria founded the first Melanesian Brotherhood, and they began work in New Guinea in 1891.

Lutheran Missions

In the 1880s two Lutheran missions started work. In the early years they faced great difficulties and made very few converts. One of the most notable Lutheran missionaries was Johannes Flierl (1831–1915), who had previously worked in Australia. He lived with the utmost simplicity, travelled widely, and believed passionately that the missions should have a sound economic basis. He therefore started plantations to provide an income, and to teach the people Western skills and the benefits of disciplined work. When he opened a school in 1887, the first students left in disgust because they were not paid for attending, and the village elders feared that the spirits of their ancestors would be angered by the school and bring trouble on them. However, Flierl's patience and skill broke through these barriers, and he was able to win a number of converts who became teachers and evangelists.

Another German missionary whose work was of great importance was Christian Keysser (1877–1961). He was an enthusiastic ethnographer, geographer, botanist, and zoologist, as well as being a brilliant linguist. He began working in the traditional way, seeking individual converts. But he soon saw that the New Guinea villages were so close-knit that the conversion of individuals created great problems, so he began to seek family and tribal conversions. When a natural group of this sort was converted, the occasion was marked by great gatherings and feasts, and the old ways were symbolically rejected and the new ways accepted. The new Christians now became members of God's clan. It was a great tragedy that Keysser was forced to leave in 1920 because he was a German. But the movement which he had begun, and his insistence on the importance of evangelism, lived on. He had begun sending out evangelists in 1908; by 1960 the Lutheran evangelists numbered 1,200.

The demands of the gospel—and their cost—were well recognized by the people of Papua New Guinea. Here is what one chief said to his people:

Friends, we all like the missionary and the evangelists. Since they came, we have been able to sell our goods. We have found work, and have been able to earn money. Not only so; when we are ill they come to our help. But they have brought all this talk about God with them. Formerly we used to be able to do as we liked. Now, if we want to do so much as steal a pig, we are told at once that God doesn't approve. If we think of starting a war, at once they say that God wants us to keep the peace. We just can't put up with this. We want to live in the way our fathers lived. What has this God to do with us? I want to make a proposal. Let us give the missionary pigs by way of compensation. Then let him go away, and take his God with him; for if this God stays here, everything will be turned upside down. Away with God! (Quoted in G. Vicedom, *Church and People in New Guinea*, p. 24.)

Some, on the other hand, were impressed by the changes that had come about. A missionary recalled the following incident:

One day a stranger who came from a remote area was sitting with me in front of my house. He introduced his remarks by saying, 'Missionary, how great your God must be!' I asked, 'What makes you say that?' He continued, 'In old times, if I had wished to come here, I would not have got as far as Ogelburg. I would have been killed on the way. I see that the people no longer carry weapons. No one has stolen from me. The folk have received me kindly. They look after me. In the old days it would not have been so. People here have been completely changed. They used to be dirty, as I am; now they are clean. They used to have nothing better than filthy huts; now they have fine houses. In all this country there used not to be a single road; now one can go everywhere on well-made roads. They used to talk about sorcery all the time; since I have been here, I have not heard the word once. They used to worship their ancestors; now the huts for offerings have fallen down, and the places for offerings are all overgrown. No man can bring about a change like that. How great your God must be, if he can help men to find the way to a new life like this. And how kind your God must be!' (Quoted in G. Vicedom, *Church and People in New Guinea*, p. 25.)

Church Growth

We have already noted many of the difficulties facing those who tried to establish the Christian Church in Papua New Guinea: the strength of clan and family ties, the lack of a common language, the difficulty of travel. When the first Roman Catholic mission plane arrived in 1935, it reduced journeys that had taken fourteen days to two-hour flights.

The Australian government had some limited authority in the coastal regions of the island, but gave very little help to the missions in their task of education and health care, and much of the interior was still unexplored by Europeans. During the 1920s and 1930s a huge population living in the highland interior of the country was contacted by the missions for the first time. The Highlanders were deeply suspicious of strangers, and two Roman Catholic missionaries were killed in 1934 and 1935. As a result, the government banned the movement of missionaries into the Highlands until their safety could be guaranteed. This meant that all the outposts established by teachers and evangelists had to be abandoned, in spite of the people's pleas.

Missionary work did not resume in the Highlands until after 1945, when there was much rebuilding to do because the invasion of the Pacific by the Japanese during World War II had caused heavy loss of mission property. The Christians suffered considerable hardship and some persecution, but the Churches were strengthened by this, as local leaders took on responsibility which had previously been held by Europeans.

The Lutherans were the first to form a locally organized Church. In 1956 the Evangelical Lutheran Church of New Guinea was formed, and by 1970 it had 550 congregations and approximately 270,000 communicant members. By 1962 the London Missionary Society Churches had been formed into the Papua Ekalesia. By 1965 the Methodists had also developed local synods to govern the Church. The Roman Catholic Church is the largest Christian community in Papua New Guinea, with over 700,000 members spread over seventeen dioceses, but it is still heavily dependent on overseas priests and religious for its leadership. Between 1964 and 1975 it grew from being twenty-two per cent of the population to being twenty-seven per cent. The first Papuan Roman Catholic bishop was consecrated in 1970.

Church and Society

The Churches have played a vital role in giving this varied and divided region a sense of unity, but the diversity of languages remains a major problem. The Roman Catholic Divine Word Fathers adopted pidgin English as their official language as early as 1931, but the other missions concentrated on the teaching of English at high-school level, using local languages in primary schools. After the end of World War II in 1945, the Australian government began to expand education, and the choice of English as a common language for all schools created enormous difficulties for the Churches, who provided the bulk of primary education. Many of their teachers were no longer able to teach. English is the language of the governing élite, but only half the primary pupils are educated in English. A common national language is an urgent priority for this country of over three million people which became politically independent in 1975.

Since 1945 the Churches in Papua New Guinea have played an important part in development. The Lutheran Economic Service set up in 1962 has given advice on economic change. Men and women trained in Christian schools occupy key roles in the government, civil service, and business community. But tribal and regional loyalties are still very strong, and the political separatist movement in the copper-rich island of Bougainville is an example of how deep these tensions run.

Since the 1960s there have been considerable steps towards Christian unity. In 1968 the United Church was founded, which brought together Methodists and the Papua Ekalesia. Eighty-five per cent of its leadership was indigenous. Roman Catholics and Anglicans set up a Joint Commission to discuss the main issues dividing their Churches, and the United Church sent observers to these talks. In 1969 the Roman Catholics set up the Melanesian Institute for research and theological development. In 1973 a Lutheran staff member was appointed, and in 1976 a member came from the United Church.

As in so many countries, the coming of political independence speeded up the development of indigenous Church leadership. All the Churches have had to improve training for the ministry and for lay leadership. The first major Roman Catholic seminary was established in 1964. The cost of establishing Western-style institutions and means of communication in a country where the majority of people live in a subsistence economy poses great problems for the future.

The Churches in Melanesia face two serious challenges. The first, secularism, is especially strong in the towns and among the better educated. Among this urban élite, tribal bonds have been weakened, and the new world of progress and technology has not been related to the building of a community based on Jesus Christ.

The second, the influence of magical ways of thinking, is still found among the poor and less educated. These people often suspect that Europeans have not told them the truth about the source of their wealth, and they believe that it depends on magical practices. Ships and planes bring goods in response to telephone calls, and Europeans do not seem to pay for these in ways that some less Westernized Melanesians can understand. Many so-called 'cargo cults' have grown up, through which people try to gain prosperity by magical means, and which often combine hope for a better future world with striking attempts to change the present. Some of these movements have led to useful political and economic change, but often they result only in disappointed hopes, and have made it more difficult for government to work towards development in more practical ways. The existence of the cargo cults has forced the Churches to look much more carefully at the relation between the gospel and the transformation of society.

AUSTRALIA AND NEW ZEALAND

Church Development

The European colonists in Australia and New Zealand brought the Churches and culture of their homelands with them, and have not so far developed a distinctive type of Christianity, so we shall treat their history very briefly.

Many parts of European culture were not really subject to the Lordship of Christ, and one of the most striking examples of this was the greed for land, and the disregard for the rights and customs of the original inhabitants of Australia and New Zealand, which the newcomers showed. In Australia the Aborigines, then living a semi-nomadic food-gathering life in widely scattered small tribal groups, were hunted down and driven off their ancestral lands. By the end of the nineteenth century most of the Aboriginal tribes had been destroyed in areas that were attractive to European colonists.

In New Zealand the situation was different, because the Maori people were organized in much larger social groups than the Aborigines. They were formidable fighters, and they quickly learnt European skills in farming, trade and technology. Even so, they found themselves in a desperate situation. In the North Island they became convinced that unless they opposed the Europeans they would lose all their land, and their spiritual identity, so they forbade any more land sales. The result was a series of bitter land wars which the colonists won, and further large areas of the Maoris' land were confiscated. By the end of the nineteenth century it looked as though the Maori community was on the verge of extinction. Although many Maoris had become Christians, Christianity had not filled the vacuum left by the loss of land and the impact of European culture.

It seemed to many Maoris that Christianity and the adoption of the European way of life were inseparable, and they wished to retain their own way of life. It was not until the 1920s that T. W. Ratana, a prophetic healer, began preaching and teaching in a way which attracted real interest among the Maoris of North Island. The Ratana Church which grew up as a result of his work is similar in many ways to some of the Independent Churches in Africa. It has played an important part in New Zealand politics, and the four members of Parliament who represented Maori electors in the mid-1970s all belonged to it.

The colonists from Europe who migrated to Australia and New Zealand found themselves both in a mission field and in a melting pot. Many of the settlers had ceased to practise their religion in the new surroundings, and needed to be reconverted. The task of evangelism was often neglected, and colonists who kept their religious faith concentrated on trying to recreate among themselves copies of the

Two missionary martyrs: *Left* John Patteson, first Bishop of Melanesia, *Right* John Williams, LMS pioneer to Samoa, Tonga, Cook Islands and New Hebrides.
Below Palm fronds decorate the riverside as the Anglican priest on Bougainville Island baptizes a group of contract workers from the Papua New Guinea Highlands.
Bottom In New Zealand Fr Henare Tate, the second Maori Catholic to be ordained priest, pronounces the blessing after Communion.

Churches in the countries they had come from, though often this was simply not possible.

Among the first Europeans to settle in Australia were convicts from Britain, many of them deported for very minor offences. The Church of England was established as part of the framework of government, and the authorities saw the Church as a counter to drunkenness, immorality and lawlessness. In 1825 the Church Schools Corporation gave Anglicans a virtual monopoly of private education.

This Anglican dominance was strongly attacked by Presbyterians, Methodists and Roman Catholics, who were also represented, and who did not want there to be an officially 'established' Church with special privileges. The same opposition to an official Church appeared in New Zealand. This had two important results. The first was that the Churches developed financial and political independence quite early. For example, the Church of England in New Zealand, led by Bishop George Selwyn, adopted a constitution in 1857 which was quite revolutionary. It gave lay members of the Church a share in its government which was far in advance of anything in Britain.

The second result of the rejection of an officially established Church was that Christians were forced to co-operate with one another. For instance, groups of Methodists who remained separate from one another in the home country, came together to form one national Methodist Church in New Zealand. The same thing happened with Presbyterians and Lutherans. By the beginning of the twentieth century they were thinking about reunion between different Churches, and talks were held in the 1920s and 1930s. But this took a lot longer to achieve. By 1964 however, negotiations had become very far advanced, and the Anglican Church joined in the Church Union discussions. The 1971 Plan for Union was the result. It was rejected by the Anglican General Synod in 1976, but local co-operation between Christians has grown steadily. In Australia, negotiations for Church Union between Presbyterians, Methodists and Congregationalists resulted in a United Church being established there in 1977, after some costly lawsuits among Presbyterians, many of whom remained outside the United Church. In addition, Councils of Churches at regional and national level in both New Zealand and Australia have played an important part in bringing the Churches together.

Education and Social Issues

Throughout Australia and New Zealand the Churches were deeply concerned about evangelism, and about providing facilities for worship and pastoral care. This was a large task. Christians were also deeply concerned to provide education for their children. Until the 1960s and 1970s the Churches played a very important role in primary education, and Christians were also active in establishing secondary schools and universities. But because there were still divisions among Christians, an increasing number of people believed that education must become secular if it was to be compulsory. It was clear that only the state had the finance to make primary education free and available for all children.

The Roman Catholic Church refused to accept this, and established its own schools throughout Australia and New Zealand. The Protestant Churches established some secondary schools, but the majority of Protestants were educated in state schools where religion had no official place. The Churches themselves were responsible for educating children in the faith, and the Sunday School Movement was an attempt to provide a substitute for Church primary schools. It was not entirely successful, though it had a deep impact on the children of Christian families. The decline of Sunday Schools and youth groups during the 1960s and 1970s has raised questions about the suitability of a secular education system.

In New Zealand the government Education Department has been re-examining the nature of the moral education which must take place in the public schools, yet even there Christians may not be able to take up the opportunities a change of government policy offers. They have been inward-looking and conservative on social and political matters. The development of cities and industry in the late nineteenth century, with the tensions between workers and employers that accompanied these changes, led to much Christian concern. But on the whole the Protestant Churches were not sympathetic to the claims of workers for economic and social justice. Sermons on thrift, and advice not to drink alcohol, were hardly enough to convince badly-paid workers with poor housing that the gospel could do anything to redeem their daily life. The ravages of alcoholism in Australia and New Zealand show the cost of this failure.

The political influence of the Protestant Churches has thus steadily declined. Many Protestants came to feel that religion had nothing to say about matters of political importance, while others have felt that Christians ought not to get involved in politics, in case the Churches become politically divided. Many Christians increasingly lived in two worlds, the private world of family and religion, and the public world of business and politics, and they kept the two separate. Roman Catholics were much more politically active in the Labour Party, and did not share Protestant attitudes. But it is generally true to say that religion has become less and less important in public life. The Churches' inability to think creatively about the social implications of the gospel came out clearly in their limited response to the economic depressions of the 1920s and 1930s, as well as to the problems of reconstruction following World War II. The reaction of Christians to radio and television has also shown the same inability to come to terms with change. Although there have been important political leaders in both countries who were deeply committed Christians, they have not changed the secular environment in which they work.

Part of this failure to see the relationship between the gospel and every area of life has been due to the lack of theological scholarship in the Australian and New Zealand Churches. Theology was imported and adapted, instead of growing out of the tensions between the gospel and the local situation. Church members clung to traditional expressions of belief, and the few scholars who tried to open up new perspectives were likely to arouse bitter resentment from fellow Christians, and be accused of denying the Bible. One Presbyterian scholar, Dr Angus, a fiery Irishman who taught at St Andrew's College in Sydney, was tried for heresy by the Presbyterian Church of New South Wales in 1934. Though the trial was a sensation, it did nothing to resolve the tensions between those who believed that the Christian faith was unchanging, and those who wished to re-state it in ways that could be understood by people who accepted the scientific advances of the twentieth century. The same tensions split the Presbyterian Church of New Zealand in the 1960s, when Principal Geering of its Theological Hall was charged with heresy for his reinterpretation of the doctrine of the resurrection. The Pacific Churches have not yet encountered these problems. Theological education there is still at a relatively early stage of development, and the main theological concerns are quite different. Although the situation shows signs of changing, as yet their primary task is to relate Christianity to their own traditional culture, rather than to the scientific culture of the West.

Interdependence throughout the Pacific Area

Although the Churches in Australia and New Zealand have not succeeded in reconverting the whole of society in those countries to the Christian faith, their influence has been important. The Churches remain valuable cultural and social centres in their communities, especially in farming districts and small towns. A network of Christian congregations covers both nations, and most people have continued to be married in Church and buried by ministers of religion. In a vague sense New Zealanders and Australians have thought of their countries as 'Christian' countries. The Churches have sent large numbers of missionaries to India, the Pacific, China, South America and Africa, but they did not always see the connection between preaching the gospel overseas and preaching the gospel at home.

Since 1945 the growing awareness of the need for partnership between sending Churches and receiving Churches has gradually changed this understanding of the Church's mission. Australians are beginning to think of themselves as part of the Pacific, and neighbours of Asia, rather than as British outposts in the South Seas. The development of very wealthy industrial Western-type societies in Australia and New Zealand is in sharp contrast to the subsistence village economies in which most Pacific Island Christians live. The small-scale subsistence economies are based on distribution: industrial societies are based on accumulation. The Churches need to subject both systems to the judgement of the gospel if the religion of commerce is not to triumph.

The interdependence of Churches in both rich and poor societies has become increasingly evident from the 1960s onwards. Formerly dependent colonial territories have become politically independent, and white Australians and New Zealanders have slowly begun to realize that the world is no longer a white man's empire. This has become particularly obvious to an increasing number of New Zealanders, now that over twelve per cent of the population of three million people are of Polynesian origin. In addition to a rapidly growing Maori population, who have migrated by tens of thousands to the cities, thousands of Pacific Islanders have also migrated to New Zealand. There are, for example, 22,000 Cook Islanders in New Zealand, and only 18,000 in the Cook Islands. The task of making a multi-cultural society a reality throughout the South Pacific has become more and more demanding. All the major New Zealand Churches now have significant Polynesian minorities among their members; they can no longer assume that Christianity for New Zealanders means continuing the inherited patterns of nineteenth-century Britain. In Australia the huge migration from Europe and Turkey has posed some of the same questions there. In Fiji, Fijians and Indians have to live together. The vigorous musical tradition of Pacific Island Christians, as well as an interest in new forms of worship, is transforming the way New Zealand Christians worship; they are no longer content only to sing hymns written by Europeans. There are signs of local hymn-writing on a considerable scale, a sure indication of religious vitality.

From the 1960s on there has been a dramatic shift in social attitudes in both Australia and New Zealand. Traditional ethics, social structures and leadership have all been questioned. Many of the people affected by these changes have moved outside the institutional Churches, but the development of a charismatic movement in all the major Churches in Australia and New Zealand suggests that change from within is also possible.

The whole issue of the relationship between the Christian faith and its surrounding culture has emerged with fresh force for Christians in the whole of this region. Many of the questions asked in Australia and

New Zealand are the same as those asked by villagers in Papua New Guinea, Fiji or Tonga. Christians in different parts of the Pacific region need to listen to one another and to seek common answers, because of the way in which their political destinies are more and more entwined. Partnership is by no means a one-way relationship. Churches in Australia and New Zealand have much to learn from their partners in Polynesia and Melanesia, many of whom see more clearly how their faith must lead to the creation of a society deeply influenced by the gospel of Jesus Christ.

STUDY SUGGESTIONS

WORDS AND MEANINGS

1. What do the names 'Polynesia' and 'Melanesia' actually mean?
2. Who or what were or are the following?
   (a) Pomare (b) Cargo cults (c) Mamaia (d) Ta'unga (e) Pidgin
   (f) Ratana (g) Sivoli

REVIEW OF CONTENT

Polynesia

3. (a) What missions to Polynesia had there been before 1900, in which islands did they start work, and at what dates?
   (b) What were the chief problems faced by the early missionaries?
   (c) What two 'advantages' brought by the missionaries eventually led the Polynesians to accept their teaching?
4. (a) In which islands were missions active in the early nineteenth century?
   (b) Name two Polynesian leaders who themselves served as missionaries to other parts of the Pacific. Which islands did they come from, and to which did they go?
5. What were some of the reforms carried out by King Taufaahau (George Tupou) in Tonga, and for what chief purpose did he eventually found the Free Methodist Church?
6. (a) What advantages did the nineteenth-century Roman Catholic missions have over the Protestant missions of the time?
   (b) Give a brief account of the work of the Roman Catholic bishop Jean-Baptiste-François Pompallier.
   (c) For what chief reason were Polynesian men unwilling to become priests in the Roman Catholic Church?
7. What were some of the characteristics of the independent Mamaia and Sivoli Churches, and where was each Church situated?

8. (a) What are some of the ways in which the role and structure of the Church in Polynesia has changed during the twentieth century?
   (b) What are some of the ways in which social change in Polynesia is leading both clergy and laity to re-examine the relationship of the gospel to the distinctive island cultures of the area?

Melanesia, Papua New Guinea

9. What have been the two great hindrances to the spread of the gospel in Melanesia?

10. In their different ways both John Geddie and Bishop George Selwyn were successful in attracting people to the faith. Give a brief description of the methods used by each, and point to the differences between them.

11. (a) What were some of the features which made the Cook Islander Ta-unga's missionary work in Loyalty Islands so successful?
    (b) What were some of the features of Christian teaching which Melanesians found particularly difficult to understand?

12. (a) What were the three 'advantages' brought to Melanesia by the missions which led to great social changes, and which of them was the most important?
    (b) What were some of the advantages and disadvantages, to Melanesians, resulting from the practice of recruiting cheap labour in the islands for plantation work in Australia? What were some of the advantages and disadvantages to the Church?

13. At what date was missionary work in Papua New Guinea begun, and by which society?

14. Describe some of the traditional customs of the region which posed particular problems and dilemmas for missionaries, including the risk of massacre, and for some expatriates, of serious misunderstanding and withdrawal of support in Britain?

15. At what dates were (a) Roman Catholic, (b) Lutheran, and (c) Anglican missions in New Guinea begun?

16. Give a brief description, with dates, of the aims and achievements of (a) Johannes Flierl and (b) Christian Keysser, and describe very briefly the varying reactions of Melanesians to the changes brought about by Christian evangelism.

17. (a) What was the effect of World War II on Church life in Papua New Guinea?
    (b) What are some of the most important changes in the role of the Church in Papua New Guinea that have occurred *since* World War II?

18. What two serious challenges are Christians in Papua New Guinea facing today, and to what extent are the Churches equipped to meet them?

Australia and New Zealand

19. (a) What were the chief differences between the character and way of life of the Aborigines in Australia, and those of the Maori people in New Zealand?
    (b) What difference if any did this make in the way the two peoples reacted to the arrival of European colonists, and the way the colonists treated them?
20. (a) Which was the dominant missionary Church in Australia, and why?
    (b) What was the relationship of that Church to the government, and what was the reaction of other Churches to this?
21. In what chief way did the development of inter-Church relations in New Zealand differ from that in Australia?
22. Give a brief account of the role played by the different Churches in the field of education in Australia and New Zealand, noting especially the changes taking place in the 1960s and 1970s.
23. What has been the standpoint of the Protestant Churches in Australia and New Zealand with regard to social and political matters, and what effect has this had on their relationships with the various sections of society as a whole?
24. What have been some of the strengths and weaknesses of the Church in Australia and New Zealand, and to what factors have these chiefly been due?
25. What has been the relationship of the Church in Australia and New Zealand to the Church in other parts of the Pacific region?

DISCUSSION

26. Give a brief account of steps taken towards ecumenical encounter and joint action by the Churches in (a) Polynesia, (b) Melanesia, (c) Papua New Guinea and (d) Australia and New Zealand. In what further ways do you think they might be working together, and what if any are the obstacles to this?
27. 'The Hawaiians believed they must modernize their community in order to retain political and cultural independence, and American missionaries helped them develop a society based on Christian principles' (p. 189). Compare this with the attitudes of Christians in (a) Melanesia, (b) Australia and New Zealand and with (c) Polynesian skill in using European religion and technology to meet new challenges on their own terms. How do these varying attitudes compare with those of the Church authorities and of Christians generally in your own country? What are your own views on this matter?
28. 'The task of making a multi-cultural society a reality throughout

the South Pacific has become more and more demanding' (p. 210). What do you see as some of the chief difficulties faced by Churches aiming to unite people of different cultures and/or different religions? What do you see as some of the most effective ways of achieving this aim?

29. 'In Melanesia "magical" ways of thinking are found among the poor and less educated . . . people try to gain prosperity by magical means' (p. 204). What are some of the 'magical' ways of thinking which are also found today among people of *Western* countries, including Christians (and not only among the poor and less educated)? To what extent do you see such ways of thinking as helping or hindering the spread of the gospel?

30. What are some of the things which the so-called 'older' Churches in Australia and New Zealand have to learn from the so-called 'younger' Churches in the Pacific region?

10
The Orthodox Churches: Eastern Europe and the East Mediterranean Region
from material contributed by Otto Meinardus

Many of the Christians living in Eastern Europe and around the eastern end of the Mediterranean Sea belong to the Churches known as 'Orthodox'. 'Eastern Orthodoxy' is a term which describes a number of Churches, some of which are separated from others for theological reasons. There are small theological differences between those Churches who accepted the decisions of the Council of Chalcedon in AD 451 and those who did not (see Vol. 1 of this TEF Church History Guide, p. 143). We shall call the Churches who accepted those decisions 'Chalcedonian Orthodox Churches', the others we shall call 'Non-Chalcedonian Orthodox Churches'. Until recently the two groups were bitterly hostile to each other, but today they understand each other much better. Roman Catholic and Protestant Christians also live in much of this area, and in the East Mediterranean region the majority of the people are Muslims. The religious scene is very complicated, and politics and religion are often interconnected.

THE CHALCEDONIAN ORTHODOX CHURCHES

The Chalcedonian Orthodox group of Churches includes the four ancient patriarchiates of Constantinople, Antioch, Alexandria, and Jerusalem; the Archbishoprics of Cyprus and Sinai; and the national Churches of Russia, Greece, Romania, Georgia, and Bulgaria. In Finland, Czechoslovakia, Estonia, Latvia, Poland, Yugoslavia, Hungary, and Albania there are non-Orthodox as well as Orthodox Christians, but even where the Orthodox Church is very small, it is self-governing in each country. The term which the Orthodox use is 'autonomous'. The autonomous Orthodox Churches are not united under one leader in the way that the Roman Catholic Church is united under the Pope, but they all pay special honour to the Patriarch of Constantinople, who is called the Oecumenical Patriarch. The Orthodox Churches are united by their acceptance of Holy Scripture, the Nicene Creed, the traditions of the early Church Fathers, and the decisions of the Seven Ecumenical Councils. They are also united by the use of liturgies translated and developed from the liturgies of St Basil and St John Chrysostom. Orthodox Christians value their autonomy quite as much as their membership of the Orthodox family of Churches, and they have a strong sense of history and tradition.

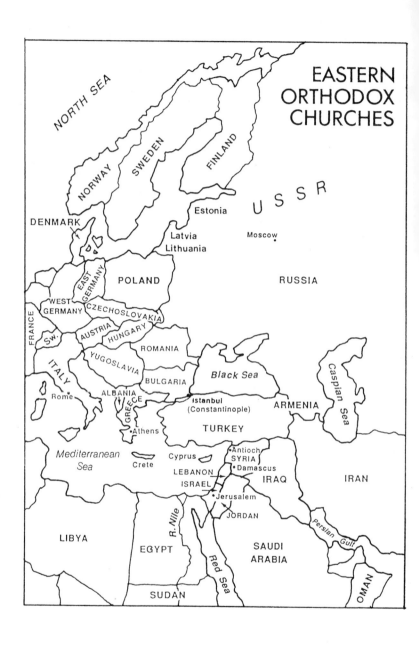

EASTERN
ORTHODOX
CHURCHES

NORTH SEA

NORWAY

SWEDEN

FINLAND

USSR

DENMARK

Estonia

Latvia

Lithuania

Moscow

EAST GERMANY

POLAND

RUSSIA

WEST GERMANY

CZECHOSLOVAKIA

FRANCE

Sw.

AUSTRIA

HUNGARY

ROMANIA

ITALY

YUGOSLAVIA

BULGARIA

Black Sea

Caspian Sea

Rome

ALBANIA

GREECE

Istanbul
(Constantinople)

ARMENIA

Athens

TURKEY

Mediterranean
Sea

Cyprus

Crete

Antioch

SYRIA

Damascus

LEBANON

ISRAEL

IRAQ

IRAN

Jerusalem

JORDAN

Persian Gulf

LIBYA

R. Nile

EGYPT

Red Sea

SAUDI
ARABIA

OMAN

SUDAN

216

The Orthodox Churches under the Ottoman Empire

In the nineteenth century much of south-eastern Europe was still under the rule of the Ottoman Turks, whose empire included most of the East Mediterranean region. Istanbul (formerly called Constantinople) was the capital of the Ottoman Empire. The Ottoman Turks were Muslims. Most of their European subjects were Christians, and there were small communities of Christians in the East Mediterranean lands.

In traditional Muslim nations Muslims form the *umma*, or community of Islam, and only they can hold office in the state. Under the *millet* system, other religious communities, or *millets*, were allowed to exist, and were given certain rights. Each *millet* appointed a leader who also had to be approved by the state, and this leader was responsible for the good conduct of the people of his *millet*. Muslims called Jews and Christians *dhimmi*, which means protected people. The Qur'an tells Muslims to respect Jews and Christians because they too are 'people of the book'. Jews and Christians living under Muslim rule were not usually persecuted, though sometimes a fanatical ruler would persecute them, but they did not have all the privileges of citizenship that Muslims had, and they paid higher taxes than Muslims did. The rule of the Ottoman Turks, however, was harsh and oppressive, because they were a small alien minority, and minority rule has to be harsh if it is to continue. However, they recognized the rights of the Patriarch of Constantinople. When Sultan Mehmet conquered the city in 1453 he said to the Patriarch, 'Continue to be Patriarch; may God protect you. I grant you my protection and support. You shall enjoy all the rights that your predecessors enjoyed.' The Ottoman Turks continued to recognize the Oecumenical Patriarchs as the chief Christian authorities in their Empire, and held them responsible for the behaviour of all Christians. We shall see one consequence of this when we study the Greek Church.

The Oecumenical Patriarchate of Constantinople

The Oecumenical Patriarch and his Secretariat have lived in Istanbul (the ancient Constantinople), near the shore of the Golden Horn, since 1601. A twelve-man synod with the Patriarch as its chairman administers Church affairs. At the beginning of the nineteenth century the Patriarch cared for all Orthodox Christians in Turkey and in the European parts of the Empire. But during the nineteenth century the Ottoman Empire began to collapse. And as the countries of south-eastern Europe regained their freedom, their Churches were granted autonomy, and this process of granting autonomy has continued almost up to the present. We can easily understand that the Patriarch has not been happy to see his influence and glory reduced, and that he has sometimes been reluctant to grant autonomy. The less power the Patriarch has, the less he is able to do for the people still left in his care, and some of the Churches have wanted autonomy for political rather than religious reasons.

The Oecumenical Patriarch now cares for the few remaining Christians in the modern state of Turkey and on the island of Crete. He also cares for Orthodox Christians in Finland, and for those who have migrated from East European countries and now live in Western Europe, the Americas, and Australia. He also has charge of the monks of Mount Athos in Greece, a major centre of monasticism in ancient times.

Since 1920 the Oecumenical Patriarch has taken part in the world-wide Ecumenical Movement. The Patriarchate joined the World Council of Churches in 1946 when it was first formed. In 1964 Patriarch Athenagoras I met Pope Paul VI in Jerusalem. The Patriarch and the Pope withdrew the anathemas of 1045 (see Vol. 3 of the TEF Church History Guide, p. 131), and in this way did something towards ending the quarrel between the Orthodox and the Roman Catholic Churches. For some years the Chalcedonian Orthodox Churches have wanted to hold a synod at which all the autonomous Churches could be represented. If the synod can be held, it will be the first such meeting for a thousand years.

The Greek Orthodox Church

Almost all Greeks belong to the Orthodox Church, and during the period of Ottoman rule their Church did much to help them survive without losing courage. The Greeks rose against Ottoman rule in 1821. In the course of the uprising, thousands of Muslims in Greece were massacred, and the Ottoman rulers held the Oecumenical Patriarch responsible. They dragged him out of his cathedral on Easter Sunday and hanged him. In 1833 the Greek Church was declared autonomous, but its autonomy was not recognized by the Patriarch until 1850.

The Archbishop in charge of the Greek Church lives in Athens, and the Church is governed by a synod. There are lively evangelistic, training, and renewal programmes in the Church. The most important is the Zoe movement. *Zoe* is the word used for 'life' in the New Testament. Some years ago it looked as though monasteries would soon die because there were so few monks, but now more young men are becoming monks, so there is new life in the monasteries. Lay people play an important part in the life of the Greek Church. Many teachers and writers of theology are lay people, and some of them preach in Church with the bishop's permission. Each bishop has only a small diocese, so he can get to know his people well. The Greek Orthodox Church is a member of the World Council of Churches, as are many of the other Orthodox Churches, and is becoming more outward-looking. For a long time Greece was too troubled by political strife and war to look outward, but now things have changed. Greek missionaries have gone to East Africa to help the indigenous Orthodox Churches there, and some African priests have been trained in Greece.

A small number of Greek Orthodox Christians live in the ancient patriarchates of Antioch, Alexandria, and Jerusalem, and there are Greek Orthodox Patriarchs in all these places, although, as we shall see later, the majority of Christians there belong to other Churches. The Orthodox Church in East Africa looks to the Greek Orthodox Patriarch of Alexandria as its ultimate spiritual authority. Some other small groups of Orthodox Christians on the African continent do so too.

The Church in Cyprus is autonomous, but is closely linked with the Greek church. Archbishop Makarios was both head of the Orthodox Church in Cyprus and President of Cyprus until his death in 1977. Religion and politics are so mixed up in Cyprus that all we can do in a short survey is to mention that there seems no easy solution to the problems of the island, which is now partitioned between Greeks and Turks.

The Russian Orthodox Church and Christians in the USSR

After the Ottoman Turks had captured Constantinople in 1453, the Russians began to think of Moscow as the Third Rome (the Second Rome had been Constantinople). The Russian Orthodox Church became autonomous in 1598; Moscow was then made a Patriarchate, and the Russian Church became the largest of the Orthodox churches.

In the eighteenth century the Czar (emperor) Peter the Great of Russia abolished the Patriarchate, and the Church was ruled instead by a synod and was strictly controlled by the state. The Czars were harsh rulers, and they tried to use the Church to strengthen their position. From 1880 to 1907 the lay official in charge of the synod was K. P. Pobedonostev, who became a Minister of State, and used the Church to put down popular unrest and support the state. He made both himself and the Church hated by all those who wanted to see Russian society reformed.

But there were other aspects of Church life in Russia. The *startsy* or elders, many of whom were monks, led a revival of spiritual life. People came to them in crowds for spiritual and personal advice and for bodily healing. St Serafim, who died in 1832, is the best known of the *startsy*. From 1808 to 1825 he lived as a hermit, seeing no one. Then he started seeing people who came to him for advice. Thousands came, he healed many, and his love and holiness brought them nearer to God. This kind of spirituality gave people the courage to endure; it was not concerned with social action. Russian theologians of the nineteenth century studied the early Church fathers anew, and this led to a revival of theology.

In the nineteenth century Russia extended her boundaries considerably, and Russian missionaries went to the people brought under Russian rule. They also went beyond, to China and Japan, and small Orthodox Churches were founded in both countries as a result of their work. From 1824 to 1868 John Veniaminov, who later became Bishop Innokenty, worked as a missionary among the Aleutian Islanders and the peoples of north-eastern Siberia and Alaska. He was a brilliant linguist, and was greatly beloved by those amongst whom he worked, and he brought many to Christ. Nikolay Ilminsky, a layman, was another outstanding Russian missionary who worked among the people of Central Asia. He made great efforts to present Christianity in the people's own languages and in terms of their own culture.

In 1905 the Russian Orthodox Church gained enough freedom from state control to begin to make reforms. This was a slow business, and a new constitution was not ready until 1917. On 31 October 1917 the Patriarchate was re-established, and a new Patriarch named Tikhon was elected. He tried to work with the Communist government which came to power through the 1917 revolution, but by 1922 he was in prison. He was released the following year after making a 'confession' of his previous faults, and neither he nor his successors have since criticized the government, although the Church has been severely hampered in its work, and the aim of the Soviet government is to abolish all religion, whether Christian or Muslim. For a few short periods the pressure on the Church has eased, especially during World War II, when the German threat was so great that the support of the Christians was needed. The worst periods of persecution were under Stalin, but serious repression also took place under Krushchev. Stalin has since been dishonoured by the USSR.

Baptists, Evangelicals, and Pentecostalists in the USSR have faced the same dilemma as the Orthodox Church. The All-Union Council of Baptists and Evangelical Christians issued *New Statutes* and a *Letter of Instruction* in 1960 in which Baptist and Evangelical leaders instructed Christians to curtail evangelistic activities and discourage baptisms among the young because, they said, the task of the Church at the time was to provide spiritual care for those already in the Church. This was contrary to all evangelical belief and practice, and the Church leaders must have been put under great pressure by the government to agree to such a document. Many Baptists and Evangelicals disagreed with the *New Statutes* and refused to accept them, and many have since been imprisoned and are in great difficulty. The All-Union Council has twice altered the *New Statutes* since then, and has taken a rather bolder

Dignitaries of the Russian Orthodox Church in procession through the streets of St Petersburg (Leningrad) in the 1840s.

Today many Greek Orthodox Christians are living in other countries—as witness the occasion in 1972 when Metropolitan Kyrilos of Chaldea, representing the Oecumenical Patriarch, officiated at a service in London to celebrate the 50th anniversary of the Archbishopric of Thyatira and Great Britain.

stand, but many Christians remain unhappy about what their leaders have done.

The Roman Catholics and Mennonites, both small Churches in the USSR, have been greatly harassed, and the Eastern Rite Catholics have had a more difficult time still. The Mennonites have been persecuted almost out of existence, but more recently there have been strong signs of revival. Most of the Roman Catholics in this region live in Latvia and Lithuania, on the north-western border of the USSR, and the Church is strongest in Lithuania. In 1971 over 17,000 Lithuanian Catholics wrote to the Secretary-General of the United Nations, and to the government of the USSR, asking to be granted religious freedom. This angered the authorities, who made the bishops sign and read out in their Churches a letter rebuking the people for doing this. The parish priests said the bishops had betrayed them. They published a statement saying they were only asking for the religious freedom promised under the Soviet Constitution, which was being denied to them.

In spite of three-quarters of a century of rule by a government which has been determined to bring to an end all 'religious superstition', at least thirty million Soviet citizens (and possibly many more) out of a total population of 250 millions are still practising Christians. There has recently been a revival of interest in religion among the younger generation, and especially among educated people. Very little Christian literature is available, but people value highly whatever there is and it is passed from one person to another. Sermons are listened to with great attention. There is also a revival of religion among Soviet Jews.

According to Marxist teaching all religions, not just Christianity, are to be seen as harmful superstition, and the aim is to get rid of them. About half a million Buddhists and forty million Muslims live in Asiatic Russia. So far it seems that the Buddhists have been much more severely repressed than the Muslims. The Muslims all live in an area to the east of the Aral Sea, forming the majority of the population in that area, and there is evidence that Islam is still practised widely.

The Churches in other Soviet Bloc Countries

There are Orthodox Christians living in all of the countries of the Soviet Bloc except the German Democratic Republic (GDR), and also in Yugoslavia, which is a communist country, but which broke away from the Soviet Bloc in 1949. However, Poland and Hungary are traditionally Roman Catholic countries, and Czechoslovakia is part Roman Catholic and part Protestant, with a few Orthodox. There are Muslims as well as Christians in Yugoslavia and Albania. Romania and Bulgaria are overwhelmingly Orthodox.

All the southern parts of this area (Hungary, Romania, Yugoslavia, Bulgaria, and Albania) were, like Greece, part of the Ottoman Empire.

They regained their independence during the nineteenth century. The Orthodox Church of Bulgaria did not become autonomous until 1964, however. The Churches of these countries enjoyed only a short time between the period of repression under the Ottoman Turks, and repression under Marxist governments.

In all these east European countries, then, Christians are under pressure. Difficulties vary from country to country and include the closure of churches, reductions in the number of clergy, obstruction of Christian education and evangelism, and the exclusion of Christians from senior jobs. In spite of these difficulties, however, Church life continues, and Christian leaders often receive permission to attend international gatherings and meet with Christians from other parts of the world.

In Poland and the GDR people are rather more free to practise their religion than elsewhere, though there are restrictions on Christians. In the GDR, for instance, hardly any Christians get placed in universities, however well they qualify to do so. Bishops in both countries have complained to the authorities on many occasions about such restrictions. Church life in both countries is vigorous, and some Poles go overseas as missionaries. The election of a Polish Pope, John Paul II, has strengthened the position of the Roman Catholic Church in Poland.

In the tiny country of Albania religion has been more fiercely repressed than anywhere else, and both Christians and Muslims have suffered. Since 1967 all religious practice has been forbidden. Mosques and churches have been taken over by the state and used for other purposes. In 1973 a seventy-year-old priest who was in prison was asked by a fellow-prisoner to baptize her baby. He did so—and was shot by firing squad for this. There are very few signs of religion in Albania today, but the Communist authorities still complain at times that religion has not yet completely disappeared from the country.

NON-CHALCEDONIAN ORTHODOX CHURCHES IN THE EAST MEDITERRANEAN REGION

In this section we consider the Non-Chalcedonian Orthodox Churches around the eastern end of the Mediterranean: Turkey, Syria, Lebanon, Jordan, Israel, and Egypt, and two countries further to the east: Iraq and Iran. Christians form only a small part of the population of this region, and they are divided among several different Churches. Some of the divisions go back to the theological controversies of the fourth to the sixth centuries. The majority of the Christians belong to Non-Chalcedonian Orthodox Churches. They follow Orthodox traditions of worship and thought, but they did not accept the decision of the

Council of Chalcedon in AD 451 that in Christ there are two natures (human and divine) in one person.

This region has a long history of invasion and conquest. Some of the earlier parts of this history are found in the Old Testament. After the Roman conquest, which took place just over a hundred years before the time of Christ, and subsequent Roman occupation, came the Arab conquests in the seventh century which brought Islam. Then in the eleventh century the Seljuk Turks invaded, followed by the Ottoman Turks in the fifteenth century. In between these two came the Crusades of the eleventh to the fourteenth centuries, which were particularly damaging. These brought great hatred between Muslims and Christians, and between Christians from the west and those in the east. In modern times the Russians, British and French have all controlled parts of the region. The creation of the state of Israel solved one problem by providing a homeland for Jewish people, but has created others, as the Palestinians were made homeless.

The Armenian Church

The homeland of the Armenian Christians is around the eastern end of the Black Sea. Armenia was converted to Christianity by St Gregory the Wonderworker around AD 300, but this Church was not represented at the Council of Chalcedon, and afterwards refused to agree to doctrines which it had taken no part in thinking out. Armenia's history has been troubled, and at the beginning of the nineteenth century the Armenian people had become widely scattered. Both Roman Catholic and Protestant missions began work among the Armenians, and the Sultan ordered that their converts should be grouped into two new *millets*. The Armenians were grateful for the medical and educational help brought by the missions, but they were unhappy about these new divisions which weakened the community.

During the nineteenth century Russia was expanding southwards into west and central Asia, and gained control of lands occupied by Turkish Muslims. Many of these were killed during the Russian conquest. The Armenians hated Turkish rule, and the Turks suspected them of disloyalty. In the 1890s the Armenians in both Russia and Turkey rose in rebellion, but their attempt to gain their independence was suppressed with much loss of life. In Turkey 300,000 Armenians were massacred, and during World War I there were further massacres. Many fled to the West.

The worst chapter in Armenian history, however occurred just before and during World War I. The Ottoman government collapsed, and a revolutionary group called the 'Young Turks' seized power. They tried to free Turkey from what they saw as the 'dead hand' of religion. They set up a secular state, and tried to get rid of all minority groups. A million and a half Armenians were killed and thousands more fled the country, many of them being helped to safety by the missions.

After the war ended in 1918, Armenia was divided between the USSR and Turkey. The Armenians who now live in the USSR have been treated rather better than most other Christians in that country, and after World War II about 75,000 Armenians from other countries where they had taken refuge joined those in the USSR. The Armenian Patriarch at the ancient Christian centre of Echmiadzin in the USSR is the head of the whole Armenian Church scattered throughout the world, except for the small group in Turkey who look to the Catholicos of Sis. The Patriarch pledged the loyalty of his Church to the Soviet Revolution in order to ensure his Church's continuance. Some Armenians think he went too far in this.

The position of Armenians in Turkey remains difficult. The Catholicos in Turkey has protested more than once that the Turks are destroying Armenian culture and treating Armenian Christians badly. In the early 1970s the USA helped Turkey, who is a member of the North Atlantic Treaty Organization, to hide from the world the truth about the Turkish Armenians, by pretending that a letter of protest from the Catholicos had never been sent, and by refusing to publish his complaints.

There are now about five and a half million Armenians in the world, the majority of whom are in the USSR, and most of the remainder in the West. They are a gifted and artistic people, who are becoming increasingly aware of their cultural heritage.

Nestorian Christians

The Nestorians, or Church of the East, are another small and much harassed Christian community in this region. (The early achievements of this once-great Church are described in Vols 1 and 2 of this TEF Church History Guide.) At the beginning of the nineteenth century all that was left of them was a small group who had taken refuge in the mountains on the borders of Iran and Iraq. The Kurds, a Muslim people, shared this mountain refuge.

Western Christians learnt of the existence of the Church of the East in 1820. Missionaries were sent, who established schools and hospitals, and helped the people to raise their standard of living. They also drew some people away from their ancient Church into the mission Churches. The Nestorians began to hope that the Europeans might help them to gain their independence from Turkey, but this led to tragedy. The Turks were angered, and encouraged the Kurds to fight against the Church of the East. During World War I the Turks were on the same side as the Germans, fighting against the British and French. The Church of the East so hated the Turks that many of them went to join the British and French forces, hoping that they might be rewarded with independence at the end of the war. But this did not happen. The Nestorians became refugees, and when Iraq became independent of the British mandate in 1933 thousands of them were massacred. Small groups escaped to exile in the USA and elsewhere, and only a few thousand remain in the Middle East, in Iraq, Iran and Syria. The head of their Church, called the Catholicos, is in the USA.

The Maronite Church

The Lebanon is a small, mountainous country, whose population was fairly evenly divided between Christians of the Maronite Church, Muslims, and Druzes whose religion has connections with Islam. Both the Maronites and the Druzes had taken refuge in the mountains of Lebanon so that they could preserve their customs and beliefs without interference. The Maronites are Arabic-speaking, but their liturgy is in the ancient Syriac language, though Arabic is being introduced. The Maronites share much of the Orthodox tradition, but for centuries they have been linked with the Roman Catholic Church.

During the first half of the nineteenth century the Maronites and Druzes lived at peace with one another under a leader called Amir Bashir, who had family links with both groups. After his death the Turks stirred up the Druzes against the Maronites, and the French had to intervene. In 1920 the Lebanon became self-governing under French protection, and in 1944 it became fully independent. In order to keep a balance of power between the different religious communities the President was a Maronite and the Vice-President a Muslim. The French continued to give educational help to the Maronites, and the Jesuit-run University of St Joseph in Beirut was a centre of Maronite culture.

Over the years the balance of power in the Lebanon has been upset by the emigration of many Maronites to the USA, and by the influx of Palestinian refugees at the time of the creation of the State of Israel. There are Christians among the Palestinians, but they are politically divided from the Maronites, because of Maronite links with the USA and with its policy of support for Israel. The Maronites tried to hold on to political power in spite of their diminishing numbers, and this has been one cause of the civil strife in the Lebanon.

The Syrian Orthodox (Jacobite) Church

In Syria the Christian minority mostly belongs to the Syrian Orthodox, or Jacobite, Church. The Jacobites, like the Copts, did not accept the decisions of the Council of Chalcedon of AD 451. They use Syriac in the liturgy, though Arabic is their language. During centuries of Muslim rule the number of Jacobite Christians declined, and it was not until late in the nineteenth century that they recognized the need to take advantage of modern education, and began to adapt to the modern world.

Missionaries from Rome, Britain and America went to help the Jacobite Church, as they went to the other ancient Churches in the region. In the seventeenth century a large group of Jacobites came into communion with the Roman Catholic Church, though they kept many of their own traditions, and only small changes were made in their liturgy. They sent their young people to St Joseph's University in Beirut for higher education. Protestant missionaries arrived in the nineteenth century with strict instructions not to draw the Jacobites away from their own Church. Later Protestant missionaries however did not refrain from making converts from the Jacobites to the mission Churches. The missions brought educational advantages to these Christians, but the inevitable result of the contact was division among the Jacobite Christians.

During World War I the Jacobite Christians suffered severely as did other Christians in the region. But after that time they greatly improved their social and economic position. They moved from the rural areas into the towns, and have benefited from modern education. The Patriarch went to live in Damascus, not Antioch as formerly, and took to travelling frequently to Beirut, because a number of Jacobite Christians settled in Lebanon.

The Coptic Church in Egypt

The name 'Copt' simply means 'Egyptian'. The Non-Chalcedonian Orthodox Church in Egypt is quite correctly named 'Coptic' because its members are descended from the original population of Egypt before the Muslim invasions of the seventh century, and also because the vast majority of Egyptians who are Christians belong to this Church—it is the national Church of Egypt. The Coptic Church is the largest Non-Chalcedonian Orthodox Church in the region we are studying, and claims a membership of four to five million people, though there has been some emigration to the West in recent years. There has been spiritual renewal in this Church since the mid-twentieth century, and the number of monks and nuns is growing.

At the end of the eighteenth century the picture was quite different. The Copts then were few in number, and desperately poor and ignorant. Christians in Europe began to take an interest in them after Napoleon's conquest of Egypt, and as a result their position began to improve. Cyril IV, known as the Reformer, who was Patriarch from 1854 to 1861, established schools for the Copts, and also encouraged them to take advantage of the schools established by the missions. The missions drew some Copts away from their own Church, but they also helped to stimulate the movement for reform within it. Coptic women as well as men benefited from the schools and colleges introduced by the missions, and better medical care was enormously important. Whilst many Coptic Christians have done well economically, however, others are among the very poor of Cairo today, living off the city's rubbish dumps.

As the number of Copts has increased, new churches have been built in Egypt, whose architecture is inspired by ancient traditions. Welfare societies have flourished, and have not limited their activities to Copts. Copts have played a part in the ecumenical movement since 1954, and have also joined in the growing dialogue between Christians and Muslims. The presence of this sizeable Christian community, many of whose women, as well as men, are educated, has been important for Egyptian development. Egyptian Muslim women have far greater freedom than Muslim women in many other Muslim countries, largely as a result of Coptic influence on society in general.

The North African Coast

Finally we must look at one area which is not part of the East Mediterranean Region: the North African coast, where ancient Christian Churches in what are now Libya, Tunisia, Algeria and Morocco disappeared during the centuries of Muslim rule. In the French (and in Libya Italian) colonial period missionaries worked in all these countries. Most of the missionaries were Roman Catholics, and the vast majority of Christians in the area were French settlers and colonial officials. Some converts were made from Islam, but most of these have emigrated since these countries won their independence. Since then, very little evangelism has been possible in this strongly Islamic area. However, some Christians remain, including some communities of the Little Brothers and Little Sisters of Jesus, Roman Catholic orders whose inspiration comes from Charles de Foucauld, who gave his life in North Africa seeking to live the hidden life of Jesus at Nazareth. The Little Brothers and Little Sisters are dedicated to lives of complete poverty among the very poor. They seek to live the love of God, placing great emphasis on prayer and adoration, and they work to earn their living, doing the same sort of work as the poor among whom they live. They believe that a life of silent witness is a necessary part of the Christian apostolate, even though they may never see the results in terms of conversion to Christianity.

STUDY SUGGESTIONS

WORDS AND MEANINGS

1. Explain the meaning of the following terms, as used in this chapter:

(a) Chalcedonian (b) autonomous (c) *millet* (d) *startsy*
(e) Catholicos (f) Coptic (g) *Zoe*

REVIEW OF CONTENT

2. (a) What is the difference between the 'Chalcedonian' and the 'Non-Chalcedonian' Churches?
(b) Where are the Chalcedonian Churches chiefly situated?
(c) Which Churches in which countries belong to the Non-Chalcedonian group?
3. What has been the role of the Oecumenical Patriarch, and in what way did it change during the nineteenth century?
4. (a) What are the beliefs and practices which unite the Orthodox Churches with each other?
(b) What has been the relationship of the Orthodox Churches to the World Council of Churches?
5. (a) What was the position of the Russian Orthodox Church in relation to the state during the nineteenth century?
(b) What 'revivals' took place in the Russian Church during the nineteenth century?
(c) What change occurred in Russia in 1905?
(d) What further changes in the situation have there been—in 1917 and since then?
6. What were the 'New Statutes' issued in the USSR in 1960?
7. In what chief ways has the situation in the following Soviet bloc countries differed from that in Russia?
(a) Poland and Hungary (b) Albania
8. (a) What was the relationship of the Church to the state under the rule of the Ottoman Turks?
(b) What was the relationship between the Armenian Church and the Turkish rulers?
(c) Who were the 'Young Turks', and what were their policies?
9. Give a brief account of events in the Nestorian Church of the East since the beginning of the nineteenth century.
10. In which country are Maronite Christians mostly living? What is their relationship with the Druzes, and in what way have the two groups been related to the government since the time of Independence?
11. With which Western Church is the Syrian (Jacobite) Church in Communion, and how did this come about?
12. In what chief ways has the history and character of the Coptic Church differed from that of other Non-Chalcedonian Churches over the past two centuries?
13. To which Church did most of the few Christians living along the North African coast belong during the latter part of the nineteenth

century, and why? In what sort of work have most of the Christians still remaining in the area since Independence been engaged?

DISCUSSION

14. Unlike most of the Churches of the West, most of the Eastern Orthodox Churches have taken little part in missionary expansion in the past two centuries. What do you think was the reason?

15. The Eastern Orthodox Churches have suffered oppression from both militant Islam and militant Atheism. Which of the two do you think it has been more difficult for them to face up to, and why?

16. Some of the Church leaders in Russia have tried to work with the Communist authorities, and to accept the limitations imposed by them, and this has angered many individual Christians. How far do you think such 'collaboration' is justified, as a means of ensuring the survival of the Church?

17. When under government pressure, the Council of Baptist and Evangelical Church leaders in the USSR has discouraged evangelism, saying the Church's immediate task is spiritual care of its existing members. Many individual members have refused to accept the ruling. But some Churches elsewhere, with no oppression to excuse them, concentrate on their own internal interests, and neglect Christ's command to 'Go ... and make disciples'. What is likely to happen to a Church that turns inward, and cuts itself off from the rest of the world in this way?

Further Reading

Latourette, K. S., *A History of Christianity*. Harper and Row, USA.

Neill, S., *A History of Christian Missions*, Vol. 6. Penguin, UK.

Neill, S. and Anderson, Gerald, *Concise Dictionary of the World Christian Mission*. Lutterworth Press, UK.

Gibbs, M. E., *From Jerusalem to New Delhi*. CLS, Madras.

Latourette, K. S., *A History of Christian Missions in China*. Harper and Row, USA.

Whyte, B., *Unfinished Encounter: China and Christianity*. Collins, UK.

Brown, G. T., *Christianity in the People's Republic of China*. John Knox Press, USA.

Germany, C. H., ed., *The Response of the Church in Changing Japan*. Friendship Press, USA.

Clark, A. D., *History of the Korean Church*. CLS, Korea.

Hong, Harold S., Won Yong Ji and Chung Choon Kim, *Korea Struggles for Christ*. CLS, Korea.

Neill, S., *The Story of the Church in India and Pakistan*. Wm. B. Eerdmans, USA.

Firth, C. B., *An Introduction to Indian Church History*. CLS, Madras.

Varghese, V. T. and Philip, P. P., *Glimpses of the History of the Christian Church in India*. CLS, Madras.

Thomas, M. M., *The Acknowledged Christ of the Indian Renaissance*. CLS, Madras.

Subramanyam, K. N., *The Catholic Community in India*. Madras.

Anderson, G. H., ed., *Christ and Crisis in South-East Asia*. Friendship Press, USA.

Manikam, R. B. and Thomas, W. T., *The Church in South-East Asia*. Friendship Press, USA.

Gowing, P. G., *Islands Under the Cross: the Story of the Church in the Philippines*. NCC, Philippines.

Sitoy, T. V., *History of Christianity in the Philippines*. New Day, Philippines.

Cooley, F., *Indonesia: Church and Society*. Friendship Press, USA.

Scopes, W., ed., *The Christian Ministry in Latin America and the Caribbean*. WCC, Geneva.

Rycroft, W. S., *Religion and Faith in Latin America*. Westminster Press, USA.

Dussel, E., *History and Theology of Liberation*. Orbis Books, USA.

Vallier, I., *Catholicism, Social Control and Modernization in Latin America*. Prentice-Hall, USA.

Hastings, A., *African Christianity*. Geoffrey Chapman, UK.

Hastings, A., *A History of African Christianity 1950–1975*. Cambridge University Press, UK.

FURTHER READING

Hastings, A., Fasholé-Luke, E., Gray, R. and Tasie, E., eds., *Christianity in Independent Africa.*

Falk, P., *The Growth of the Church in Africa.* Zondervan Publishing House, USA.

King, N. Q., *African Cosmos, an Introduction to Religion in Africa.* Wadsworth Publishing Co., USA.

Ndiokwere, N. I., *Prophecy and Revolution: Prophets in the African Independent Churches.* SPCK, UK.

Clarke, P. B., *West Africa and Christianity.* Edward Arnold, UK.

Anderson, W. B., *The Church in East Africa, 1840–1974.* Central Tanganyika Press.

de Gruchy, J. W., *The Church Struggle in South Africa,* 2nd edn. Collins, UK/Eerdmans, USA.

Tutu, Desmond, *Hope and Suffering.* Collins, UK.

Hope, M. and Young, J., *The South African Churches in a Revolutionary Situation.* Orbis Books, USA.

Head, B. *Serowe, Village of the Rain Wind.* William Heinemann, UK.

Vicedom, G., *Church and People in New Guinea.* Lutterworth Press, UK.

Tippett, A. R., *Solomon Islands Christianity.* Friendship Press, USA.

Koschade, A., *New Branches on the Vine. From Mission to Church in New Guinea.* Augsburg Publishing House, USA.

Keysser, C., *A People Reborn.* William Carey Library, USA.

Le Guillou, M. J., *The Tradition of Eastern Orthodoxy.* Burns & Oates, UK.

Atiya, A. S., *A History of Eastern Christianity.* Methuen, UK.

Meyendorff, J., *The Orthodox Church.* St Vladimir's Seminary Press, USA.

Bourdeaux, L. and M., *Ten Growing Soviet Churches.* Marc Europe, UK.

Beeson, T., *Discretion and Valour.* Collins, UK.

Key to Study Suggestions

This Key relates to Word study and Review of Content questions only. It does not provide 'answers', but gives page and paragraph and/or line references to show where in the text answers can be found. When checking their answers to Word study questions, readers may find it helpful to consult a dictionary.

Introduction

1. (a) P. 1, last 7 lines and 2, lines 1–3.   (b) (i) P. 1, lines 7–2 from foot of page and p. 2, lines 2–3 and 20–24; (ii) P. 5, para. 2.   (c) P. 4, paras 2–4 and p. 5 lines 1–26 and numbered para. 1.
2. P. 4, last line and p. 5, lines 1–5.
3. P. 2, last para. lines 1–7.
4. P. 1, last para. and p. 2, paras 1 and 2.
5. P. 2, last para. and p. 3, lines 1–15.
6. P. 3, last 2 paras.
7. P. 4, para. 1.
8. P. 2, last 6 lines; p. 3, lines 1–8 and p. 4, lines 11–19.
9. P. 4, paras 2 and 3.

Chapter 1. Western Europe and North America

1. (a) P. 16, para. 1.   (b) P. 17, lines 4–end and p. 18, lines 1–14. (c) P. 20, paras 1 and 2.
2. P. 10, last para. and p. 11, lines 1–3.
3. Whole of pp. 9–12.
4. P. 10, lines 21–31 and p. 11, para. 2.
5. (a) P. 11, last 6 lines and p. 12, lines 1–9 and 23–29.   (b) P. 12, lines 12–14.
6. (a) P. 13, lines 4–22.   (b) P. 14, last 4 lines and p. 15, lines 1–3.
7. P. 13, last para. and p. 14, lines 1–18.
8. (a) and (b) P. 15, paras 2 and 3.
9. P. 16, para. 1.
10. (a) P. 17, lines 5–8.   (b) P. 17, paras 3, 4 and 5.   (c) P. 18, para. 2. (d) P. 20, para. 1.
11. P. 20, last 2 lines and p. 21, lines 1–17.

Chapter 2. North-East Asia
China

1. (a) P. 26, line 12 from foot and p. 29, lines 5–7.   (b) P. 26, lines 13–7 from foot.   (c) P. 29, lines 11–13.   (d) P. 31, lines 5–12. (e) P. 30, lines 10–16.

KEY TO STUDY SUGGESTIONS

2. (a) and (b) P. 27, last 2 paras and p. 28, lines 1–7.
3. P. 24, last 2 paras and p. 26, paras 1 and 2.
4. (a) and (c) P. 26, last 16 lines and p. 27 lines 1–13.
5. (a) P. 27, lines 18–30.   (b) P. 27, last 5 lines and 28, lines 1–9.
6. P. 28, para. 1 lines 9–end and para. 2.
7. (a) P. 27, last 3 lines and p. 29, lines 1–3.   (b) P. 29, lines 3–25.
   (c) P. 28, last 6 lines; p. 29, last para.; p. 30 and p. 31, paras 1 and 2.
8. P. 29, lines 5–26 and p. 31, para. 4.
9. P. 29, lines 13 from foot and 5–2 from foot.
10. (a) P. 29, last 2 lines and p. 30 para. 1.   (b) P. 30, para. 2.
    (c) P. 30, last para. and p. 31, lines 1–5.
11. P. 31, lines 5–11.
12. (a) P. 31, last 6 lines and p. 32, para. 1.   (b) P. 32, paras 2 and 3;
    p. 33 and p. 34, para. 1. (c) P. 34, paras 2 and 3 and p. 36 lines 1–4.
13. P. 33, lines 10–37.

Taiwan

1. (a) P. 36, para. 1 of section on Taiwan last 4 lines. (b) P. 36, para. 4
   lines 1–5 and p. 38, numbered para. 2. (c) P. 38, numbered para. 2
   lines 1 and 2. (d) P. 36, last line and p. 37, lines 1–5 and 14–4 from
   foot.
2. P. 36, para. 3 of section on Taiwan.
3. P. 37, paras 2 and 3 and p. 38, para. 1.
4. P. 36, para. 1 of section on Taiwan.
5. (a) P. 36, para. 3 of section on Taiwan lines 1–8. (b) P. 36, para. 3 of
   section on Taiwan lines 8–13. (c) P. 37, para. 2 lines 9–16.
6. Pp. 38 and 39, numbered paras 1–4.

Hong Kong

1. (a) P. 36, para. 3 of section on Taiwan and p. 39, paras 1–3 of
   section on Hong Kong. (b) P. 39, lines 11–5 from foot.
2. (a) P. 39, para. 3 of section on Hong Kong lines 1 and 2. (b) P. 39,
   para. 3 of section on Hong Kong lines 3–6.
3. P. 39, para. 1 of section on Hong Kong and p. 40, para. 2 lines 1–6
   and 9–13.
4. P. 39, last para. and p. 40, lines 1–5.
5. (a) P. 39, line 9 from foot. (b) P. 40, para. 3 lines 1 and 2. (c) P. 40,
   para. 3 lines 6 and 7.
6. P. 40, para. 2 last 3 lines and paras 3 and 4, and p. 41 lines 1–4 and
   para. 2.
7. P. 40, para. 4 and p. 41, para. 3 lines 1–6.

Japan

1. (a) P. 42, last para. lines 1–5.   (b) P. 43, para 2 lines 4–6.
(c) P. 45, last line and p. 46, line 1.   (d) P. 43, para. 3.
2. P. 42, para. 2 and para. 3 lines 1–7.
3. P. 42, last para. and p. 43, lines 1–4.
4. P. 43, para. 2.
5. P. 43, last line and p. 45 para. 2.
6. (a) P. 45, para. 4.   (b) P. 46, para. 3 lines 1–8.
7. (a) P. 45, last line and p. 46, lines 1–7.   (b) P. 46, para. 2.
8. P. 46, para. 3 lines 8–12.

Korea

1. (a) P. 47, para. 1 of section on Korea lines 3–7.   (b) P. 47, para. 1
of section on Korea lines 7–9.   (c) P. 48, para. 3 lines 1–8.
(d) P. 48, last para. and p. 49, lines 1–5.
2. (a) P. 47, lines 16–14 from foot.   (b) P. 47, lines 14–12 and 7–4
from foot.
3. (a) P. 48, para. 1 lines 1–4.   (b) P. 48, para. 1 last 7 lines.
4. P. 48, para. 2.
5. P. 48, para. 3.
6. P. 37, last line; p. 38, para. 1; p. 48, last para and p. 49, lines 1–5.

Chapter 3. The Indian Sub-Continent, Sri Lanka and Nepal

1. (a) P. 57, para. 3.   (b) P. 59, para. 4.   (c) P. 64, para. 1.   (d) P. 66,
lines 16–18.   (e) P. 67, para. 1.   (f) P. 69, last line and p. 70, para. 1.
(g) P. 63, last para.   (h) P. 70, para. 4.
2. P. 58, para. 3 lines 1–6.
3. (a) P. 55, para. 3 lines 1–15.   (b) P. 57, para. 3.   (c) P. 57, paras 1
and 4.
4. P. 57, last para.
5. (a) P. 58, paras 2, 3 and 4 and p. 59, paras 1, 2 and 3.   (b) P. 58,
para. 2.   (c) P. 58, paras 3 and 4 and p. 59, paras 1 and 2.
6. P. 60, para. 2 lines 1–4 and p. 61 last para. lines 8–6 from foot.
7. P. 63, para. 1.
8. (a) P. 58, para. 3 lines 9–18.   (b) P. 59, last para and p. 60, lines
1–7.   (c) P. 60, last para. and p. 62, caption 2.   (d) P. 61, para. 4,
lines 1–5.   (e) P. 66, last para. and p. 70, para. 3.   (f) P. 69, last
para.   (g) P. 76, para. 3.
9. (a) P. 64, last 16 lines and p. 65, lines 1–8.   (b) P. 65, lines 9–11 and
25–31 and p. 66, lines 11–15.
10. (a) and (b) P. 66, para. 3 and p. 67, para. 1.
11. (a), (b) and (c) P. 64, last para.; p. 65, para. 1 and p. 71, paras 3
and 4.

12. P. 71, last 21 lines and p. 72, paras 1 and 3.
13. (a) P. 63, last para.; p. 64, para. 1; p. 70, last 3 lines and p. 71, para. 1. (b) P. 69, para. 1.
14. P. 72, last para. and p. 73 lines 1–3 and para. 4, lines 1–3.
15. (a) P. 73, paras 2 and 3. (b) P. 73, last 15 lines and p. 74 paras 1 and 2.
16. (a) Para. 1 of section on Sri Lanka. (b) P. 74, last para. and p. 76, lines 1–3.
17. (a) P. 76, last para. (b) and (c) P. 77, paras 2 and 3.

Chapter 4. South-East Asia

1. (a) P. 94, lines 3–9. (b) P. 96, last 6 lines and p. 97, lines 1–6. (c) P. 63, para. 1 and p. 90, para 4. (d) P. 90, para 3 last 7 lines. (e) P. 91, last 4 lines and p. 92 lines 1–4.
2. (a) and (b) P. 81, para. 2.
3. (a) P. 83, para. 1. (b) P. 83, para. 2 lines 1–5.
4. (a) and (b) P. 84, para. 1 of section on Burma lines 2 and 3 and 4–7. (c) P. 84, para. 2 of section on Burma.
5. P. 83, para. 3 including quotation and p. 84, last para. lines 1 and 2.
6. (a) P. 85, para. 1. (b) P. 85, para. 2 and para. 3 first sentence.
7. (a) P. 85, last 2 paras and p. 86. (b) P. 85, last 4 lines. (c) P. 86, paras 2 and 3.
8. (a) P. 87, para. 1. (b) P. 87, para. 2. (c) P. 87, paras 3 and 4.
9. (a) P. 87, last para. (b) P. 89, para. 1, lines 1–4. (c) P. 89, lines 4–11 and para. 2 lines 5–10.
10. (a) P. 89, para. 1 of section on the Philippines. (b) P. 89, last 4 lines and p. 90, paras 1, 2 and 3.
11. (a) P. 89, last 4 lines and p. 90 paras 1 and 2. (b) P. 90, paras 3 and 4.
12. (a) P. 90, last para. and p. 91 lines 1–6. (b) P. 91, para. 2.
13. (a) P. 91, last 4 lines. (b) P. 91 last 4 lines; p. 92, lines 1–8, 18–22 and 7–4 from foot; P. 93, paras 2 and 3 and p. 94, lines 2–8. (c) P. 92, lines 20–22 and 13–7 from foot and p. 94, lines 6–9. (d) P. 92, para. 2 and para 3 lines 4–8; p. 93, para. 2 and p. 94, para. 3.
14. (a) P. 92, para. 4 lines 1–5. (b) P. 93, para. 2. (c) P. 92, last 7 lines and p. 93, lines 1–4.
15. (a) P. 93, para. 3 and p. 94, para. 2. (b) P. 93, paras 4 and 5 and p. 94, lines 1 and 2. (c) P. 94, para. 3.
16. (a) P. 96, lines 4–6 (b) P. 94, last 2 paras and p. 96, paras 1–4. (c) P. 94, last 6 lines and p. 96, lines 1–3.
17. (a) P. 96, para. 3. (b) (i) and (ii) P. 96, para. 3 lines 1–6; (iii) P. 96, para. 3 lines 7–10; (iv) P. 96, para. 4.
18. (a) P. 96, last 6 lines and p. 97, lines 1–6. (b) P. 97, paras 2 and 3.

Chapter 5. Latin America and the Caribbean

1. (a) P. 102, numbered para. 2.   (b) P. 102, numbered para. 3, lines 1 and 2.   (c) P. 104, numbered para. 3 line 3.   (d) P. 108, last 3 lines.   (e) P. 121, last para.
2. (a) P. 102, numbered para. 2 lines 1 and 2.   (b) and (c) P. 102, numbered para. 2.   (d) P. 102, numbered para. 1 lines 2–6 and numbered para. 3.
3. (a) and (b) P. 104, numbered para. 5.
4. P. 104, last para.
5. P. 105, paras 3 and 4 and P. 106, paras 1 and 2.
6. (a) P.106, last para. and p. 107, para. 1.   (b) P. 109, paras 2, 3 and 4 and p. 110, paras 1 and 2.
7. (a)–(g) P. 110, para. 4 lines 1–12 and p. 111, lines 4–9; and see also (a) P. 108, para. 2;   (b) P. 108, para. 3;   (d) P. 108, para. 4;   (e) and (f) P. 108, last 3 lines and p. 109, lines 1–6.
8. (a) P. 109, last para. and p. 110, lines 1–6.   (b) P. 109, para. 3.
9. (a) P. 110, last 9 lines and p. 111, lines 1–3.   (b) P. 111, paras 3 and 4.   (c) P. 111, para. 5.   (d) P. 111, para. 7 lines 1–3.
10. P. 111, paras 6, 7 and 8 and p. 112, lines 1–3.
11. (a) P. 112, para. 3; p. 113, last 3 lines and p. 115, lines 1 and 2.   (b) P. 112, paras 3 and 4 and p. 113, lines 1–3.   (c) P. 113, paras 3, 4 and 5 and p. 115, lines 2–8.
12. (a) P. 115, lines 9–19.   (b) P. 115, lines 19–25.   (c) P. 115, lines 25–34.
13. P. 118, paras 1 and 2.
14. P. 118, last 16 lines and p. 119, lines 1–28.
15. P. 119, last para. and p. 120, paras. 1 and 2.
16. P. 121, para. 2 lines 1–15.
17. P. 122, para. 1 lines 1–10.
18. (a) P. 120, last para.; p. 121, para. 1 and para. 3 lines 1–3 and p. 122, para. 3 lines 1–3.   (b) P. 122, para. 3 lines 4–8.

Chapter 6. Africa: The Nineteenth Century

1. (a) P. 128, lines 1–3.   (b) P. 128, lines 6–4 from foot.   (c) P. 133, section numbered 3 lines 1–3.   (d) P. 134, para. 2 last 3 lines.   (e) P. 134, last para. line 1.   (f) P. 134, para. 3 lines 6–8.
2. (a) P. 126, lines 2–4.   (b) P. 128, lines 1 and 2 and para. 3.   (c) P. 126, last 2 paras.
3. (a) P. 128, last line and p. 129, lines 1–19.   (b) P. 129, lines 19–23.
4. (a) P. 128, last para.   (b) P. 129, last line and P. 130, para. 1.   (c) P. 130, para. 3.   (d) P. 132, para. 4, lines 1–7.
5. (a) P. 132, para. 2.   (b) P. 132, para. 3.
6. (a) P. 132 last line and p. 133, para. 1.   (b) P. 133, paras 2 and 3.   (c) P. 133, para. 4.

7. (a) P. 134, para. 2 lines 1–3 and para. 4 and p. 135, lines 1–3. (b) P. 134, para. 3.
8. (a) P. 135, para. 2.   (b) P. 135, para. 3.
9. (a) P. 136, line 5 to line 5 from foot.   (b) P. 136, last 4 lines and p. 137, para. 1.   (c) P. 138, para. 2.   (d) P. 138, para. 3.   (e) P. 138, last para. and p. 139, line 1.
10. (a) P. 135, last 11 lines.   (b) P. 137, para. 3.   (c) P. 137, para. 4.
11. P. 137, last para. and p. 138 lines 1–3.
12. P. 139, para. 2.
13. P. 139, last para. and p. 140, lines 1–12.
14. (a) P. 140, last para. and p. 141, lines 1–5.   (b) P. 141, para. 2. (a) and (b) P. 141, para. 3.
15. (a) P. 140, para. 3 lines 1–6 and 8–12 and para. 4 lines 1–3. (b) P. 140, para. 3 lines 7–9 and para. 4 lines 3–10.
16. (a) P. 141, para. 4.   (b) P. 141, last 2 lines and p. 143, lines 1–5.
17. (a) P. 143, line 6–end.   (b) P. 144, paras 1 and 2.
18. (a) P. 144, para. 3 lines 1–8.   (b) P. 144, para. 3 lines 8–15. (c) P. 144, para. 4.   (d) P. 144, para. 3.

Chapter 7. Africa: 1900–1950

1. (a) P. 149, para. 2.   (b) P. 151, para. 2.
2. (a) P. 151, paras 3 and 4 and p. 152, line 1.   (b) P. 152, lines 2–14.
3. P. 152, paras 2 and 3 and p. 153, paras 1 and 2.
4. (a) P. 153, last para.   (b) P. 153, last para. and p. 154, para. 1.
5. (a) P. 154, paras 3 and 4 and p. 155, lines 1–6.   (b) P. 155, lines 7–end of para. 1.   (c) P. 155, para. 2 and p. 157, lines 1 and 2.
6. (a) P. 157, para. 2.   (b) P. 157, para. 3 lines 4 and 5.
7. (a) P. 157, last para. and p. 158, paras 1–3.   (b) P. 158, last para. and p. 159, lines 1–12.
8. P. 159, para. 2 and para. 3 lines 1–9 and p. 160, lines 2–7.
9. (a) P. 159, para. 3 line 6–end. (b) P. 159, last line and p. 160, lines 1–7. (c) P. 160, lines 7–19.   (a), (b) and (c) P. 161, last para. and p. 162, para. 1.
10. (a) P. 160, para. 2 lines 3–12.   (b) P. 160, para. 2 line 12 to p. 161, line 1.   (c) P. 161, lines 2–17.   (d) P. 161, para. 2.
11. (a) P. 162, last para. (b) P. 163, paras 1 and 2.   (c) P. 163, paras 2 and 3.   (d) P. 163, paras 2 and 3; p. 164, last 3 lines and p. 165, para. 1.
12. P. 163, para. 1 lines 6–12 and para. 2 and p. 165, lines 6–19.

Chapter 8. Africa Since 1950

1. (a) P. 168, lines 1–4.   (c) P. 168, para. 1 lines 7–12.   (d) P. 168, para. 1 lines 13–17; p. 173, last 5 lines; p. 174, lines 1–13 and last 5 lines and p. 176, lines 1–9.

2. P. 170, para. 3 lines 5–9 and last para. and p. 171, lines 1–3.

3. (a) P. 170, last para. and p. 171 paras 1–3.   (b) P. 171, paras 4 and 5 and p. 172 paras 1–3.   (c) P. 179, last 5 lines; p. 180; p. 181, para. 1 and para. 2 lines 1 and 2 and p. 183, para. 4.

4. P. 172, last para. and p. 173, paras 1 and 2.

5. P. 174, lines 15–37.

6. (a) P. 168, para. 2 and p. 176, para. 2 lines 1–8.   (b) P. 176, para 2 lines 8–end.

7. (a) P. 177, para. 2; p. 178, paras 2 and 3 and p. 179 lines 1–20. (b) p. 180, numbered paras 1 and 2; p. 181 and p. 182, paras 1 and 2.

8. (a) P. 183, para. 3.   (b) P. 183, paras 4 and 5 and p. 184, lines 1–24.

Chapter 9. The South Pacific, Australia and New Zealand

Polynesia

1. P. 188, para. 1.

2. (a) P. 188, last line and p. 189, para. 1 and para. 2 lines 1–10. (b) P. 204, last para.   (c) P. 195, para. 4.   (d) P. 198, last 2 paras and p. 199, lines 1–3.   (e) P. 203, para. 4 lines 1–6.   (f) P. 205, para. 4.   (g) P. 195, para. 4.

3. (a) P. 188, para. 2 lines 1–5.   (b) P. 188, para. 2 lines 5–9 and para. 3. (c) P. 188, last line and p. 189, para. 1.

4. (a) P. 189, paras 2, 3 and 4; p. 192, para. 2; p. 194, paras 2 and 4 and p. 195, para. 1.   (b) P. 192, paras 3 and 4.

5. P. 192, last 2 paras and p. 194, lines 1–4.

6. (a) P. 194, para. 3.   (b) P. 194, last para.   (c) P. 195, para. 2.

7. P. 195, para. 4.

8. (a) P. 196, paras 2, 3 and 4 and p. 197, lines 1–6.   (b) P. 197, para. 2.

Melanesia, Papua New Guinea

9. P. 197, para. 3 and p. 200, para. 2 lines 4–7.

10. P. 197, last para. and p. 198, lines 1–20.

11. (a) P. 198, paras 3 and 4 and p. 199, lines 1–3.   (b) P. 199, para. 2.

12. (a) P. 199, para. 4.   (b) P. 199, last para. and p. 200, lines 1–6.

13. P. 200, para. 2 lines 1–3.

14. P. 200, para. 2 lines 6–end.

15. (a) P. 200, last 3 lines.   (b) P. 201, para. 2 line 1.   (c) P. 201, lines 4–7.

16. (a) P. 201, para. 2.   (b) P. 201, para. 3.   (a) and (b) P. 201, last 6 lines and p. 202, lines 1–31.

17. (a) P. 203, paras 2 and 3.   (b) P. 203, paras 4 and 5 and p. 204 lines 1–5.

18. P. 204, paras 4 and 5.

Australia and New Zealand

19. (a) and (b) P. 205, paras 2, 3 and 4.
20. (a) and (b) P. 207, para. 2 and para. 3 lines 1–4.
21. P. 207, para. 3 lines 4-end and para. 4.
22. P. 207, last 3 lines and p. 208, paras 1 and 2.
23. P. 208, paras 3 and 4 and p. 209, lines 1–5.
24. P. 209, paras 2 and 3.
25. P. 209, last 2 lines; p. 210 and p. 211, lines 1–9.

The Orthodox Churches

1. (a) P. 215 para. 1. (b) P. 215, para. 2. (c) P. 217, para. 2 lines 1–6. (d) P. 219, last para. and p. 220, lines 1–3. (e) P. 225, paras 2 and 3. (f) P. 227, para. 4. (g) P. 218, para. 5 lines 1–10.
2. (a) P. 215, para. 1. (b) P. 215, para 2 lines 1–8. (c) P. 223, last para. lines 1–4 and see pp. 224–227.
3. P. 217, last para. and p. 218, paras 1 and 2.
4. P. 215, para. 2 line 9-end. (b) P. 218, para. 3.
5. (a) P. 219, para. 5. (b) P. 219, last para. and p. 220, lines 1–15. (c) and (d) P. 220, para. 3.
6. P. 220, para. 4 and p. 222, lines 1 and 2.
7. P. 222, paras 5 and 6 and p. 223, paras 1 and 2; (a) P. 223, para. 3. (b) P. 223, para. 4.
8. (a) P. 217, paras 1 and 2. (b) P. 224, para. 4 and p. 225, para. 3. (c) P. 224, last para. and P. 225, lines 1 and 2.
9. P. 225, last 2 paras and p. 226, para. 1.
10. P. 226, paras 2, 3 and 4.
11. P. 226, last para. and p. 227, lines 1 and 2 and paras 2 and 3.
12. P. 227, last 2 paras and p. 228, paras 1 and 2.
13. P. 228, para. 3.

Index

INDEX

McDougall, Bp F. T., 93
Medellín Conference, 112, 113, 118
Media, use of, 3, 5, 209
Medical Missionaries of Mary, 157
Medical missions, 4, 63, 69, 81, 83, 153, 156, 157, 228; training, 63
Mekane Jesus Church, 152
Melanesia, 188, **197–204**
Melanesian Brotherhoods, 201
Melanesian Mission, 198
Menelik, Emperor, 149
Mennonite Churches, 222
Methodist Churches, 47, 48, 60, 72, 73, 108, 128, 130, 160, 194, 203, 207; missions, 47, 92, 110, 121, 128, 194, 199, 200
Methodist Church in Ghana; 128; in New Zealand, 207
Methodist Missionary Society, 128
Mexico, 106, 107, 109, 110, 112, 116, 119
Micronesia, 188, 196
Mikael, Bp, 151
Milne, William, 92
Missions, missionary societies, 3–5, 11, 16–18, 20; & see *under denominations, sending countries, society names*
Mizeki, Bernard, 142, 145
Modernism, 11, 189
Moffat, Robert, 131, 138
Moluccas, 96
Mondal, D. A. K., 73, 74
Moravian missions, 121, 135
Morelos, José Maria, 106
Morocco, 170, 228
Morrison, Robert, 24, 26, 35, 92
Moscow Patriarchate, 219
Moshweshwe, Chief, 138
Mota Is., 198
Mott, John R., 29
Mozambique, 139, 145, 170, 181, 182
Mugwanya, Stanislaus, 144
Mukasa, Victoro, 158
Mukyokai ('No-Church Church'), 45, 46
Munyagabyanjo, Robert, 143
Music, 176, 177, 197, 210
Muslims, 57, 60, 72, 73, 215, 217, 222
Mutesa, King, 141, 143
Muzorewa, Bp Abel, 182
Mwanga, King, 143, 144

Naluba, Mother Cecilia, 158
Namboze, Dr Josephine, 157
Namibia, 139, 165, 168, 182, 184
Nath, Golak, 68
National Association of Evangelicals (Korea), 49
National Christian Conferences

& Councils of Churches, 28, 30, 31, 33, 49, 67, 74, 173, 174, 207
National Church (India), 71
National Conference of Christian Students in China, 31
National Missionary Society (India), 64
National Union of Catholic Students (Peru), 119
Nationalism, 6, 67, 83, 89
Naudé, Dr Beyers, 175, 183
Neesima, J. H., 43
Nepal, 55, 76, 77
Nepalese Christian Fellowship, 77
Nestorian Christians, 225, 226
Neto, Fr Pereira, 115
New Britain, 199, 200
New Caledonia, 195, 198
New Georgia, 199
New Guinea, **200–204**
New Hebrides, 199
New Zealand, 188, 194–196, 198, **205–211**
Ngo Dinh Diem, 86
Ngqika, 136
Njau, Elimo, 177
Nguyen van Binh, Abp Paul, 86
Niger, 133
Nigeria, 130, 132, 133, 155, 164, 176, 178
Nihon Kirisuto Kokwai (Japanese Church of Christ), 42, 43
Niles, D. T., 76
Niue Is., 185
Njau, Elimo, 177
Nkrumah, Kwame, 170, 180
'No-Church Church' (Japan) 45, 46
Nommensen, L., 96
Non-Chalcedonian Orthodox Churches, 215, 223
Northern Rhodesia, 155, 170
Nott, Henry, 188, 193
Ntsikana, 136, 160
Nukapu Is., 198
Nyasaland, 154, 155, 170

Oecumenical Patriarchate of Constantinople, 215, 217, 218
Oldham, Dr J. H., 163
Oldham, William, 92
Olive Tree Church, 48
Orders, Religious, 4, 69, 70, 90, 104, 106, 109, 194, 201, 228
Orthodox Churches, 17, 18, 28, 45, 215, 219, 222
Ottoman Turks, 217, 219, 222
Overseas Missionary Fellowship, 83, 87
Owen, W. E., 163
Oxford Movement, 93

Pacific region, **185–204**
Padim, Bp Candido, 117

Padroado, 63, 106
Pak, Elder, Tae-son, 48
Pakistan, 55, 69, 72, 73, 75; Church of, 73
Pallegoix, Bp, 83
Panama, 110
Pandita Ramabai, 62–64
Papacy, see Vatican
Papeiha, 192
Papua Ekalesia, 203, 204
Papua New Guinea, 188, 197, 200–204, 206
Paraguay, 115
Paris Evangelical Mission, 138
Paris Foreign Missionary Society (MEP), 87
Partnership in mission, 81, 211
Patronato real, 83, 90, 102, 105–107
Patteson, Bp J. C., 198, 206
Paul, K. T. 67, 70
Peace movements, 14, 199
Penang, 91–93
Pentecostalism, 5, 120, 122, 220
Perak, 92
Periah, Yerraguntla, 58
Persecution, 32, 34, 42, 47–49, 85, 109, 110, 115, 180–182, 217, 220, 222, 223
Peru, 113, 118, 119
Petitjean, Fr, 42
Petros, Bp, 151
Philip, Dr John, 135
Philippine Indpendent Church (PIC), 89–91
Philippines, 81, **88–91**
Pietism, 2, 38
Pironio, Bp, 113
Pluralism, 106, 210, 211
Pobedonostev, K. P., 219
Polygamy, 26, 161
Polynesia, 199–197, 210; Polynesian missionaries, 192, 195, 198, 200
Pomare, Chief, 189
Pompallier, Bp J-B-F., 194
Popes, authority of, 4, 11, 85; Gregory XVI, 107; John XXIII, 18; John Paul II, 223; Leo XII, 107; Paul VI, 143, 218; Pius VII, 107; Pius XII, 85
Portugal, 57, 63, 102–107, 162, 170, 171; Portuguese missions, 55, 57, 63, 91, 126, 171
Poverty, 117, 228
Prayer, prayer groups, 12, 159, 226
Presbyterian Churches, 36, 38, 47, 60, 72, 73, 172, 207; missions, 36, 38, 83, 92, 93, 110, 121, 199
Presbyterian Church in Canada, 198; of New South Wales, 203; of New Zealand, 209
Presses, printing, 2, 3, 36, 40, 104, 138

244

INDEX